W9-BJB-136

3 6153 00040527 9

WITHDRAWN
JEFFERSON COMMUNITY COLLEGE
LIBRARY

QM
23.2   Palmer
P28   Anatomy for speech and
1972   hearing

12/05/75 DATE DUE			
~~DEC 19 80~~			
~~DEC 1 2 1988~~			
MAY 1 0 '94			

Melvil Dewey Library
Jefferson Community College
Watertown, New York 13601

ANATOMY FOR SPEECH AND HEARING
second edition

under the advisory editorship of J. Jeffery Auer

ANATOMY FOR SPEECH AND HEARING

second edition

John M. Palmer
University of Washington

Melvil Dewey Library
Jefferson Community College
Watertown, New York 13601

Harper & Row, Publishers
New York, Evanston, San Francisco, London

ANATOMY FOR SPEECH AND HEARING, second edition
Copyright © 1972 by John M. Palmer

Printed in the United States of America. All rights reserved. No part of this book may be
used or reproduced in any manner whatsoever without written permission except in the
case of brief quotations embodied in critical articles and reviews. For information ad-
dress Harper & Row, Publishers, Inc., 49 East 33rd Street, New York, N.Y. 10016.

Standard Book Number: 06-044971-3
Library of Congress Catalog Card Number: 71-181549

CONTENTS

TABLES

FIGURES

PREFACE TO THE FIRST EDITION

Anatomic studies are, often to the despair and confusion of the student, analytic studies. The despair and confusion result when the student, immersed in the process of analysis to the fullest extent possible, is expected to apply his information through the use of undirected and perhaps unexpected synthesis. A student is often qualitatively measured by his ability to generalize, to make wholes from the parts, to induce rather than to deduce; in short, by the ideal standards of an individual who can engage in the simultaneous processes of analysis and synthesis.

Studies in human anatomy are designed to make more or less complete investigations of the detailed components of a gross structure that is ultimately more than the sum of those component parts. This concept that the whole is more than the sum of its parts is not novel, nor is the concept of studying the parts in order to better understand the whole a new idea. Both concepts are stressed here particularly because the student may find it easy to lose sight of the total organism in the study of the detailed parts. The nature of the human body can be better understood in the normal or abnormal state when one has complete understanding of its various component parts.

It is hoped that this text will enable the student to secure a better understanding of the related parts involved in the specialized process of oral communication, important in the civilized life of the total human organism. The text emphasizes those anatomical parts that constitute the mechanisms *immediately* responsible for *speech* and *hearing*. Thus, although the speech and hearing mechanisms could not operate without the support of a heart, for example, our concern is restricted to the understanding of muscles, nerves, and tissues that play a more direct role in speech and hearing.

The organismic doctrine, or holism (or *gestalt,* as some psychologists prefer) is extremely useful to the student of speech and hearing phenomena. Such a student enjoys the unique position of working in an area of behavior that is an admixture of a number of other areas; it, too, is more than the mere sum of its parts. The study of speech and hearing is somewhat like the study of many physical phenomena. In chemistry, for example, one studies the properties of elements in isolated as well as in combined forms. The student chemist soon learns that sodium chloride, commonly known as table salt, is really more than just a combination of two ions, sodium and chlorine, and that its properties are variable, depending upon the environment in which the two ions, or the sodium chloride, exist. Likewise, man varies. Specifically, his speech and his hearing vary according to the composition of the speech and hearing mechanisms, of the whole organism, and of the environments in which the mechanisms and the organism operate.

The intent of this text is to present in readily available form information on speech and hearing anatomy that is not now available in composite form; it has been written with the following in mind:

> The chief objective of anatomic studies is the accumulation of structural knowledge which will enable us to understand the functioning of living tissues.[1]

The text presents the anatomic structures *directly* related to the functions of speech and hearing. The opening chapters are aimed at transmitting background information concerning the nature of the human organism in general, specific information on the structural elements of the organism, and terminology explanations; some attention is focused on the vegetative nature of the basic structures and the vital role they play in maintaining life as well as the overlapping role they play in speech and hearing. To facilitate better understanding:

1. The material is organized and presented from the anatomic point of view, primarily. There is definite and deliberate delimitation of discussion of function.
2. The material is presented, overall, from an anterior-superior orientation, proceeding from there down and back. Thus, the first topics will have to do with the bones and tissues of the skull, the nose, the mouth, to the pharynges, larynx, and so on. The ear and nervous mechanisms are treated differently.
3. Occasional illustration of the anatomy is made through clinical notes, relating the structures under discussion to definite speech or hearing pathologies.
4. Outline drawings of anatomic areas under discussion are offered so that students may label noted landmarks and enter whatever details are suited to their study.
5. The glossary is included to assist students in understanding the technical terminology.

John M. Palmer
Dominic A. LaRusso

---

1 F. R. Bailey, *Textbook of Histology* (14th ed.), Baltimore: Williams and Wilkins, 1958.

PREFACE TO THE SECOND EDITION

The first edition of this text was the product of a number of years of experience teaching the basic anatomy of speech and hearing to beginning students. The present edition represents additional years of such experience, plus the added advantage of the welcome suggestions, criticisms, and protest of several hundred students exposed to the first edition.

Although the same general orientation pertains, the present edition presents corrections in both text and illustrations that were badly needed. It attempts to clarify some far-from-clear descriptions. It offers some additional materials to both student and instructor. It contains completely rewritten sections.

Certain of the illustrations were omitted largely because of their relatively less important role to the purpose of the text. Other illustrations were improved and clarified. A third group of illustrations was added to fill gaps. The illustrations were left unlabeled, against the sage advice of some critics, so that they might be utilized as exercises for the students in their study.

The suggested references and bibliographies were generally eliminated, leaving such materials to the instructor to provide, depending upon his emphasis and predilections in teaching such a course. Previous reference lists were a complicated gathering of general, overly technical, outdated and mainly unusable sources for beginning students.

The text material was carefully scrutinized. In many places only minor changes were required. In others, reorientation and rewriting on a more general basis was utilized. Some material, for example the chapter on the nervous system, was completely rewritten in a more practical way. And, lastly, some overly detailed material was removed; for example the extreme detail on dental structure and embryologic development, which might best be left for advanced courses.

There was also added a suggested list of anatomic landmarks for each of the illustrations. At the discretion of the instructor, this list might be used by the student to find those landmarks on each illustration and to submit them as evidence of having grasped the necessary understanding of those structures. Obviously, this is no guarantee of such understanding, but it acts as a teaching device that might assist in its development.

The second edition retains the same philosophy and goal as the first edition: the key to understanding the functioning of the speech and hearing mechanisms is a solid understanding of their structures. This points up another possible disadvantage of this text: the delimitation of physiology. It is thought by this author that this area might be provided by the lecturer with appropriate assignments in supplementary writings. It is also a reasonably common practice to follow a beginning anatomy course with a series of courses devoted to the specific physiology and pathology of regions and systems for which the student of communication disorders will ultimately be responsible. For example, there are many courses in the anatomy, physiology, and pathologies associated with cleft lip and palate, dysarthria, and those associated with dentition, among others.

Omitted from the first edition was any recognition of persons who directly and indirectly contributed to it. Certainly those many students who studied from it and made suggestions as well as complaints deserve first acknowledgment in this second edition. Certain colleagues in the field also added considerably, especially those who read it carefully for the purpose of criticism. Lastly the contribution of Professor Dominic LaRusso, who has withdrawn as coauthor because of the pressures of his present work, must be acknowledged and appreciation given for his editorial and artistic expertise in the first and thus to this second edition.

To those who do use this text—student or teacher—comments, suggestions, and criticisms would be welcome.

John M. Palmer

chapter 1

PHILOSOPHY AND INTRODUCTION

Spoken words and heard sounds flow into and out of the body of man. The body producing those words or accepting those sounds has a number of characteristics in common with other such bodies, and the study of the exchange of acoustic symbols as communication might just as well start with the study of the bodies associated with them. Thus, the study of the pertinent anatomy of the human body might well be a precursor to the further detailed study of the processes of communication. Admittedly, to study anatomy is to study only a part of the total process. Like the study of words and sounds as communication, the study of the parts of the human body is but a partial study of the whole. Doubtless, it is an important activity with which to begin a fascinating exploration of the science of communication.

COMMUNICATING MAN: AN ORGANISMIC APPROACH

The definition of a "normal organism" is not easily derived. According to Dorland, an organism is *"any organized body of living economy;* any individual animal or plant."[1] Further searching leads us to Webster, who describes economy as *"an orderly management or arrangement of parts;* organization or system; as, the economy of the human body." Of some import is the fact that both sources stress *organization* as being of prime interest when considering the parts of the subject under study, which are here the parts of a human body directly concerned with the functions of speech and hearing. The term "organism" refers, obviously, to an entity—a living body—whose parts are sufficiently organized or ordered as to preserve the unity of that body.

The behavior patterns of man are dictated by his anatomic mechanism as well as by the social milieu of which he is part. In other words, as a physiologic entity, he has certain needs—some social, some individual; these must be satisfied, or the organism does not fit or adapt into that environment—it becomes abnormal. Many sciences and arts are concerned with the fitting or adapting processes through which man passes in order to be normal.

Communication is of extreme importance to the social being that is man, and it is foremost among the characteristics that differentiate man from other organisms. Man's needs encompass every aspect of animal behavior, from so-called biologic acts to others of a more highly specialized nature. This behavior, or functioning, is frequently determined by, and based upon, information gathered by the individual through communication with an environment of a special type. Knowledge of the needs to be fulfilled, in a real and concrete sense here, is

[1] W. A. H. Dorland, *Dorland's Illustrated Medical Dictionary* (23rd ed.), Philadelphia: Saunders, 1957.

initiated and maintained through speech and hearing, through the body parts utilized in these processes.

Speech as an interorganismic function remains an essential and primary process as long as man remains a social, communicating organism. It is not an essential, or primary, function if man becomes asocial. Man has other, truly vital needs that must be satisfied to sustain life. Yet it must be obvious that by far the majority of men are not asocial but are gregarious animals of highly specialized natures, depending heavily upon oral communication for existence. One might define normal speech, here, as that which aids the individual to serve efficiently in his role as a social animal.

Breakdowns in communication, either in the sending or receiving ends of the system, may have two results. First, they may inhibit the accomplishment of the objective of the communication. Second, and perhaps more important to students of speech and hearing, the organisms involved—the individuals concerned—may become disturbed psychologically, and thus become more "abnormal" than "normal."

Defective speech and defective hearing, then, interfere with successful communication and thus interfere with normal satisfaction of the needs of the individual and of the group. Defective speech, alone, may be defined as speech that is sufficiently different from that of other individuals in the same environment as to lessen the efficiency of communication and ultimately to disturb the individual possessing such deviant processes. Defective hearing might be defined similarly with respect to the reception of the communication.

TERMINOLOGY

Students of speech and hearing often have difficulty with the foreign terminology associated with the study of body parts. In the field of anatomy, as in any science or art, special terminology has developed. Compounding the confusion, these specialized terms become archaic with time; or they become "popular" and lose their technical and specialized meaning; or they are replaced by other terms; or they retain their foreign nature. This loss of specialization by terms reflect what most students of communication and language well know: the more abstract a symbol is, the better the chance of a communication breakdown. In other words, a term that does not have a single, concrete referent has a better opportunity for being misunderstood during a communicative act than a term that has a definite, specific meaning.

Thus, the science of anatomy (the study of the structure and form, or *morphology,* of an organism) has been forced to restrict its language symbols for purposes of general understanding. It is somewhat different from other sciences because of the fact that anatomy is one of the oldest of the sciences, and thus has something of an international flavor. International efforts have been made to standardize the terminology.

The student of anatomy will find it important to understand clearly the various terms used in describing the position, direction, or relationship of structures. He will find that some of these terms are foreign to him; others will have been used differently under other circumstances; and some of them have a popular usage that will interfere with the understanding of the special utilization made in anatomic study. The terms of spatial orientation are illustrative.

Body Planes

In considering the body planes, it must be assumed that the body is erect; the arms are hanging at the sides; the head, the eyes, and the palms of the hands are directed forward. The three major planes of the body are the *sagittal, coronal,* and *transverse.* (See Figure 1–1.) The sagittal is also known as the *midsagittal*

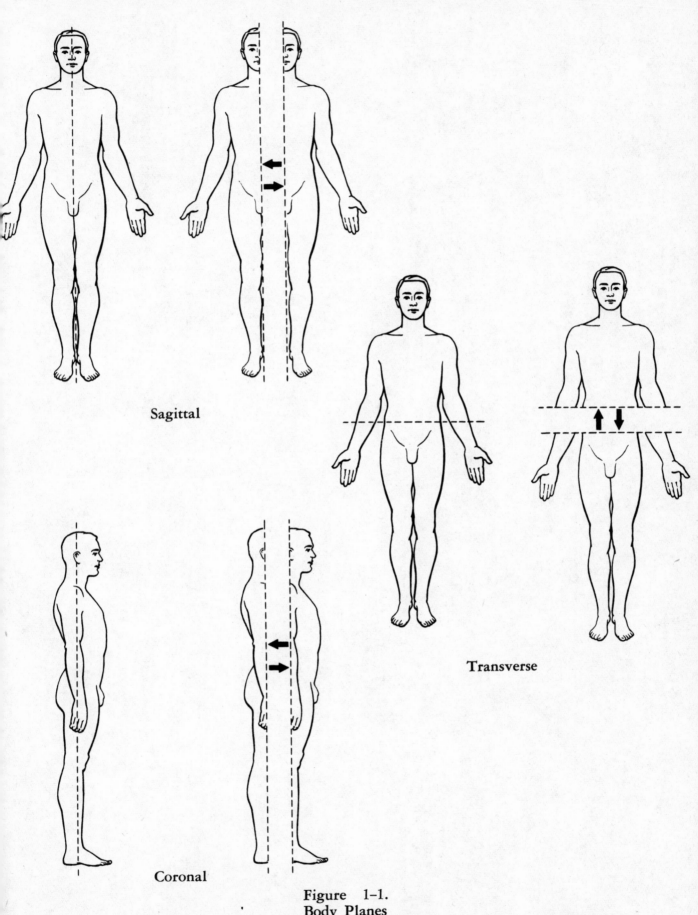

Sagittal

Coronal

Transverse

Figure 1–1.
Body Planes

when at the midline of the structure; the coronal as the *frontal;* and the transverse as the *horizontal.*

As can be seen in Table 1.1, the *sagittal* plane, or section, refers to a plane from front-to-back, or anteriorly-posteriorly, dividing the body structure into right and left parts. When the parts are equal, the plane is a *median* or *midsagittal;* when the two parts are unequal, it is a *lateral sagittal,* or simply a *sagittal* plane.

TABLE 1.1   **ANATOMIC PLANES**

PLANE	DIRECTION OF PLANE	DIVIDING INTO
Sagittal	Front-to-back (anterior-posterior)	Right and left parts (sections)
Coronal (Frontal)	Side-to-side (lateral)	Front and back parts (sections)
Transverse (Horizontal)	Across	Upper and lower parts (sections)

The plane dividing the body into front and back parts is known as the *coronal* plane. It is obviously at right angles to a sagittal section, or plane. The The third plane, *transverse,* is at right angles to both of the others, dividing the body or structure into upper and lower parts. This is sometimes ambiguously referred to as a *cross section.*

Table 1.2 lists terms of direction and location that should be known fully and thoroughly by the student of anatomy. The list is not exhausive, and a glossary of such terms to assist in spatial orientation might prove of value to the beginning student. Such a glossary is found in Appendix I.

TABLE 1.2   **TERMS OF DIRECTION AND LOCATION**

TERM	SYNONYM	MEANING
Anterior	Ventral	Toward the front or belly side
Posterior	Dorsal	Toward the back or rear side
Superior	Cranial, cephalad	Toward the head or upper end
Inferior	Caudad	Toward the tail or lower end
Medial	Mesial	Toward the midline or median plane
Lateral		Away from the midline
Proximal		Toward the point of attachment
Distal		Away from the point of attachment

Latin Nomenclature

With the great weight placed upon it during the early years of recorded science, Latin has remained the official language in the science of anatomy. The reason for this is clear. There were serious problems in nomenclature, what with the poor communications and coordination of study in past centuries:

> At an earlier time there was much confusion in the anatomical nomenclature, due to the multiplicity of names and the lack of uniformity in using them. Various names were applied to the same organs and great diversity of usage prevailed, not only between various countries, but also even among authors of the same country. Comparatively recently, however, great improvement was made by the formulation of a comprehensive system of anatomical nomenclature. This system was first adopted by the German Anatomical Society at a meeting in Basle (Basel), in 1895, and is hence called the Basle Nomina Anatomica, or briefly, the BNA. The

BNA provides each term in Latin form, which is especially desirable for international usage. Each nation, however, is expected to translate the terms into its own language, wherever it is deemed preferable for every-day usage.[2]

Since the Basel meeting anatomists have met repeatedly to standardize the nomenclature further. Revisions in terminology are identified by the place or date of the meeting; for example, JNA refers to the meeting that took place in Jena, Austria. More recently the International Congress of Anatomists, meeting in Paris in 1955, agreed on further revisions. The identifying signature to terms coming from that meeting is now NA or NAIC, referring simply to *Nomina Anatomica* or *Nomina Anatomica* of the International Congress.

Students beginning their studies of anatomy will meet with terms derived from any of those meetings. Older texts, for example, use an older terminology. Professors and clinicians trained in an older terminology tend to retain those terms in their everyday usage. And, occasionally, references will provide the reader with all alternatives. The most recent references appear to be moving away from nomenclature of the eponym variety, that is, those terms using the proper name of an individual; for example, the student of speech and hearing will encounter the Eustachian tube, the organ of Corti, the ventricle of Morgagni, and so on. In this text, a goodly portion of the terminology attempts to follow that pattern, without complete success, in that it uses a large proportion of BNA terminology, with a liberal sprinkling of newer terms, with Anglicized forms, and with retention of a few of the original Latin forms that have yet to be Anglicized.

One serious error frequently committed by students could be avoided easily by following this suggestion: When in doubt, never guess as to the meaning of a word or term—always look it up in the proper reference. It is suggested that a medical dictionary be available during this study, for it is the rare student who has sufficient background in languages to discern the meaning and pronunciation of all the terms used. For quick reference to definitions of terms used herein, along with guides to their pronunciation, the student should use the Glossary in Appendix I of the present book.

TYPES OF ANATOMICAL STUDY

Applied anatomy is the study of the structure of the organism, in terms of the specific functioning of mechanisms, as it affects the behavior of the organism. The student of applied anatomy evaluates not only the theoretical aspects of anatomy, but also the practical aspects, with regard to the living organism in normal and abnormal states. Such an approach is a blending of other means of studying anatomy. *Systematic anatomy* undertakes the study by emphasizing the various systems of the body: respiratory, digestive, nervous, and so on. *Regional, or topographic, anatomy* concentrates on special areas or sections and considers every aspect of each area under study, including its structure, the relationships of all the parts, and the relationships of the area to others. *Sectional anatomy* is the study of the body as it has been divided into morphologic planes or sections, relating all structures found within this plane.

In this text all approaches are used insofar as they pertain to speech and hearing, although the emphasis is on applied anatomy. Systematic anatomy is used especially in considering speech production; regional anatomy is the major approach to hearing. Sectional anatomy is used in discussing pathology and clinical application of the information gleaned from other approaches.

[2]J. B. Schaeffer, *Morris' Human Anatomy* (11th ed.), New York: McGraw-Hill, 1953.

chapter 2

STRUCTURAL COMPOSITION
OF THE ORGANISM

To help in the understanding of the differing structural components of the human body it is important to understand as much about each of those components as possible. Yet with obvious limitations upon the student, the teacher, and the text, exploring in great depth and detail is impossible. Perhaps, as an analogy, it could be said that to appreciate and understand your own home, it is not necessary to understand the complete chemical and physical nature of the wood, the wire, the pipe, the glass, the nail, and so on, which go into the making of that home. To be sure, one must know the limitations and capabilities of those components. So it is in the study of the anatomy for speech and hearing: there is much to know in depth and detail but it will have to suffice to present but a survey and overview of the structural characteristics of the tissues of the body.

GENERAL NATURE OF THE STRUCTURE

The structural and functional unit of the organism is the cell. The study of cells is known as *cytology;* the study of cells in groups is known as *histology;* and the study of the growth of cells into the form the organism finally takes is known as *embryology.* Groups of cells acting harmoniously together form what is known as *tissue,* which is an aggregation of similarly specialized cells united in the performance of a particular function. Such cells need not be retained within the confines of a circumscribed area, but may represent a fairly widely distributed aggregation. Examples of tissues with which the speech and hearing specialist has to deal are *muscular tissue, connective tissue,* and *nervous tissue.*

Muscular Tissue

In general, muscular tissue has one function: It performs mechanical work by contracting, that is, by becoming shorter and thicker. In so doing, the muscle approximates its two ends and thus controls the position and movement of various structures. Some muscles in the hollow viscera, in the vascular system, and in various ducts of the body control the lumen of the passages in such a way as to propel the contents of the passages in a single direction.

There are two major classes of muscular tissue: (1) *smooth,* or *involuntary* and (2) *striated,* or *voluntary.* A third type, *cardiac,* is a combination of these two, being striated in structure but involuntary in function. We shall be concerned with the striated variety, sometimes called "skeletal" because of its control of the skeleton of the body.

Connective Tissue

Connective tissue is represented by a number of subclasses; for example, connective tissue "proper," cartilage, and bone. The common characteristic among these subclasses is the abundance of intercellular material, which differs from class to class, accounting for the physical condition of the type under consideration. For example, in cartilage the material is generally characterized by fibers of some type that furnish the rigidity and firmness required.

Among the types of connective tissue proper found in speech and hearing mechanisms are loose, dense, regular, and connective tissue with special properties. Loose connective tissue can be described as being collagenous, strong, and white; dense connective tissue is a thicker, more compact, and more elastic material than the loose type.

Regular connective tissue is structured of parallel, collagenous bundles of fibers that give great resistance to stretching. It is appropriately found in tendons, ligaments, and other fibrous membranes. Connective tissue with special properties is structured in relationship to its location and function, and varies considerably. Included in this category are mucous membrane tissue, elastic tissue of the vocal folds, reticular tissue, adipose (fat) tissue, and others.

CARTILAGE TISSUE

Characteristically, cartilage has as firm a mass as its intercellular material, and thus retains its shape under various conditions. There are three types of cartilage (depending upon the composition of the interstitial substance): *hyaline, elastic,* and *fibrous.* Hyaline cartilage is the most common. It is somewhat flexible and elastic. It makes up the majority of the embryonic skeleton and is permanently located at the ventral ends of the ribs, on the surfaces of bones within joints, and in the skeleton of the respiratory tract. Elastic cartilage is considerably more flexible and elastic and is typically found in the epiglottis, the eustachian tube, the external auditory canal, and in the corniculate and cuneiform cartilages of the larynx. Fibrous cartilage is composed of interlacing strands of fiber firmly bound together to absorb shock and to cushion skeletal units from damage. It is found in locations at which extreme stress can be focused, such as in the intervertebral discs and at the symphysis pubis.

> CLINICAL NOTE
>
> Changes in the phonatory abilities often are related to laryngeal cartilage changes, an occurrence common in man's aging process. Changes in the structure of the cartilage from one type to another, or even to a type of bone tissue, restrict the flexibility and mobility of laryngeal structures, having distinct effects upon the phonatory act. Also, the cartilage of the eustachian tube changes in structure and in location as the individual ages. The growing child presents a horizontally oriented tube; the adult generally has one with a decided slope from ear to throat.

BONE TISSUE

The skeletal support of the body is provided by bone. It further protects organs found in the skull and thorax: the brain, the heart and the lungs, among other organs. Bone houses the marrow, so vital in its relationship to the blood. In this type of shape-retaining tissue, the interstitial substance is extremely hard, being composed mainly of inorganic salts. Bone is often classified according to its type: spongy or compact. The spongy variety is irregular in cellular arrangement, simpler, and developmentally previous to the compact type. The compact type is more regular in arrangement and more complex. All bone, however, is plastic and responsive to changes in its environment and health.

Classification is made also according to shape: flat, long, short, and irregular. The flat bones are found in the skull, the long bones in the extremities, and the short and irregular bones in the hands, feet, and vertebrae. Mobility of bones is provided through joints. The articulation of a bone with another, at a true joint, is known as a *diarthrosis*. Where bones articulate, but where no movement is present, the joining is known as a *synarthrosis*.

Thus, it can be seen that connective tissue is an important part of the organism. Certainly, cartilage and bone are obvious supporting structures to the organs and tissues so importantly related to speech and hearing. Also, connective tissue proper must be recognized for its importance in the protection and the interconnection of other types of tissues.

Nervous Tissue

The functions of nervous tissue are to receive stimuli from the environment, to transform these stimuli into nervous excitations, and to transmit them to nervous centers; this tissue is further obligated to transmit nerve impulses from important neural centers to muscles and glands, as well as to integrate and coordinate the sending and receiving of all impulses throughout the body. Nervous tissue allows the organism to maintain its integrity and economy by coordinating the functions of the various organs and systems in adjusting to events, to stimuli. Further detailed description of nervous tissue will be found in Chapter 8, "The Nervous Mechanism."

ORGANS AND SYSTEMS

The cells and tissues of the organism are the building units from which are formed parts of the body having special functions: the organs and the systems. There remains some difference of opinion regarding the nature of organs, and classification of them varies according to location and function, illustrated by labeling the tongue as the organ of speech to a more restricted use in labeling the nose as the organ of olfaction. Other such organs germane to this text include the throat, the ear, the larynx, the bronchial tree, and the lungs. This list, obviously, is not intended to be exhaustive. The speech and hearing behavior of an organism is not the product of one organ nor a series of organs, but of the organism in its totality. There is no simple one-to-one relationship between normal or abnormal communication and a single organ. Each operates in synergy with others of its system, and each system in synergy with others of the body, to produce the behavioral characteristics of that individual.

The term "organ-system" denotes the expansion of the organ concept beyond simple structure to include acknowledgment of function. In fact, in considering an organ-system, one considers a series of structures that performs one of the very fundamental and basic biologic acts. Thus, we find the respiratory organ-system, the digestive organ-system, and the reproductive organ-system. The two major organ-systems of respiration and digestion play the predominant roles in the speech act. The digestive system is of importance for the health of the organism, of course. But because it provides many of the organs involved in the speaking and listening processes, the cephalad portion above the esophagus bears the main burden in any act of oral communication. On the other hand, the entire respiratory system plays a most important role in the speech behavior of the individual.

CLINICAL NOTE

In the respiratory organ-system, pathologies affecting oral communication frequently lie in the larynx, the voice-producing apparatus. Voice defects such as hoarseness or breathiness result when there is tissue change or new growth on the vocal folds. In the digestive organ-system there may be a structural defect in the roof of the mouth, the hard palate, in clefts of the palate. A defect in communicative abilities may result, especially in the resonance characteristics of the voice.

Relationships of other organ-systems to speech and hearing behavior have been suggested by speech and hearing experts down through the years, but up to the present the strength of these relationships has not been demonstrated. It is plausible, however, to consider the endocrine system, for example, as having an important relationship to speech. Illustrative of such a condition might be a thyroid deficiency, which affects the organism generally and the mechanism of phonation specifically. Other systems might be mentioned, but, again, the complexities and interrelationships are not directly pertinent to the purposes of this text. Further study and research by both student and experimenter should expose the strength of those relationships.

THE RESPIRATORY ORGAN-SYSTEM

The respiratory organ-system, in providing oxygen to the body, must supply a continuously changing body of air from the environment. This air traverses the passageways from nose and mouth through the pharynx into the larynx, trachea, bronchi, and the elements of the lungs, and is subsequently utilized in the voice-producing, or phonatory, process that occurs in the larynx. Although the speech and hearing student concentrates on the actions of the larynx in voice production, he must never lose sight of the more fundamental and vital function of the larynx: As part of the respiratory system it provides a passageway for the column of air, controls its ingress and egress, acts as a defense mechanism for the lower respiratory structures, and serves as a valve inhibiting the flow of air when the body so demands.

CLINICAL NOTE

The individual who has had a laryngectomy (surgical removal of the larynx) has not only a speech defect because of his inability to produce sound, but also other difficulties that are as debilitating. He finds it difficult or impossible to blow his nose, to smell, and to blow out matches, and he may have trouble lifting heavy objects.

THE DIGESTIVE ORGAN-SYSTEM

The digestive system presents infrequent pathologic instances in which a speech defect may result. The deglutition (swallowing) apparatus is of vital importance, of course, in providing means for passing ingested food into the pharynx and esophagus for life-maintaining purposes. This same mechanism is also used for the communicative acts of articulation (the formation of different acoustic symbols used to represent the message) and of resonance (the acoustic adaptation of the laryngeal tone to produce the characteristic voice quality as well as certain of the speech symbols).

CLINICAL NOTE

A tongue that is either partially or totally defective may produce inaccurate articulation and slovenly speech. The nasal quality of cleft-palate speakers is another example of defective digestive-system structures. Edentulous (toothless) persons have problems in making certain speech sounds and, in a more complicated way, tongue-thrusting may produce different articulation of speech sounds as well as aberrant occlusal relationships of the dental arches.

The speech clinician, or pathologist, should determine the state or condition of the two vital organ-systems in the case of a speech or voice defect. Although it is an oversimplification, the old expression that speech is an overlaid function is basically useful. Detailed information on the organ-systems is essential to an accurate impression of the structure and function of the mechanisms so important to speech and hearing.

CLINICAL NOTE

As examples of the interdependent relationship between the two organ-systems, speech pathologists may find occasional cases having both pathologies. Cancerous conditions of the oral cavity that require extensive surgical excision, traumatic events that involve the pharynges, and paralyses of common musculature are examples. These affect both the digestive system (swallowing and mastication, for example) and the respiratory tract; further, they would have effects upon the resonance characteristics, if not the phonatory characteristics, of the voice. Also, in many of such examples, we find occasional overlap into the auditory system, where the means of transmission is the eustachian tube into the middle ear.

chapter 3

THE ORO-NASAL REGION

The anatomical and physiological importance of the oro-nasal region to the functions of speech and hearing is so obvious that it sometimes overshadows the importance of other closely related areas. It is in the oro-nasal region that the mechanisms offer the beginning and the end of the processes related to speech; it is this region that provides the ingress for air en route to its pulmonary destination; and it is this same region that provides the resonance and articulatory functions for the sound resulting from control of this air as it returns to the environment.

CONNECTIVE TISSUE

The most important type of connective tissue in the oro-nasal region is bone tissue. Some cartilage is present to provide additional skeletal support. Even though predominant attention will be focused upon the oral regions, the importance of the entire *skull,* in which the oro-nasal region is located, should not be overlooked, and the student is urged to familiarize himself with those structures of the skull which are simply listed or indicated, but for which detailed descriptions are lacking owing to space limitations.

The bony skull is divided into two areas: the *cranium* supporting and protecting the brain, and the *facial skeleton* more closely associated with the speech production region. (See Figures 3–1 and 3–2.)

The Cranium

The *cranium* is composed of eight bones: one occipital, two parietal, two temporal, one sphenoid, one frontal, and one ethmoid. Besides containing and protecting the brain, this part of the skull houses the hearing mechanism and contributes to the area affecting speech. The cranium itself is supported directly by the vertebrae and blends effectively with the facial skeleton with little sign of differentiation or demarcation.

Although the importance of their function cannot be denied, the bones of the superior region (vertex) are not of primary interest to the present discussion. Further, though the occipital and the parietal bones comprise large portions of the cranium region, they do not pertain as importantly to speech and hearing as do the other bones. Thus, primary attention will be placed upon the *frontal, ethmoid, sphenoid,* and *temporal* bones at this time.

THE FRONTAL BONE

The *frontal bone* provides the smooth, convex surface of the forehead. Inferiorly, it extends from the superior margin of the orbit of the eye; laterally, it extends through the temporal fossa (temple); and superiorly, it extends to the vertex (crown) to articulate with the parietal bones. From front to back, this bone articulates also with the nasal, maxillary, lacrimal, and zygomatic bones of the facial skeleton group, and with the sphenoid, ethmoid, and parietal bones of the cranium. The greater wing of the sphenoid bone, on the lateral surface of the cranium, intervenes between the frontal and temporal bones, so that there is no connection between these two bones.

The frontal bone is significant because (1) it houses the frontal sinus, which is of some importance to the functioning of the nasal area and ultimately to the health of the individual, and (2) it serves as attachment for muscles related to speech activities.

The frontal sinus is a part of the sinus system of the skull. The system is actually a series of spaces within the skull bones (mainly those of the facial skeleton), but its function has been the subject of considerable debate. Outstanding among the suggested purposes of the sinuses are (1) lightening the skull, (2) providing for better balance of the skull, (3) resonance for the voice, (4) expanding the area served by the nose in warming, moistening, and perhaps filtering the incoming air.

CLINICAL NOTE

Although little is known about the actual contributions of the sinuses to normal speech, it has been believed that their main contributions are to the resonance of the voice, producing a chamber that either vibrates sympathetically or as a *cul-de-sac* chamber. More important, however, are the pathologic aspects of the sinuses: Inflamed, infected, and structurally defective sinuses are major contributors to various speech and hearing disorders. It is a commonplace to find "sinus trouble" in the histories of individuals who suffer from loss of hearing as well as among those with some type of speech defect, especially voice problems.

The frontal sinus itself is composed of paired spaces located one at each side of the midline and extending to various heights in the frontal bone. The total effect is pyramidal; one wall of this pyramid separates the right from the left frontal sinus. The frontal sinus communicates with the nasal fossa through the frontonasal duct and opens into either the frontal recess or the middle meatus of the nose.

As in all the paranasal sinuses, this structure is lined with mucous membrane that is continuous with the lining of the nasal mucous membrane, and has a similar composition, histologically speaking, including the cilia of the epithelium. The beating of the cilia here and elsewhere serves to remove foreign matter from the sinus as well as to cause the outflow of natural secretions, normal and pathologic, produced by actions of the tissues. These cilia are microscopic structures. They are of great importance to normal functioning of both the sinuses and the nasal (and other ciliated) passages; removal in disease and surgery generally results in malfunction and thus a defect in warming, filtering, and especially, moistening the air and passageways.

THE ETHMOID BONE

The *ethmoid bone* is found immediately inferior and posterior to the frontal bone. It is a single midline bone, light in weight, spongy in composition, and cuboidal in shape. (See Figure 3–3.) This bone forms important surfaces of the cranial floor, the roof of the nose, and the two eye orbits. The bone is composed of four parts: a horizontal or cribriform plate (forming part of the cranial floor), a perpendicular plate (contributing to the structure of the nasal septum), and the two lateral labyrinths (containing the ethmoid air cells).

The ethmoid air cells are sinuslike spaces that are lined with mucous membrane. They occupy the space between the orbits as extremely variable cavities. They may number as few as three or as many as eighteen; the larger the

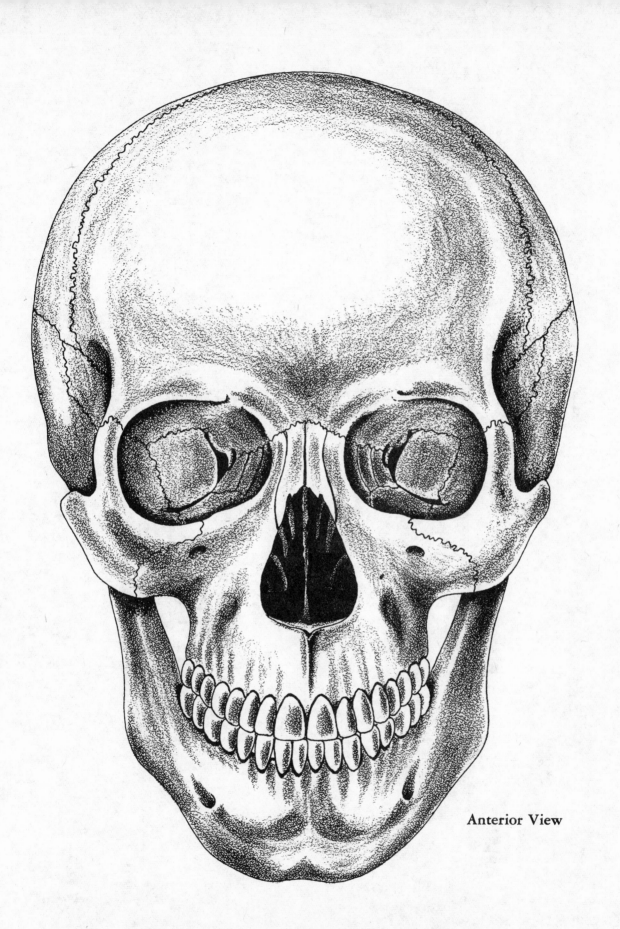

Anterior View

Figure 3–1.
Bones of the Skull: Anterior View

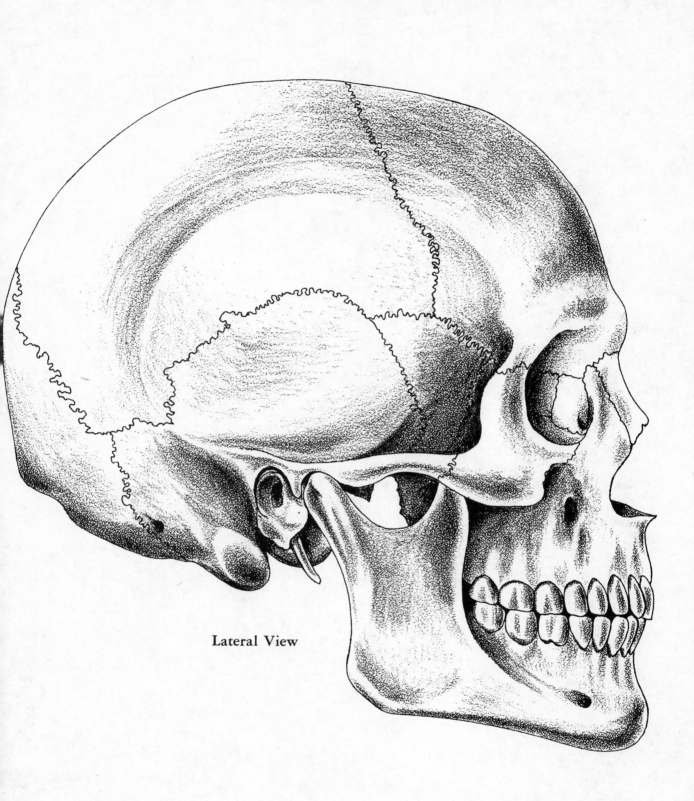

Lateral View

Figure 3-2.
Bones of the Skull: Lateral View

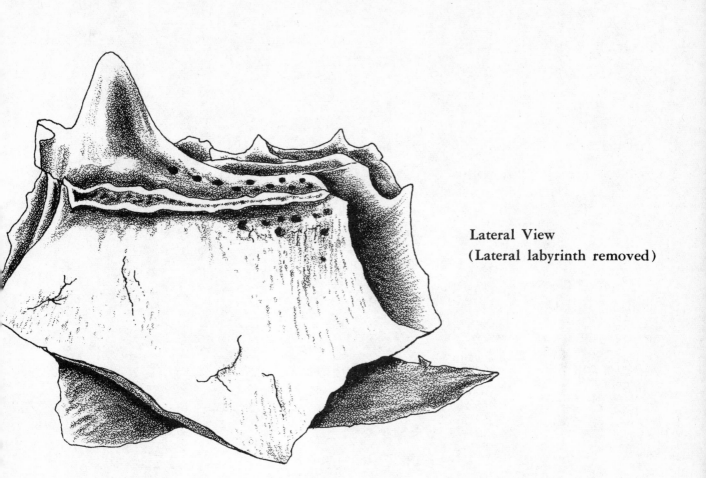

Lateral View
(Lateral labyrinth removed)

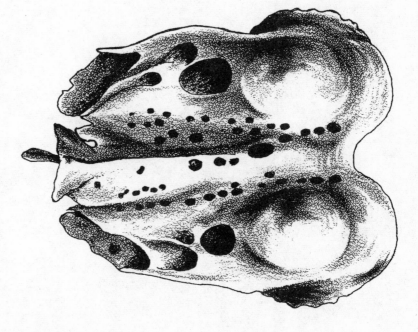

Superior View

Figure 3-3.
Ethmoid Bone

number, however, the smaller are the individual cells. Occasionally, a cell will invade a bordering bone; as a result, such spaces as the anterior ethmoid cell may well be named the posterior frontal sinus because of its location in the frontal bone. Other examples occur in other neighboring bones, but with irregularity.

CLINICAL NOTE

The ethmoid air cells—or ethmoid sinuses, as they are sometimes called —act structurally and physiologically much as the other sinuses of the skull. Sinusitis may localize in the ethmoid area, for example, providing signs and symptoms similar to those of the other sinuses, and providing the same general sequelae, but necessitating special technics for treatment and surgery because of the uniqueness of location and relationship to both the central nervous system and the eye. Speech and hearing problems rarely develop from the single source, but commonly involve the ethmoid sinuses.

THE SPHENOID BONE

The *sphenoid bone* (Figure 3–4) is immediately posterior to the ethmoid bone. This complex and irregular bone is situated at the base of the skull, just anterior to the temporal as well as to the basilar part of the occipital bones. The sphenoid bone is a relatively large midline structure, with projections from it oriented so as to give the entire bone a strong resemblance to a bat with its wings outstretched, each side having a greater wing and a lesser wing. There are two pterygoid processes projecting inferiorly that are of considerable importance to structures and tissues affecting speech and hearing.

The body of the sphenoid is cuboidal and, to a great extent, it is hollowed into two separate spaces: the sphenoid sinuses. These sinuses have their openings into the nasal passages. The superior surface of the body of the sphenoid bone is a smooth surface, deeply indented for housing the pituitary body, articulating anteriorly with the cribriform plate of the ethmoid bone, and posteriorly with the basilar part of the occipital bone. The lateral surfaces of the body are united with the great wings as well as with the medial pterygoid plate on either side. The anterior surface, forming a part of the roof of the nasal cavity, is divided at its midline by the sphenoidal crest, a vertically oriented ridge of bone which articulates with the perpendicular plate of the ethmoid and forms a part of the nasal septum. Further articulation with the ethmoid bone is provided by the lateral margins which are roughly associated with the ethmoid labyrinth. Inferiorly, the body of the sphenoid presents a rough surface for the soft tissues of the pharynx, along with a ridge—the sphenoidal rostrum—with its projecting lamina (the vaginal processes) directed medialward from the medial pterygoid plates.

The great wing of the sphenoid is attached to part of the lateral surface of the body, and extends first laterally, then superiorly. The wing comprises part of the floor of the cranium, supporting the convolutions of the temporal lobe of the brain. It is penetrated by numerous foramina and canals, providing access to the brain for various nerves and blood vessels. The greater wing articulates at various positions along its perimeter with both squamous and petrous portions of the temporal bone, with the parietal bone, with the frontal bone, and with the zygomatic bone. In addition, the greater wing serves, in part, as a portion of the orbit, as the container for the cartilaginous part of the eustachian tube, as points of attachment for the sphenomandibular ligament and the tensor veli palatine muscle, and as an extension to the attachment for the external pterygoid muscle.

The lesser, or small, wing of the sphenoid bone is comprised of two thin, triangular plates of bone arising from the upper and anterior parts of the body, and projecting laterally or horizontally. As in the case of the greater wing, the superior surface of this structure is flat and serves to support part of the frontal lobe of the brain. The inferior surface forms a part of the roof of the orbit. The anterior surface articulates with the frontal bone. The posterior border is smooth and rounded, and is received into the lateral fissure of the brain. The optic foramen pierces the foot of the small wing dividing it into two roots that attach to the body; through the optic foramen pass the optic nerve and the ophthalmic artery.

Descending inferiorly from the juncture of the body and great wing on either side are the pterygoid processes, each with its two pterygoid plates. These two plates, the lateral and medial, are fused superiorly and anteriorly (in their upper regions), diverging posteriorly to create a V-shaped space, the pterygoid fossa. It is this fossa that gives rise to the internal pterygoid and the tensor veli palatine muscles.

The lateral pterygoid plate is a broad, thin, everted sheet forming a part of the infratemporal fossa on its lateral surface and part of the scaphoid fossa on its medial surface; its lateral surface also gives origin to the external pterygoid muscle and its medial surface (forming the pterygoid fossa) gives rise to the internal pterygoid muscle. The medial pterygoid plate, on the other hand, is a longer and narrower sheet of bone than the lateral plate; it curves sideways at its extremity into a hooklike process, the pterygoid hamulus, around which the tensor veli palatine muscle tendon glides. The lateral surface of this plate forms part of the boundary for the pterygoid fossa, and its medial surface constitutes the lateral boundary of the posterior choana of the nasal passage. Superiorly, the medial plate is prolonged into the vaginal process that articulates with the sphenoidal process of the palatine bone and with the ala (wing) of the vomer. The posterior border of this plate provides attachment for the pharyngeal aponeurosis as well as the superior constrictor muscle that arises from its inferior one-third. At about the middle of this border is a projection, the processus tubarious, that supports the pharyngeal end of the eustachian tube.

CLINICAL NOTE

Although specific attention has not been drawn to the sphenoid bone in speech and hearing pathologies, it does demonstrate some few deviations indirectly related to these functions. Perhaps more common is the sinusitis that involves the sphenoid sinus. In some surgical procedures for palatal defects, the hamular process is fractured or severed, or the tensor veli palatine muscle is removed, so that tension is no longer applied to the repaired palate.

TEMPORAL BONES

On either side of the cranium are the two *temporal bones,* contributing to the lateral walls of the skull and to a portion of the base of the skull. (See Figure 3–5.) Each temporal bone contributes significantly to speech and hearing processes, affording attachment to muscles of mastication, of the neck, tongue, and pharynx; it also houses the major portion of the peripheral hearing mechanisms. It is thus a bone of considerable importance to the anatomist and to the speech clinician. The temporal bone is typically studied as a five-part bone; these parts are the *squamous, mastoid, petrous, tympanic,* and *styloid* portions.

The *squamous* portion of the temporal bone is the relatively large, fan-shaped, thin part that also forms part of the temporal fossa. This smooth and convex area provides origin for the temporal muscle, a muscle of mastication. Projecting ventrally from the lower part of the squama is the long and arched zygomatic process; the inferior border of this process provides origin for the masseter muscle, another masticatory muscle. The end of the zygomatic process is rough and serrated for articulation with the zygomatic (malar) bone, an important member of the facial skeleton. The entire squamous portion of the temporal bone articulates with the parietal bone, as well as with the greater wing of the sphenoid bone.

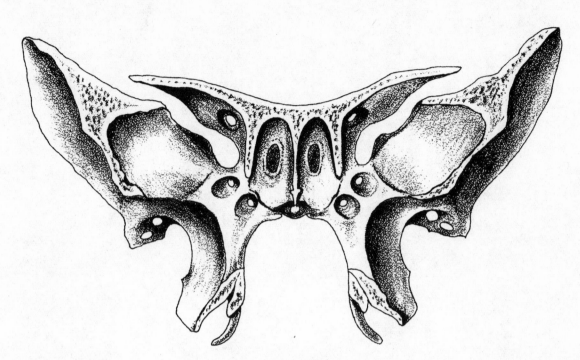

Anterior View

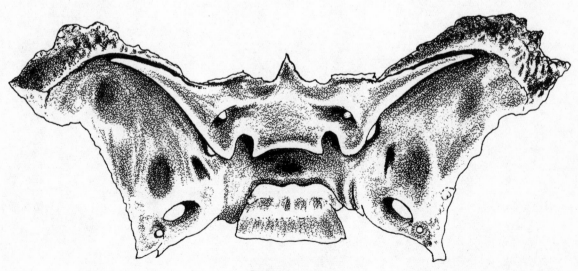

Superior View

Figure 3–4.
Sphenoid Bone

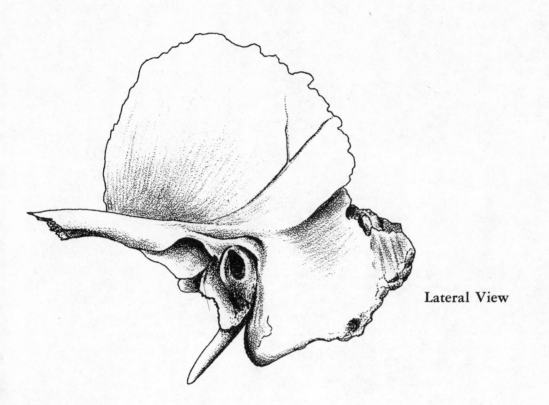

Lateral View

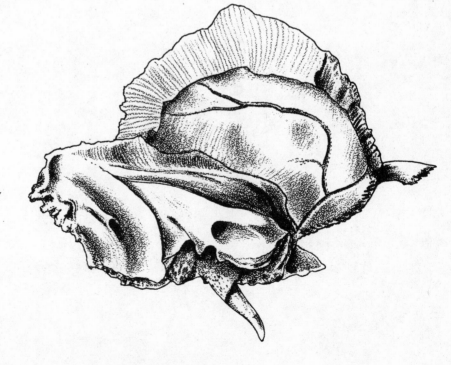

Superior View

Figure 3-5.
Temporal Bone

Inferior to the preceding portion is the large and bulky *mastoid* portion of the temporal bone; this is the most posterior part of the bone. A large conical projection beneath this portion is the mastoid process, giving attachment to several muscles among which are the digastric of the suprahyoid group and sternocleidomastoid of the cervical region. The mastoid process is composed of many air cells of irregular size, shape, and number; near the apex of the process, these air cells are small, but become larger at the upper portion. At the uppermost region is a larger- and irregular-sized cavity—the *tympanic antrum*—communicating with the mastoid air cells in one direction and with the middle ear cavity in the other. All of these cavities are lined with mucous membrane.

The *petrous* portion of the temporal bone is a pyramidal structure that is found at the base of the skull projecting medially between the occipital and the sphenoid bones. It is, of course, fused with the squamous and mastoid portions of the temporal bone. The sides of the pyramid are oriented somewhat anteriorly and posteriorly; the anterior surface presents marks for the convolutions of the brain, a prominence—the *arcuate eminence*—under which is found the superior semicircular canal of the vestibular system, and a very thin portion of bone—the *tegmen tympani*—beneath which is the tympanum, or middle ear, of the hearing system. The posterior surface of the petrous portion presents orifices of importance, including the opening to the internal auditory canal, which is the largest, and the tiny and difficult-to-find vestibular aqueduct.

The internal auditory meatus, or canal, carries the facial (Cranial VII) and the auditory (Cranial VIII) nerves, the nervus intermedius to the chorda tympani nerve, and the internal auditory branch of the basilar artery. This canal extends laterally and posteriorly about one centimeter (less than half an inch) uninterrupted. There is then a bony shelf, oriented horizontally, dividing the canal into a smaller upper and a larger lower portion; this shelf is the crista falciformis. The upper area—the area cribrosa superior—opens into two further canals, one leading nerves into the utricle and the superior and lateral semicircular canals of the vestibular mechanism, and the second but much larger canal being the opening of the Fallopian aqueduct, which transmits the facial nerve. Below the crista falciformis are three groupings of openings: the nerves from the saccule leaving through the area cribrosa media; the nerves from the posterior semicircular canal, through the singular foramen; and the nerves from the auditory receptor, the cochlea, arranged spirally around the central canal of the cochlea.

The inferior surface of the petrous portion of the temporal bone forms a part of the exterior surface of the base of the skull, along with the occipital and sphenoid bones. Its rough and irregular surface presents the origin of the levator veli palatine muscle and a part of the cartilaginous auditory tube (of Eustachius), the carotid canal for the internal carotid artery, the jugular fossa for the bulb of the internal jugular vein, and the styloid process.

At the angle of joining of the petrous and squamous portions of the temporal bones are two canals that pass into the tympanum (middle ear cavity). The upper one carries the tensor tympani muscle, which is housed within this canal and is attached through its tendon to the malleus bone. The lower canal is larger; it is the bony portion of the auditory tube, connecting tympanum with nasopharynx.

The *tympanic* portion of the temporal bone is a thin, everted, and somewhat curled structure that forms all of the anterior and inferior, and part of the posterior, walls of the bony portion of the external auditory meatus (canal). The remainder of the canal wall, the superior and part of the posterior wall, is composed of the temporal squama. At the lateral border of the tympanic portion it is roughened and free to provide attachment for the cartilaginous portion of the external auditory canal. More medially, the canal is grooved through part of its circumference, the tympanic sulcus, which receives the tympanic membrane. Its very thin anterior-inferior surface contacts a part of the parotid gland.

The external auditory meatus is composed of both cartilaginous and bony sections. The former is discussed in Chapter 7 in association with other cartilaginous structures of the external ear. The bony portion of the canal is about two-thirds of the entire canal, oriented forward and somewhat downward, and narrowest at its medial or internal end. The cutaneous lining of the canal, unlike the cartilaginous portion, does not have any hairs, nor are there any glands. This lining continues over the lateral surface of the tympanic membrane, forming one of its layers.

The *styloid process* of the temporal bone is a slender, cylindrical spur projecting downward and forward from the inferior aspect of the temporal bone. Its length varies, from 5 mm (about ⅜ inch) to 50 mm (about 2 inches); it may even approximate the hyoid bone. The process may be literally engulfed by the vaginal process of the tympanic portion or it may be quite lengthy, as indicated. This process gives attachment to three muscles and two ligaments: the stylohyoid, styloglossus, and stylopharyngeal muscles, and the stylohyoid and stylomandibular ligaments.

The Facial Skeleton

The *facial skeleton* is formed by fourteen bones of the skull which surround the nose and mouth and which, together with the cranial bones, provide for the reception of the eye. These fourteen exclude the more movable bones of the middle ear (ossicles) and the hyoid, all of which are discussed in some detail in Chapter 7. Those specifically under consideration and upon which some emphasis will be placed herein are the *zygomatic, nasal,* and *lacrimal* bones—which are somewhat less important for speech purposes but important as far as skeletal structure is concerned—and the *vomer, inferior nasal concha, palatine, maxilla,* and *mandible.* All but the vomer and mandible are paired.

The *zygomatic* (malar, cheek) *bone* is quadrangular and forms the prominence of the cheek; it articulates with the maxilla, the temporal, and the frontal bones and forms a large part of the floor and lateral wall of the orbit. The *nasal bones* are two small oblong bones placed together at the bridge of the nose; they articulate with the frontal, ethmoid, and maxillary bones. The *lacrimal bone* forms part of the antero-medial wall of the orbit; it is the smallest and most fragile of the facial bones and articulates with the ethmoid, frontal, maxillary, and inferior nasal concha.

The *vomer* (Latin: *plowshare*) is an unpaired bone that forms the lower and posterior part of the septum of the nose. (See Figure 3–6.) It is a midline structure, thin, roughly quadrilateral, and frequently bent or deflected to one side at its anterior end. The long sloping anterior border articulates in its lower portion with the triangular septal cartilage and in its superior portion with the perpendicular plate of the ethmoid bone. Its superior border, which is the thickest part of the bone, divides into two alae with an intervening groove to receive the sphenoid rostrum. Its posterior border is free and forms the operating wall between the posterior choanae (nares). The inferior border is received into the groove formed by the two halves of the maxillary bones and the palatine bones; this groove is part of the nasal crest.

The *inferior nasal concha* (inferior turbinate) is a scroll-like bone horizontally oriented along the lateral wall of the nasal cavity, separating the inferior from the middle meatus. (See Figure 3–7.) The concha itself is a thin, spongy type of bone having a convex medial surface and a concave lateral surface. It is more pointed at its posterior end than at its anterior. This bone is attached by its superior border with the conchal crest of the maxilla, as well as with the ethmoid, lacrimal, and palatine bones.

The *palatine bone* is an L-shaped bone situated at the posterior end of the nasal cavity between the maxilla, which is forward, and the medial pterygoid plate of the sphenoid, which is behind. (See Figure 3–8.) It has two parts: the

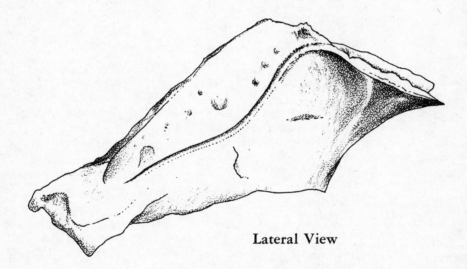

Lateral View

Figure   3–6.
Vomer Bone

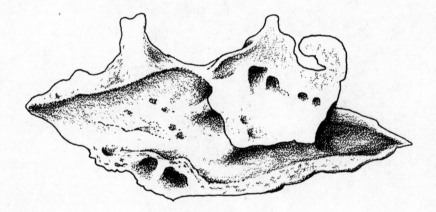

Lateral View

Figure   3-7.
Inferior Nasal Turbinate Bone

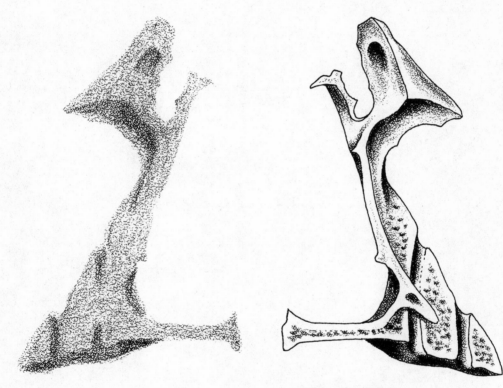

Posterior View

Figure 3–8.
Palatine Bones

vertical, or perpendicular, and the horizontal. There are also three processes: the pyramidal, orbital, and sphenoidal. The perpendicular part of the palatine bone is long and thin and presents two surfaces: lateral and medial. Its lateral surface (maxillary surface) is roughened for articulation with the nasal surface of the maxilla; its medial (nasal) surface is smooth and has three shallow depressions corresponding to the three nasal meatuses. It is this perpendicular portion of the L-shaped palatine bone which forms the major part of the posterior portion of the nasal cavity, although the latter is continued to its completion by the medial pterygoid plate of the sphenoid.

The horizontal part of the palatine bone, on the other hand, forms the posterior part of the floor of the nasal cavity, which causes it to compose the posterior portion of the roof of the oral cavity. Its superior, or nasal, surface is smooth and concave. Its inferior, or oral, surface is likewise concave but roughened. It forms the posterior extension of the hard palate. The anterior border of the horizontal part is roughened, and articulates with the palatine process of the maxillary bone. Its medial border is roughened for articulation with its fellow of the opposite side and is thickened to provide a continuation of the nasal crest (to receive the vomer), which prolongs posteriorly into the posterior nasal spine (for the attachment of m. uvula). The lateral border of the horizontal part of the palatine bone is united with the lower margin of the perpendicular part. The posterior border of this part is concave and free, and forms the source of attachment for the soft palate (velum).

The three processes of the palatine bone provide for articular surfaces with other facial and cranial bones. The pyramidal process (tuberosity) projects posteriorly and laterally to articulate with the tuberosity of the maxilla. The sphenoidal process is directed upward and medially to contribute to the wall of the nasal cavity and to articulate with the medial pterygoid plate, the pterygoid process (root), and the ala of the vomer. The orbital process is directed toward the orbit forming part of its floor as well as articulating with the maxilla, sphenoid concha, and ethmoid labyrinth.

The *maxilla* (upper jaw) is, next to the mandible (lower jaw), the largest of the facial bones. (See Figure 3–9.) The fusion of the two maxillae provides boundaries of three cavities: the roof of the mouth, the floor and lateral wall of the nose, and the floor of the orbit. The maxilla has a body and four processes, one of which supports the upper (maxillary) teeth. The pyramidal body has its base pointed toward the nasal cavity and contains the maxillary sinus. The four surfaces of the body meet, or articulate, with the opposite maxilla and the palatine bone, and form large parts of the floor of the orbit and the lateral wall of the nasal cavity.

Of some significance to speech are the four maxillary processes: frontal, alveolar, zygomatic, and palatine. The frontal process forms part of the lateral boundary of the nose and articulates with the frontal, nasal, and lacrimal bones. The alveolar process, thick and spongy, is crescentic in shape and contains eight alveoli (cavities) in which the upper teeth are lodged. The zygomatic (malar) process is small, rough, and triangular, articulating with the zygomatic (malar) bone.

The fourth maxillary process—the palatine—forms the greater portion of the floor of the nose and the roof of the mouth in its horizontal and medial projection from the sides of the crescent. This part forms about three-fourths of the hard palate. (See Figure 3–10.) The horizontal plate of the palatine bone completes it. The medial border of this process is roughened or serrated for articulation with its opposite; this suture line commences anteriorly at the incisive fossa. Extending laterally and anteriorly from this point to the space between the second incisor and the canine teeth is the suture line separating the palatine process of the maxilla from the premaxilla (incisive bone). The posterior border articulates with the horizontal plate of the palatine bone; this line of articulation is called the transverse suture. The previously mentioned midline suture continues through the palatine bone (horizontal process) and terminates in the posterior nasal spine. Superiorly along this suture, a raised portion presents the nasal crest, receiving the vomer; the crest extends forward to form the anterior nasal spine.

CLINICAL NOTE

Some of the people seen by speech and hearing therapists are those with palatal defects. These defects stem from embryologic developmental failure of fusion of the lines (sutures) of articulation. More commonly, clefts are found along the midline suture, with one process failing to grow to fuse with the opposite side; also occurring are clefts along the maxillary-premaxillary suture line, unilaterally or bilaterally separating the premaxilla (and its soft tissues) from the rest of the structures. Concomitant defects, such as dental or nasal deformities, frequently accompany the basic palatal failure. Further related problems result from faulty skeletal support of various muscle groups, so that deglutition, respiration, and even auditory difficulties may develop.

The *mandible* (lower jaw or inferior maxillary bone) is the largest and strongest of the bones of the face. (See Figure 3–11.) Its major biologic function is to support the teeth. The mandible is made up of a body shaped somewhat like a horseshoe; from each end a ramus ascends at nearly right angles to articulate with the temporal bone at the mandibular fossa. The two halves of the mandible fuse at the ventral midline at the symphysis menti, which is elevated at the point of the chin to form the mental protuberance. There are two lines on the mandible: the oblique line, which is a slight ridge running externally from low anteriorly to high posteriorly, and the mylohyoid line, running on the internal surface upward and backward toward the ramus. The lower, or mandibular, teeth are found on the alveolar border of the mandible, with its eight cavities.

The ramus (perpendicular portion) extends upward, ending in two prominent processes: the coronoid and the condyloid processes. The coronoid process is the most anterior of the two, and provides attachment for the temporalis and masseter muscles. The condyloid process rises to meet the articular disc of the temporomandibular joint at the mandibular fossa. The external pterygoid muscle attaches to the neck of this process. Inferiorly, the ramus terminates in the angle of the mandible, an important landmark.

The *hyoid bone,* located in the anterior part of the neck between the larynx and the mandible, is not considered a part of the facial skeleton; it is considered here because of its important association with structures commonly related to the bones discussed. It is sometimes called the lingual bone because it is the major supporting structure for the tongue. (See Figure 3–18). This bone is a U- or horseshoe-shaped bone, the bottom of the U being directed horizontally anteriorly and the two pairs of processes directed laterally and dorsally. Not only is the hyoid bone intimately related to the tongue, but it is of considerable importance in that it provides attachment for numerous muscles of the laryngeal region. It is suspended in its position by two thin bands from the tips of the styloid processes of the temporal bones. It has a body and two pairs of processes, the greater and the lesser cornua.

The body of the hyoid bone is roughly quadrilateral and is oriented across the ventral midline of the neck. The anterior surface is flattened and tilted, presenting a convex appearance. In the upper portion of the anterior surface is a transverse ridge running from side to side, dividing the body into two unequal portions. Infrequently, there is another ridge—perpendicular to the transverse ridge—which further divides the anterior surface, so that there are formed four areas to which muscles are attached. The posterior surface of the body of the

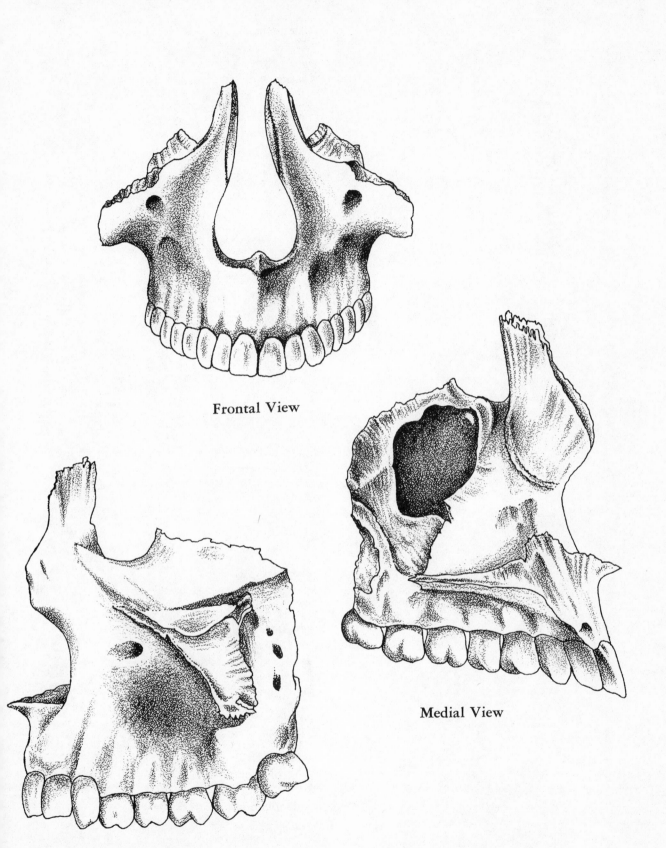

Frontal View

Lateral View

Medial View

Figure   3–9.
Maxillary Bone

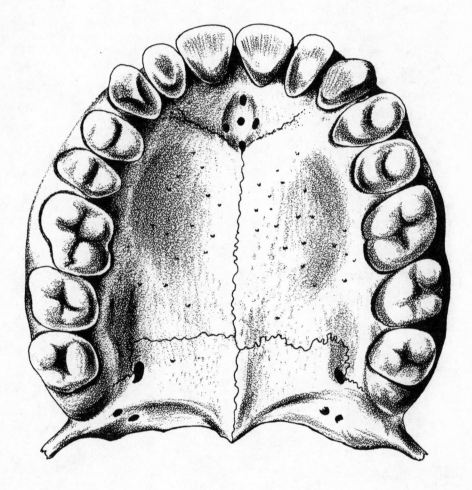

Figure 3–10.
Bony Palate

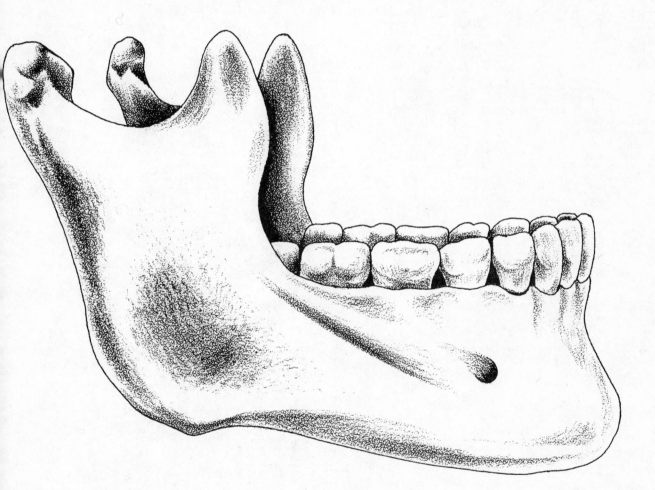

Figure   3-11.
Mandible with Adult Dentition

hyoid bone is deeply concave and is separated from the nearby epiglottis by the hyothyroid membrane and by loose areolar tissue. That membrane is attached to the hyoid bone at its superior border; the inferior border of the hyoid provides attachment for various muscles.

The larger of the two processes of the hyoid is the greater cornu, or horn. This pair is directed laterally and posteriorly, tapering from front to back, and ending in a tubercle. Until middle life, the connection between the greater cornu and the body of the hyoid is cartilaginous; ossification occurs thereafter.

The lesser cornua are smaller, conical bodies that project upward and backward from their points of attachment, at the junction of the body and the greater cornu. This attachment is usually fibrous in nature, and some authorities feel there is a true diarthrodial joint with the body and/or the greater cornu. The apex of the lesser cornu serves as the point of attachment for the stylohyoid ligament.

CARTILAGE

The *cartilages* of the facial skeleton are few, having only slight relationship to communication. The outstanding exceptions to this, insofar as speech and hearing may be concerned, are the nasal cartilages. The cartilaginous portions of the ear and eustachian tube, although a part of the facial skeleton, are discussed in Chapter 7.

The supporting structure of the nose is composed of both bone and cartilage; the bony structures have been described. There are five larger cartilages of the nose and several smaller cartilages. These vary considerably from individual to individual and determine the characteristic facial profile. There are two *lateral nasal* cartilages, two *greater alar* cartilages, and the single *midline nasal septal* cartilage. There are, also, the *lesser alar,* the *vomernasal,* and the *sesamoid* cartilages.

The *greater alar* cartilages form the medial and lateral walls of the anterior nares on each side. (See Figure 3–12 and Figure 3–13.) These cartilages are thin and flexible; each of the pair joins the other at the midline, and a curved portion of each circles laterally to form the outer walls of the nasal entrance. A part of these walls is formed by the lesser alar cartilages continuing the wall until the alveolar process of the maxilla is approached. Interceding are fibrous and fatty tissues to complete the apex of the nose.

Immediately superior to the preceding and somewhat dorsally is the *lateral nasal* cartilage on either side. This cartilage is interposed between the greater alar cartilage inferiorly and the nasal bone superiorly. (See Fig. 3–13.) It is thin and flexible, and is attached to the two related structures as well as to the midline nasal cartilage.

The *central nasal septal* cartilage is an unpaired midline structure that continues the separation of the two nasal passageways in an antero-posterior direction. (See Figure 3–12.) Although quite varied in size and shape, because of ossification of the nasal bone as well as genetic and injurious influences, it is generally quadrilateral in shape. The septal cartilage runs antero-inferiorly from the nasal bone forward between the two lateral nasal cartilages and thereafter between the two greater alar cartilages. The posterior portion of the septal cartilage is attached to the vomer and the nasal crest of the maxilla.

The *lesser alar* cartilages are three or four in number, and form a part of the lateral wall of the nares, along with the greater alar cartilages. The *vomernasal* cartilage is a variable structure, generally considered to be a part of the septal cartilage; it runs on either side of the inferior border of the septal cartilage, attaching to the vomer posteriorly and to the maxilla and the septal cartilage anteriorly. The *sesamoid* cartilages are structures that vary in occurrence, number, and size, but are generally found as small, thin plates interposed between the lateral nasal cartilage and the greater alar cartilage.

DENTITION

The two jaws in which the teeth are found are the maxilla and the mandible. In each of these, the alveolar processes house the dentition; the term alveolus refers to the socket or hole in which the teeth normally reside. These alveolar processes, in both instances, are crescent-shaped, with the closed end of the crescent oriented anteriorly and the open end posteriorly toward the pharynx. Normally, the teeth are arranged around this crescent, differing from anterior to posterior in number and type; but bilateral symmetry is maintained.

As is well known, the developments of the dentition vary considerably from individual to individual. However, at the time of birth, the child having any erupted teeth is sufficiently rare to be a news item, and certainly the parents of the newborn with even one or two erupted teeth publicly announce the advanced development of their infant.

It is generally agreed, however, that by the sixth month the second molar enlargement occurs, and by the fifth year the third molar enlargement occurs. Eruption of these molars and other teeth varies among individuals.

The first teeth of the two sets the human being develops are generally temporary and are replaced by the second or more permanent set. These first dental structures—the milk, or deciduous, teeth—are twenty in number. Eruption generally starts around the seventh month; the deciduous teeth are shed between six and fourteen years of age.

TABLE 3.1   **DECIDUOUS TEETH**

	Molars	Canines	Incisors	Incisors	Canines	Molars
			MIDLINE			
Maxilla	2	1	2	2	1	2
Mandible	2	1	2	2	1	2
			TOTAL: 20			

A glance at Table 3.1 shows that there are only three types of deciduous teeth, repeated in various patterns in the upper and lower jaws. The most anterior teeth, the cutting and slicing teeth, are appropriately named the incisors; there are two of these in half of each jaw, making a total of eight for the individual. There is a tearing and ripping tooth in half of each jaw, which is aptly termed the canine tooth; obviously, there are four of these in the individual. And there are two grinding teeth—the molars—in each jaw half, giving a total of eight molars.

The more-or-less permanent teeth number thirty-two because of the addition of one more molar and two more premolar teeth inserted between the canine and the molars. These teeth, of course, gradually replace the deciduous teeth between the ages mentioned above, so that by the time adolescence is well started there should be a reasonably full complement of teeth. Certainly, in this

TABLE 3.2   **PERMANENT TEETH**

	Molars	Pre-molars	Canines	Incisors	Incisors	Canines	Pre-molars	Molars
				MIDLINE				
Maxilla	3	2	1	2	2	1	2	3
Mandible	3	2	1	2	2	1	2	3
				TOTAL: 32				

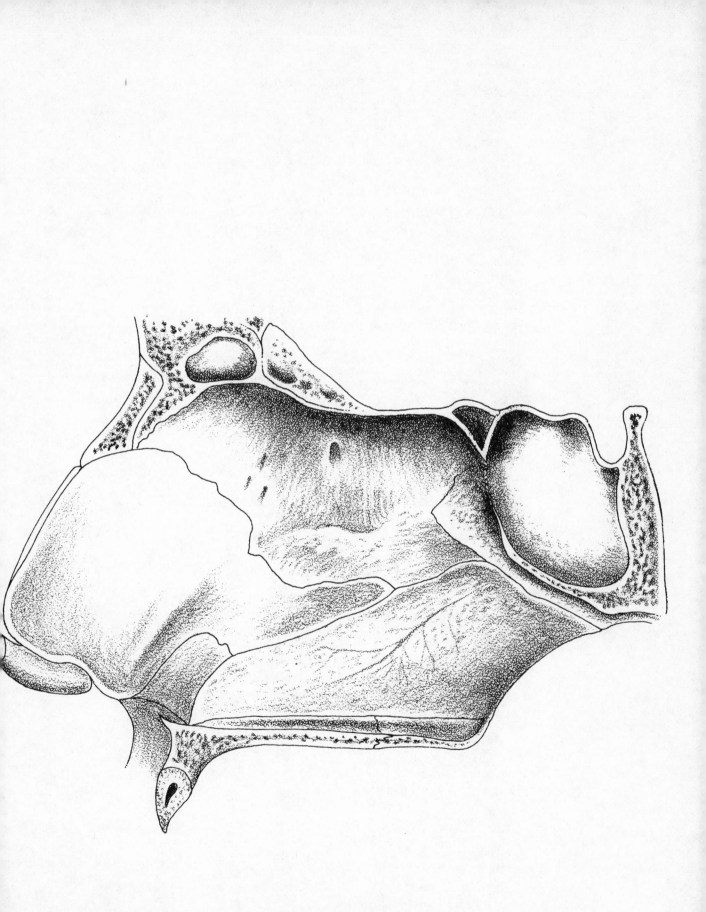

Figure 3–12.
Nasal Septum

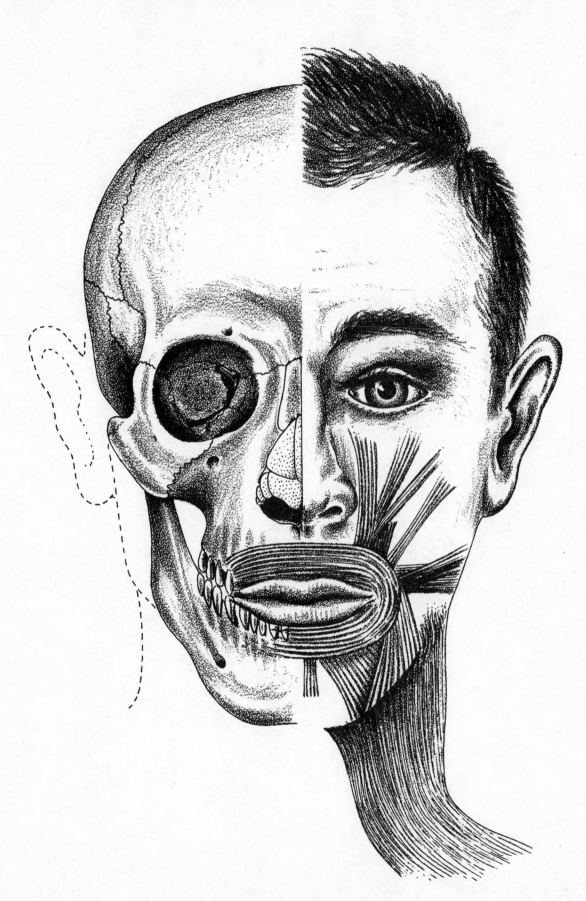

Figure 3-13.
Muscles of Facial Expression

respect—as in all others mentioned—individual variations and hereditary characteristics play a major role in any generalizations made. However, a standard chart (Table 3.2) may be safely used to evaluate the young adult and the adult. Some individuals never erupt a third molar, or "wisdom" tooth.

> CLINICAL NOTE
> The speech examiner would be interested in the number, alignment, and condition of teeth present in his clients. Reliability of diagnoses based solely upon number of teeth is not good, for normal speech and normal functioning often occur even with missing teeth. Certainly, the contribution of that particular omission in that individual remains the evaluative task of the practicing clinician.

MUSCULATURE

Muscles of Facial Expression

There are ten muscles of the oro-nasal region which together form the commonly accepted grouping called the muscles of facial expression. (See Figure 3–13.) Some authorities ascribe specific emotional expressions, as seen by facial contortion, to each of these muscles; others prefer to attribute expression to the combined action of several of these muscles. It is indeed convenient to think of the individual muscles described in this section as being responsible for the facial expression of emotions such as laughing, smiling, pouting, and so on.

These muscles are those associated with the mouth. As such, they play a role in the vegetative functions such as maintaining the closure (fixing the oral aperture), in assisting retention of the bolus of food, as well as producing the typically human facial expressions. Generally, these muscles have their origins in the bones of the facial skeleton; they are inserted in the soft tissues (e.g., other muscles, connective tissues) of the mouth and lips.

The ten muscles discussed are *quadratus labii superior, canine, zygomatic, risorius, quadratus labii inferior, triangular, mental, orbicularis oris, buccinator,* and *platysma muscles.* All are supplied by the facial nerve (Cranial VII). See Table 3.3.

> CLINICAL NOTE
> In certain pathologies in which the speech therapist plays a rehabilitative role, the muscles (all or part, bilateral or unilateral) are direct effectors of the speech defect. As an example, certain of the neurologic defects (palsies, Parkinson's disease, etc.) are exemplified by facial paralysis. The muscles cannot make the fine movement required for the articulation of many of the speech sounds. As a result, speech is often slurred, slovenly, and even unintelligible. When the lips cannot be moved to make an /f/ or /v/, or certain vowel sounds, the speech defect is then obvious and disturbing.

Quadratus labii superior is the most median of the superior lip muscles in its origin; actually, it has three heads, some of which are so separated from the others that some anatomists label them as entirely separate muscles. The origin of these heads is, in general, from the side of the nose, which is the frontal process of the maxilla, the lower margin of the orbit, and the zygomatic bone. The three muscle bundles run inferiorly to insert into the upper lip close to its midline and along the upper boundary. It is felt that this is the muscle of contempt or disdain, as it elevates the lateral half of the upper lip.

The *canine* muscle has its origin in the canine fossa just below the infraorbital foramen of the maxilla. Its fibers descend into the angle of the mouth near the upper lip in a nearly vertical direction, so that when it contracts it elevates the lateral portion of the upper lip and produces a sneering expression.

The *zygomatic* muscle begins at the zygomatic bone, lateral to the origin

TABLE 3.3   MUSCLES OF FACIAL EXPRESSION

MUSCLE	ORIGIN	INSERTION	ACTION	NERVE
Quadratus Labii Superior	Frontal process maxilla; lower margin of orbit; zygomatic bone	Upper lip at midline	Elevates upper lip	Cranial VII
Canine	Canine fossa of the maxilla	Angle of mouth, upper lip	Elevates portion of upper lip	Cranial VII
Zygomatic	Zygomatic bone	Angle of mouth, upper lip	Draws corner of mouth up and back	Cranial VII
Risorius	Fascia over masseter	Skin at angle of mouth	Retracts corner of mouth	Cranial VII
Triangular	Oblique line of mandible	Angle of mouth, lower lip	Depresses angle of mouth	Cranial VII
Quadratus Labii Inferior	Oblique line of mandible	Lower lip at angle of mouth	Depresses and retracts lower lip	Cranial VII
Mental	Incisive fossa of mandible (anterior)	Integument of chin	Raises and protrudes lower lip	Cranial VII
Orbicularis Oris	(A sphincteric muscle, deriving from others of the area, with no definite origins or insertions)		Closes mouth and puckers lips	Cranial VII
Buccinator	Alveolar ridges of maxilla and mandible; pterygo-mandibular raphe	Angle of the mouth mingling with fibers of mm. forming upper and lower lips	Flattens cheek	Cranial VII
Platysma	Thoracic fascia over pectoralis major, deltoid, and trapezius mm.	Mental protuberance of the mandible, skin of cheek, and corner of mouth	Depresses mandible; aids in pouting reaction; depresses corner of mouth; wrinkles skin of neck and chin	Cranial VII

of the canine muscle, with its fibers descending rather obliquely into the upper lip at the angle or corner of the mouth. It draws the corner of the mouth up and backward; thus it is the laughing muscle.

The *risorius* muscle originates in the fascia (connective tissue) overlying the masseter muscle, still lateral to the previous muscles listed. It runs horizontally, superficially to the platysma, into the skin at the angle of the mouth. Its action is to retract the angle of the mouth; thus together with the zygomatic muscles, smiling is accomplished.

The *triangular* muscle of facial expression has its origin in the oblique line of the mandible, but somewhat lateral to the origin of the quadratus labii inferior muscle (discussed next). Its fibers radiate into the lower lip at the angle of the mouth, so that upon contraction it depresses the angle; thus it is a frowning muscle.

The *quadratus labii inferior* muscle originates from the oblique line of the mandible, anteriorly. Because it is below the level of the mouth in its origin, its fibers pass medialward and upward into the lower lip, as do those of the triangular muscle. Its action is to draw the lateral portion of the lower lip directly down; thus it is a muscle that helps express irony or perhaps terror.

The *mental* muscle is close to the midline of the mouth and below it. It derives its origin from the incisive fossa of the mandible (close to the level of the lower lip), with its fibers descending (*not* ascending) into the integument or skin of the chin. It acts to protrude the lower lip, when the integument is fixed, or to wrinkle the skin of the chin, and therefore might be called a muscle of doubt or disdain. It is a variable muscle, more so than most of this group; it is sometimes considered a major part of the platysma muscle.

Orbicularis oris muscle is a much more complex muscle of the mouth area. It is essentially a layer of muscle fibers derived from the other muscles that are inserted into the lips and, technically, is said to have no origin or insertions. These muscle fibers continue on from their original muscle group, bypassing the insertion location at which other fibers stop, and pass along the border of the lip. In this way a circular muscle group is formed, encompassing the periphery of the mouth. Upon contraction it acts somewhat like a drawstring, closing the mouth and, upon extreme contraction, pursing or puckering the lips.

The *buccinator* muscle is the principle muscle of the cheek, the lateral wall of the buccal cavity. Its origin is in the outer surfaces of the posterior alveolar processes of the maxilla and mandible as well as in the pterygomandibular raphe. The fibers pass forward in a converging fashion to insert or blend with the deeper stratum (layer) of muscle fibers of the corresponding lip. Its action, then, is to compress the cheek, forcing air from the mouth; in performing this compression act, it also acts as an accessory muscle of mastication, keeping the food from slipping out from between the teeth, while the tongue operates from within, holding the food between the chewing surfaces of the teeth.

The *platysma* muscle is the last and most variable of the muscles of facial expression. It is composed of scattered aggregates of muscle bundles found along the sides of the neck from the upper thorax to the sides of the chin and mandible. It is a superficial muscle, originating in the superficial fascia (tela subcutanea) covering the muscles of the thorax (pectoralis major, deltoid, and trapezius muscles), with its fibers running obliquely upward and medially over the side of the neck. They insert into the mental protuberance of the mandible, the skin of the lower cheek, and the corner of the mouth (with quadratus labii inferior and orbicularis oris mm.). The action of these muscle bundles is to wrinkle the skin of the neck and chin, to depress the corner of the mouth, and to assist in lowering the mandible (along with the external pterygoid m.).

CLINICAL NOTE

Defects and differences in the muscles of mastication occur in certain paralytic conditions as well as in some congenital musculoskeletal deformities. In Bell's palsy, for example, a unilateral paralysis of the facial musculature leads to an easily observable facial asymmetry, often accompanied by a speech defect as a form of dysarthria. A similar condition, although bilateral in effect, is Parkinson's disease, which often attacks more than just the facial structures. The facial configuration of the upper lip region is often disturbed in congenital cleft lip, usually of the left side, and extending variously from nares to lip.

Muscles of Mastication

The muscles of mastication, sometimes known as the craniomandibular muscles, are four in number, and are paired. In general, they originate on the bones of the cranium and insert into the mandible. (See Figure 3–14.) Their actions are to cause masticatory (chewing) movements, essentially up-and-down and back-and-forth (grinding) movements of the mandible against its opposite bone: the maxilla. The four pairs of muscles are *temporal, masseter, internal (medial) pterygoid,* and *external (lateral) pterygoid.* Each is supplied by the trigeminal (Cranial V) nerve. (See Table 3.4.)

The *temporal* muscle has as its origin the whole of the temporal fossa of the temporal bone and its covering fascia. The muscle fibers radiate and converge downward, forming a tendon that passes beneath the zygomatic arch. This tendon inserts on the anterior borders of the coronoid process and the ramus of the mandible. The action of this muscle is to elevate and retract the mandible, which closes the jaw.

The *masseter* muscle is a two-part muscle, having a superficial and a deep portion. The superficial portion arises from the lower, and the deep portion from the medial, edge of the zygomatic arch. Its superficial fibers pass downward and backward; the deep fibers pass downward and forward. The two portions insert into the lateral surface of the ramus and of the angle of the mandible, respectively. The action of masseter is to raise the mandible (close the jaw) against the maxilla.

The *internal (medial) pterygoid* muscle has its origin at the lateral pterygoid plate, with slips from the palatine bone and the tuberosity of the maxilla. Its fibers pass downward, laterally, and backward, to insert in the ramus and angle of the mandible. This muscle elevates the mandible (closes the jaw) and protrudes it.

The *external (lateral) pterygoid* muscle arises by two heads. One comes from the infratemporal fossa of the greater wing of the sphenoid bone, and the other from the lateral surface of the lateral pterygoid plate of the sphenoid. They run horizontally to insert into the neck of the condyle of the mandible and the articular disc. The action, upon contraction, is to depress the mandible (open the jaw), to protrude the mandible and, when operating singly, to provide for lateral movement (grinding) of the mandible, along with others of the masticatory group.

As a group, the muscles of mastication function to slice, bite, grind, and chew food. Closing the jaw is accomplished by temporal, masseter, and internal pterygoid muscles working together. Biting is performed mainly by masseter and internal pterygoid muscles, whereas chewing requires all three. Opening the jaw is accomplished by gravity as well as external pterygoid muscle contraction, by its forward pull of the condyle moving the mandible about an axis located at the angle.

CLINICAL NOTE
Weakness, paralysis, or injury of these muscles will initially produce a defect of mastication, of course, but one could expect accompanying speech disturbances. In some cases, such as a cerebral vascular accident, of unilateral paralysis, a dysarthria may result, evidenced by more or less severe articulatory as well as resonance differences that draw

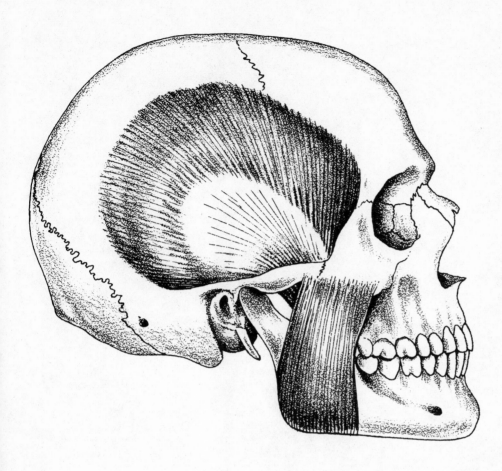

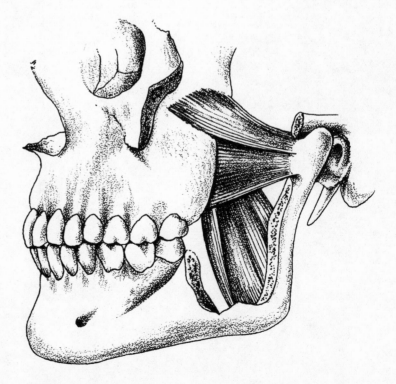

Figure 3–14.
Muscles of Mastication

TABLE 3.4   **MUSCLES OF MASTICATION**

MUSCLE	ORIGIN	INSERTION	ACTION	NERVE
Temporal	Temporal fossa and the whole of the covering fascia	Anterior borders of mandibular ramus and coronoid process	Raises and retracts the mandible	Cranial V (Mandibular Division)
Masseter	Lower edge of the zygomatic arch (superficial); medial edge of the zygomatic arch (deep)	Lateral surface of the angle of the jaw; lateral surface of the ramus	Raises the mandible against the maxilla	Cranial V (Mandibular Division)
Internal Pterygoid	Lateral pterygoid plate; slips from the palatine bone; maxillary tuberosity	Ramus and angle of mandible	Raises the mandible and protrudes jaw	Cranial V (Mandibular Division)
External Pterygoid	Upper head arises from the infratemporal fossa and greater wing of the sphenoid bone; lower head arises from lateral aspect of the lateral pterygoid plate of the sphenoid bone	Mandibular condyle and the disc of the joint of the jaw	Depresses mandible and draws mandible forward and sideways	Cranial V (Mandibular Division)

attention to themselves. Fairly good jaw closure must be available to produce many of the speech sounds (e.g., the plosives and some of the fricatives), and the size and shape of the oral cavity is one of the prime determinants of vowel characteristics, that is, the resonance aspects thereof; tongue and lip movements also are involved in this determination.

Muscles of the Soft Palate

The soft palate, or velum, is essentially a soft-tissue extension of the hard palate, further dividing the oral from the nasal cavity. (See Figure 3–15 and Figure 3–20.) This extension is a musculo-membranous shelf that is mobile into several planes, thus providing for changes in the volume and shape of the two cavities, as well as being largely responsible for the action separating the nasal from the oral pharynx: velopharyngeal closure.

This mobile structure is composed, in the main, of various muscles entering the palate from skeletal structures in the immediate vicinity. Because of the various origins—some superior, some inferior, and some posterior—it is possible for the palate to be moved cephalad, caudad, and dorsad, or a combination of these. Five muscles make up the major part of the palate, with a sixth muscle bundle that is considered to be present but that is not universally recognized as a separate muscle. The five muscles discussed in this section are *levator veli palatine, tensor veli palatine, uvula, glossopalatine,* and *pharyngopalatine.* (See Table 3.5.)

The *levator veli palatine* muscle derives its name from its action upon the soft palate. It has its origin in two heads, the first coming from the petrous part of the temporal bone and the second from the pharyngeal end of the eustachian tube cartilage. The muscle fibers then pass downward and medially to insert into the midline of the velum, the palatal aponeurosis; some of the fibers do cross this midline to blend with the fibers of the opposite muscle. This muscle contracts to raise the velum toward the posterior pharyngeal wall, to narrow the pharyngeal isthmus in velopharyngeal closure, and to widen the orifice of the eustachian tube. The nerve supply comes from the pharyngeal plexus, indirectly from the vagus (Cranial X) nerve.

The *tensor veli palatine* muscle (also named by its action) has usually been described as having a twofold origin: the medial pterygoid plate and the lateral wall of the eustachian tube. More recent investigation indicates a threefold origin: the medial pterygoid plate spine, the scaphoid fossa, and the posterior border of the hard palate. This last origin indicates a reversed origin-insertion relationship, as compared to the others. In this case, the fibers run from the hard palate to the hamulus of the medial pterygoid plate, curve around the hamulus, and pass to the lateral wall of the eustachian tube. The other fibers from the superior origins pass forward and downward, pass as a tendon around the hamulus, and then enter the velum to terminate at its aponeurosis, much as the levator muscle does. The action of the tensor is to make the velum taut and to dilate the orifice of the eustachian tube. The nerve supply comes from the mandibular division of the trigeminal (Cranial V) nerve.

The *uvula* ("little grape") is the most posterior of the velum; paired bands of muscle fibers pass dorsally through the soft palate. Their origin is the posterior nasal spine as well as the palatal aponeurosis, anteriorly. The two muscle bundles pass as two narrow strips of muscle fibers along each side of the midline until they terminate in, or insert into, the uvula itself. It is believed that this free-swinging, pendulous structure is vestigal, and serves no important function in man. Usually it does swing upward and backward upon contraction. Its nerve supply comes from the pharyngeal plexus from the vagus nerve.

The *glossopalatine* (palatoglossal) muscle passes from the tongue to the palate along the sides of the oral cavity, making a large bundle called the *anterior*

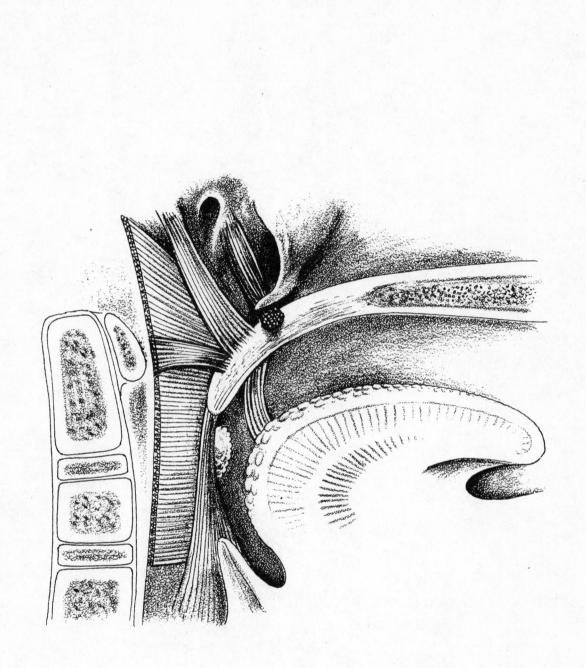

Figure 3–15.
Muscles of the Soft Palate

TABLE 3.5   MUSCLES OF THE SOFT PALATE

MUSCLE	ORIGIN	INSERTION	ACTION	NERVE
Levator Veli Palatine	Apex of the petrous portion of the temporal bone; eustachian tube	Aponeurosis of soft palate	Raises soft palate to meet posterior pharyngeal wall; dilates eustachian tube orifice	Cranial X (Pharyngeal Plexus)
Tensor Veli Palatine	Scaphoid fossa; medial pterygoid plate spine; posterior border of hard palate	Palatine aponeurosis; eustachian tube	Tenses the soft palate; opens the eustachian tube during swallowing	Cranial V (Mandibular Division)
Uvula	Posterior nasal spine; palatal aponeurosis (anterior)	Mucous membrane of uvula	Raises and shortens uvula	Cranial X (Pharyngeal Plexus)
Glossopalatine	Merges with transversus and superficial mm. of side and undersurface of tongue	Palatine aponeurosis	Raises posterior portion of tongue; constricts isthmus of fauces; depresses side of palate	Cranial X (Pharyngeal Plexus)
Pharyngopalatine	Posterior thyroid cartilage; aponeurosis of pharynx	Aponeurosis of the soft palate	Depresses soft palate; aids in elevating larynx and pharynx; constricts faucial isthmus	Cranial X (Pharyngeal Plexus)

pillar of the fauces. Its origin is in the superficial layer of muscles of the side and undersurface of the tongue and from the transverse (intrinsic) muscle of that structure. The fibers pass from the side of the tongue in the bundle mentioned beneath the mucous membrane of the mouth up toward the palate. They enter its side to finally insert into the palatal aponeurosis, again with some fibers crossing the midline to blend with fibers of the opposite muscle. Upon contraction, this muscle draws down the sides of the soft palate or draws up and back the sides of the tongue, depending upon which end of the muscle is the more fixed end. The nerve supply comes from the pharyngeal plexus of the vagus nerve.

The *pharyngopalatine* (palatopharyngeal) muscle is similar to the glossopalatine muscle in that it has an attachment inferior to the velum and forms a noticeable bundle beneath the mucous membrane lining of the oro-pharynx. Its origin is considered to be the posterior border of the thyroid cartilage near the base of the superior cornu and a broad expansion of the fibrous layer of the pharynx at its lowest part. The fibers pass up the lower part of the pharynx, along with the stylopharyngeal, until they form a compact bundle known as the *posterior pillar of fauces.* From here the bundle divides into two fasciculi: a lower and an upper one. The lower band of muscle fibers follows the posterior curve of the soft palate; the upper one enters the palate directly. Both sets insert into the midline of the soft palate at the palatal aponeurosis. This muscle acts to constrict the pharyngeal isthmus, to depress the soft palate, and to elevate the pharynx and larynx. It is supplied by the pharyngeal plexus of the vagus nerve.

A sixth muscle, the *velopharyngeal sphincter* muscle, is described later (in Chapter 4) because of its intimate relationship to the superior constrictor muscle of the pharynx.

CLINICAL NOTE

Knowledge of the palatal muscles is basic to any therapeutic procedures applied to a number of clinical defects. In many cases of dysarthria, of resonance problems, and of cleft palate, it is important to evaluate the position of and the functioning of these muscles, individually and as a group. In illustration, one might point to the postsurgical cleft palate that demonstrates defects because of the original malplacement of muscles as well as the surgical disturbance that may have occurred. It is not uncommon in some surgical procedures to fracture the pterygoid hamulus (to provide relaxation for the soft palate post-surgically), and thus remove the tensor muscle from its usual operation. In other cases, muscles are paralyzed, injured, or disturbed in such a way as to require the therapist's specific attention, both in evaluation and therapy.

THE TONGUE

The next major structure of importance in the oro-nasal region is the tongue (lingua or glossus). It is variously called the major organ of speech, taste, and swallowing; it has been reasonably established that, although of great importance, the tongue is not solely responsible for any of these actions. In structure, the tongue is almost entirely muscular. Four muscles are found to make up the majority of the intrinsic structure. Four others, which come from adjacent skeletal areas, make up the extrinsic group. The intrinsic muscles provide for changes in the shape of the tongue, and the extrinsic muscles are largely responsible for its movement within the oral cavity.

The overall structure of the tongue varies from individual to individual, of course, but in general there are locations and landmarks that every tongue demonstrates. The root of the tongue is directed dorsally, and connects with the hyoid bone (studied earlier in this chapter under "The Facial Skeleton") through the hyoglossus muscle and the genioglossus muscle. The tongue's anterior end is

TABLE 3.6   INTRINSIC MUSCLES OF THE TONGUE

MUSCLE	ORIGIN	INSERTION	ACTION	NERVE
Vertical	Superior surface of tongue near tip edges	Inferior surface of tongue	Widens and flattens tongue tip	Cranial XII
Transverse	Tongue septum, median portion	Mucosa at sides of tongue	Elongates, narrows, thickens tongue; lifts sides	Cranial XII
Inferior Longitudinal	Hyoid bone; inferior surface of base of tongue	Apex of tongue	Widens, shortens tongue; creates convex dorsum; depresses tip	Cranial XII
Superior Longitudinal	Septum of tongue; submucosa near epiglottis	Sides of tongue	Widens, thickens, and shortens tongue; raises tongue tip and edges; forms concave dorsum	Cranial XII

the apex, or tip; it is thin and narrow, directed forward against the lingual surfaces of the lower incisors. The inferior surface of the tongue is connected with the mandible through the genioglossus muscle; it is also attached to soft tissues at its inferior margin through the lingual frenulum—a vertical elevation or fold of mucous membrane—which is sometimes considered responsible for tongue-tie. The superior surface of the tongue is called the dorsum (see Figure 3–16). Its anterior two-thirds is roughened and contains papillae. It is oriented toward the oral aperture, and its relatively smooth posterior one-third is oriented dorsally.

CLINICAL NOTE
Defects of either, or both groups of tongue muscles may cause speech defects. These defects may be caused by paralyses or injuries or they may result from congenital or hereditary anomalies. Should the paralysis, for example, disturb the innervation of the intrinsic muscles, it would become very difficult for the tongue to be molded or formed in the precise shape for the production of some of the speech sounds. As an example, the /s/ sound requires a very fine control of the tongue to produce a narrow groove through which the air stream passes prior to its striking the central incisors for the friction effect. The extrinsic muscles may also produce an articulatory defect should they have a faulty nerve supply. In this instance, one would hear resonance changes in the voice, because of problems in changing the shape and size of the oral cavity, as well as articulatory problems around the sounds requiring movement of the tongue to meet with other structures such as the palate or teeth (e.g., the /t/, /d/, /k/, and /g/ sounds). Vowel sound differences may well be the result of intrinsic muscle defects, as well as those of the extrinsic muscles.

Intrinsic Muscles of the Tongue

The intrinsic muscles of the tongue are named by their planes of direction within the tongue. Thus, there are the *vertical,* the *transverse,* the *inferior longitudinal,* and the *superior longitudinal* muscles. (See Table 3.6.) These are largely separate muscle bundles or layers, except that some parts of each are composed of fibers entering the tongue from certain of the extrinsic muscles, making for a firm yet flexible coordination between the shape and the position of the tongue.

The *vertical* tongue muscle is found at the borders of the tongue, near the forepart. It runs from the upper to the under surface of the structure, interlacing its fibers with those of other intrinsic muscles. The *transverse* tongue muscle's fibers pass horizontally laterally between the two longitudinal muscles. The origin of this muscle is considered as the median portion of the lingual septum (a connective tissue midline structure), and its insertion is the mucosa of the dorsum and lateral margins of the tongue. The *inferior longitudinal* muscle is a narrow band of fibers on the under surface of the tongue between genioglossus and hyoglossus, running from root to apex; the fibers at the apex of the tongue blend with styloglossus, and the posterior fibers often pass inferiorly to attach to the hyoid bone. The *superior longitudinal* muscle is a thin layer of superficial fibers running from base to apex beneath the mucosa which arise from a submucous layer close to the epiglottis and insert along the sides of the tongue as they pass anteriorly.

The actions of these four muscles should be fairly clear and self-evident. The vertical muscle contracts to flatten and broaden the tongue; the transverse muscle narrows and elongates the tongue and elevates its lateral borders; the inferior longitudinal muscle shortens the tongue, turns the tip down, and makes a convex dorsum; and, the superior longitudinal muscle shortens the tongue, turns the tip and sides upward to form a concave dorsum. The hypoglossal (Cranial XII) nerve serves as motor innervator to these muscles.

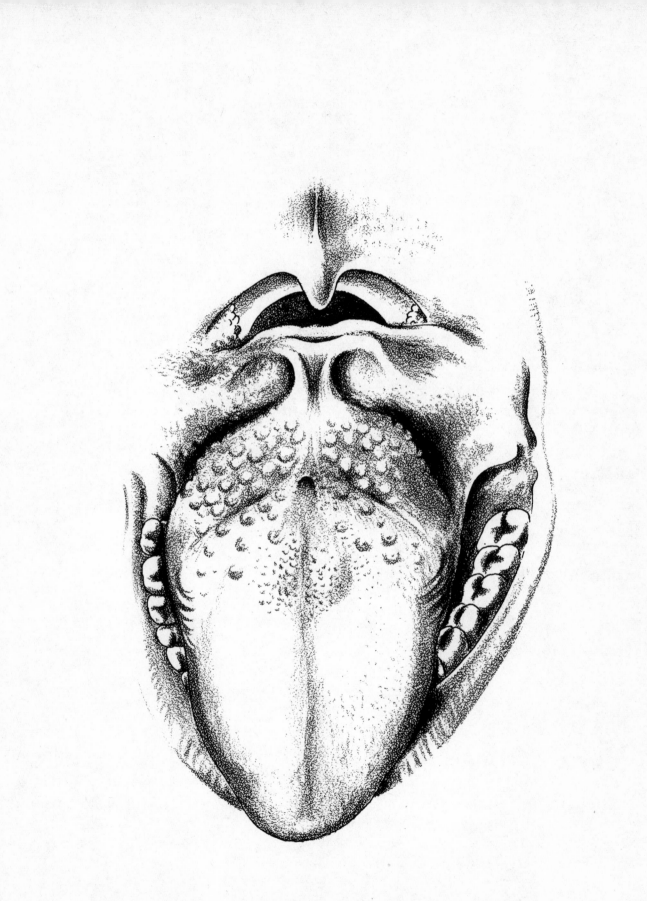

Figure 3-16.
Tongue Dorsum

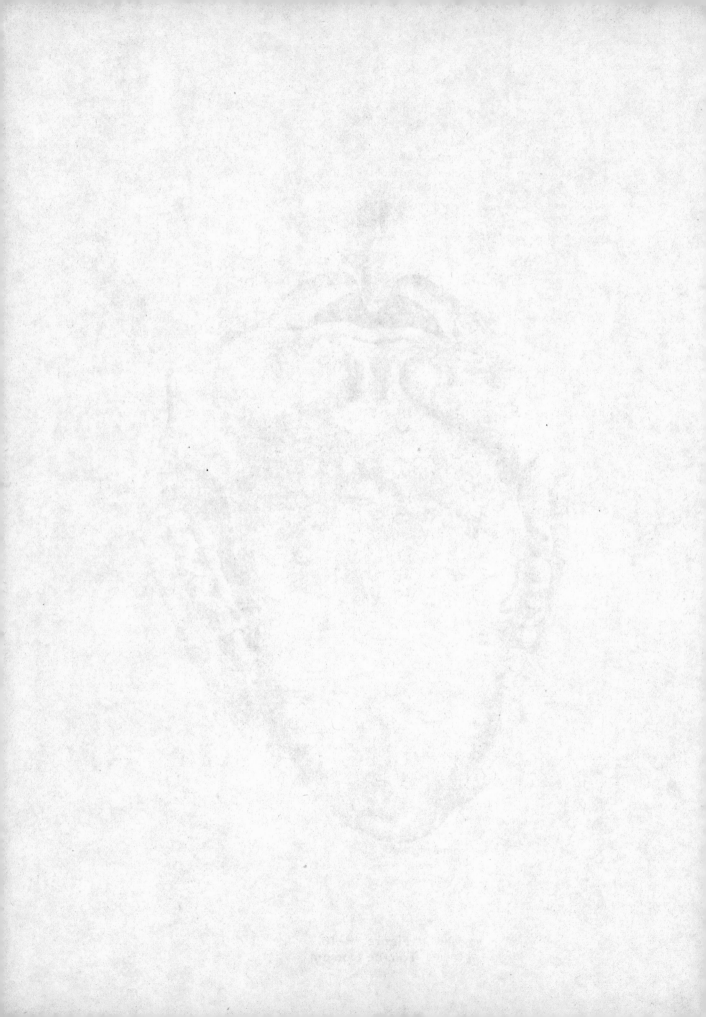

Extrinsic Muscles of the Tongue

The extrinsic muscles of the tongue are responsible for the movement of the tongue from place to place within the oral cavity. They function together with the intrinsic muscles; the latter change the shape or contour of the tongue as it is moved about, certainly actions of great importance to the various speech activities. These extrinsic muscles are attached to the skull and to the hyoid bone to effect the necessary positional changes. (See Figures 3–17 and 3–18.) All tongue muscles are innervated by the hypoglossal nerve.

There are three extrinsic tongue muscles, excluding a fourth—the palatal muscle (glossopalatine)—described earlier in the chapter, in the section "Muscles of the Soft Palate." These three are *styloglossus, genioglossus,* and *hyoglossus.* (See Table 3.7.)

The *styloglossus* muscle runs from its posterior position on the styloid process of the temporal bone obliquely forward and downward (and somewhat medially) to the lateral border of the tongue. Here it divides into a longitudinal and an oblique portion. The longitudinal portion enters the side of the tongue and runs to the tip along the lateral border, blending with the fibers of the longitudinal inferior muscle, and inserting its fibers into the mucosa of the sides along the length of the structure. The smaller, oblique portion of styloglossus enters the tongue transversely in a number of small muscle bundles that penetrate the hyoglossus muscle to finally reach the midline of the tongue. Here they decussate (cross) and terminate with their fellow muscle fibers from the opposite side. The *styloglossus* muscle retracts the tongue and draws its sides upward, thus raising both the base of the tongue and the hyoid bone below.

The *genioglossus* muscle forms a large part of the tongue; its shape and position resemble that of a vertically oriented fan. (See Figure 3–19.) Its origin is near the midline of the lingual surface of the mandible, at the superior mental spine just above the origin of the geniohyoid muscle. Its fibers fan out from this point along either side of the midline fibrous septum of the tongue. The most anterior fanning fibers curve upward and forward to the tip of the tongue to be inserted into the lingual fascia; middle fibers pass up and back to insert along the dorsum; and, the inferior fibers curve back and downward to insert into the upper part of the body of the hyoid bone.

The majority of the activity of the tongue is provided by the *genioglossus* muscle, with its threefold fan-shaped fiber bunches. The most anterior portion, running to the tip of the tongue, withdraws the tip into the mouth and depresses it. This portion, acting with the middle portion, draws the entire superior surface of the tongue downward into a concave shape, producing a channel from front to back; this is used for sucking purposes, basically, but it is also used in certain speech sound formations. The middle portion, acting alone, draws the base of the tongue forward and thus protrudes the tip through the teeth—also an important speech act. The inferior group of fibers acts upon the less fixed end, the hyoid bone, to elevate it and move it forward—a process important in deglutition.

The *hyoglossus* muscle is a thin sheet of muscle extending from the upper borders of the greater cornu of the hyoid bone upward into the posterior half of the sides of the tongue. These fibers pass medially and interlace with the intrinsic muscle fibers to insert into the fibrous septum of the tongue. Penetrating the hyoglossus are some of the oblique fibers of the styloglossus muscle. The *hyoglossus* muscle will act, when the hyoid bone is fixed, to depress the sides of the tongue as well as contribute to its retraction.

CLINICAL NOTE
Although exaggerated, the use of the term "organ of speech" as applied to the tongue indicates its general position in popular conceptions of the speaking acts. Defects of speech are many times thought

TABLE 3.7   **EXTRINSIC MUSCLES OF THE TONGUE**

MUSCLE	ORIGIN	INSERTION	ACTION	NERVE
Styloglossus	Inferior portion of the styloid process of the temporal bone	Lateral border of the tongue	Elevates rear of the tongue; retracts protruded tongue	Cranial XII
Genioglossus	Upper mental spine on lingual surface of mandible	Lingual fascia, dorsum of tongue and body of hyoid bone	Alternate fibers work to depress, retract, and protrude tongue	Cranial XII
Hyoglossus	Greater cornu of hyoid bone	Posterior half of the side of the tongue	Depresses and retracts tongue	Cranial XII

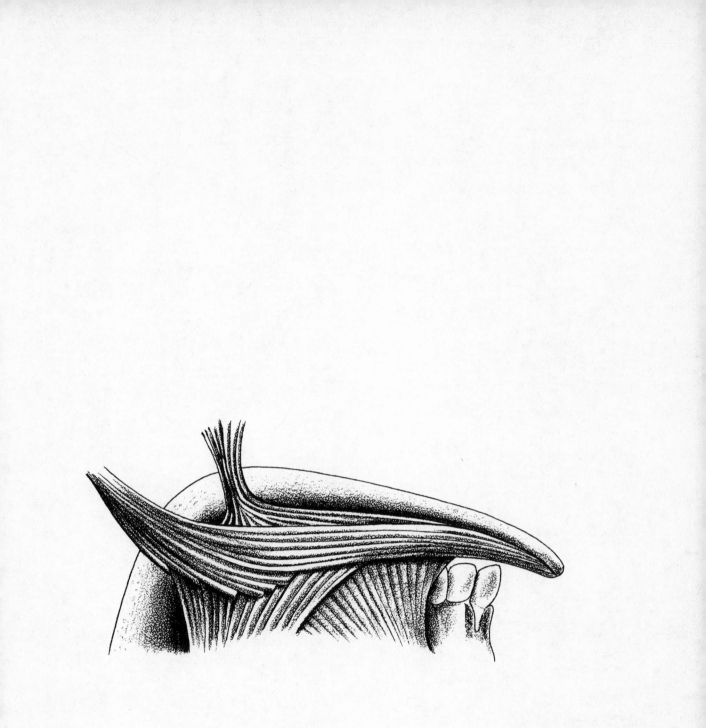

Figure 3–17.
Extrinsic Tongue Muscles: Lateral View

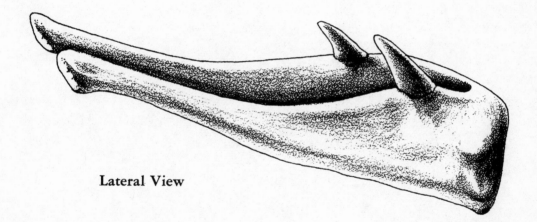

Lateral View

Figure 3–18.
Hyoid Bone

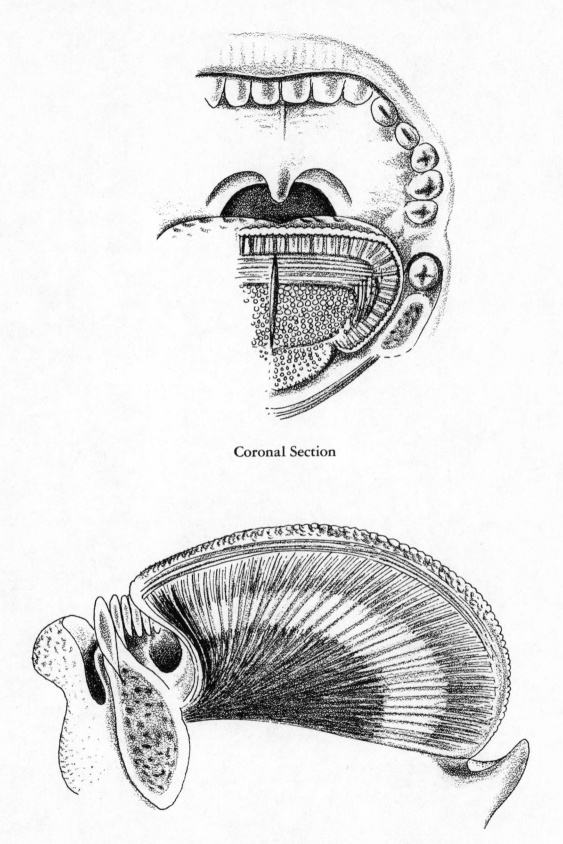

Coronal Section

Sagittal Section

Figure 3–19.
Tongue

to arise from defects of the tongue, a relationship that is not always supported by anatomic or physiologic evidence. For example, the lingual frenum, connecting the inferior surface of the tongue with the floor of the mouth, is often considered to be "too short" and is frequently clipped by physicians. This shortened lingual frenum may be, but rarely is, the actual cause of a speech defect. More serious speech problems that do arise from tongue deviations are those that stem from neurologic problems giving rise to paralyses or pareses of the tongue musculature; in these instances the clinician will see failures in such acts as tongue protrusion, deviations of the tongue from the midline, tremors and the like. In some rare instances, the clinician may see a tongue defective in size and shape, either congenitally or rising from pathologic or traumatic processes. Macroglossia (enlarged tongue) is one of these rare conditions that occur, and for which little surgical treatment is recommended. Actually the clinician must always consider not the tongue size and shape alone but that size and shape within the space it occupies, for sometimes it is not defective when viewed in that circumstance.

SURFACE LANDMARKS

The surface landmarks of the oro-nasal region draw attention to themselves, not only because they are sometimes abnormal in cases where the subcutaneous skeletal or muscular tissues may be structurally deficient, but because attention is paid to this area culturally and otherwise. It may be that such deficiencies are not importantly related to a communication disorder; it may be that they are concomitants to a more important speech disorder; it may be that they are primary etiologic agents to speech disorders.

The Nose

The external nose represents in man only a small portion of the internal spaces served by this entryway to the respiratory tract. The *bridge of the nose,* formed by the two tiny nasal bones, is interposed between the bones of the skull surrounding the eye orbit and the cartilaginous external skeleton of the nose. This midline bridge continues to the *tip* of the nose, usually a somewhat thin and relatively pointed termination. From this landmark, bilaterally, flare out the two nasal alae, arcing down from the tip to attach to the skin of the face. These are supported by the greater alar cartilages, which maintain the patency of the *anterior nares (choanae),* which give entryway to the *nasal vestibule* within. The entryway is protected to some extent by the presence of hairs, especially in postadolescent individuals.

The two anterior nares are separated by the single midline *columella.* This is the skin-covered termination of the nasal septal cartilage within. The columella is continuous above with the nasal tip and below with the integument of the upper lip.

The Lip

The skin of the upper lip generally is common to that of the remainder of the facial integument. The central region of this lip is formed embryologically from the prolabium, which fuses with the lateral regions to form the entire lip. In the center of this region, running vertically from the columella to the border of the lip, is the grooved indentation called the *philtrum.* Its lowermost end is common to the midportion of the *cupid's bow.*

At the lip border, the skin of the upper lip changes its form into a reddish *vermilion,* which is a continuation, in adapted form, of the mucous membrane lining the internal mouth and throat regions. The vermilion is found on both lips, and is highly variable in its extent from individual to individual. It is more generously abundant at the midportion of the lips, and narrows considerably to the lateral boundaries—the *angles* of the mouth. From here, the *cheeks* extend bilaterally to cover the sides of the mouth or oral cavity within.

The Mouth

The oral aperture, the *mouth,* gives entryway to the *oral vestibule.* (See Figure 3–20.) This is the space between the mouth and cheek structures and the teeth. It is generally a potential space, but it can be moved to form a real space. It is lined with mucous membrane. Between the lips and the membrane covering the external surfaces of both alveolar processes are the midline *labial frenula.* The frenum of the upper lip is generally more prominent than that of the lower lip, sometimes being externally visible. Other labial frenula may occur laterally between the lips or the cheek lining and the alveolar process. And, further into the oral cavity, another frenum—the *lingual frenum*—is generally found from the floor of the mouth at midline to the under surface of the tongue apex. In the normal individual this is a thin, highly flexible strand of mucous membrane, rarely reaching as far as the end of the tip.

The mucous membrane of the mouth continues to line the oral cavity posteriorly. Some outstanding landmarks to be viewed include the *palatal rugae (plicae).* These folds of tissue, found immediately behind the incisor teeth, represent four bony waves running laterally across the midline; they tend to smooth out with increasing age. At the midline of the bony palate the external evidence of the longitudinal suture might be found: the *palatine raphe.* It commences at the tiny projection, *incisive papilla,* continues posteriorly along the palatal midline to disappear at about the juncture of the bony and soft palates.

Laterally, the walls of the oral vestibule may show the opening for the parotid (Stensen's) duct, which carries saliva to the mouth. This duct and the ducts from the other, primarily submandibular (sublingual) salivary gland provide the first digestive system materials to convert ingested food into available nutritive substances.

Farther posteriorly along the lateral boundaries of the mouth internally, the mucous membrane may form a thin ridge, indicating the external landmark to the *ptergomandibular raphe*—the adjoining of the buccinator muscle of the cheek and a portion of the superior constrictor muscle of the pharynx. Behind this raphe a more prominent ridge, the *anterior pillar of the fauces,* may be found. This ridge is often a continuation of the posterior border of the velum, running in a slight arch downward and forward to disappear beneath the lateral borders of the tongue. This pillar, of course, is external evidence of the palatoglossus (glossopalatine) muscle. Posterior to these pillars on either side is an indentation, the tonsillar fossa, which in childhood houses the important portion of the protective lymphoid ring known here as the tonsils. The back portion of this fossa is formed by the *posterior faucial pillar,* which derives from the posterior border of the soft palate near the midline, then curves outward and downward to disappear behind the root of the tongue in the lateral pharyngeal walls. This pillar houses the palatopharyngeal (pharyngopalatine) muscle. The pillars, and tonsillar pads when present, along with the dorsum of the tongue root and the end of the velum, form the entryway to the pharynx called the *faucial isthmus*. Beyond that is found the pharynx, especially the oropharynx, which receives the bolus of food in swallowing to carry it downward to the esophagus and stomach.

SUMMARY OF FUNCTIONS OF ORO-NASAL REGION

Although emphasis has been placed in this chapter on the structures surrounding and including the mouth and nose, many structures of the entire head have been covered; thus, to provide a concise and short summary would be impossible. To

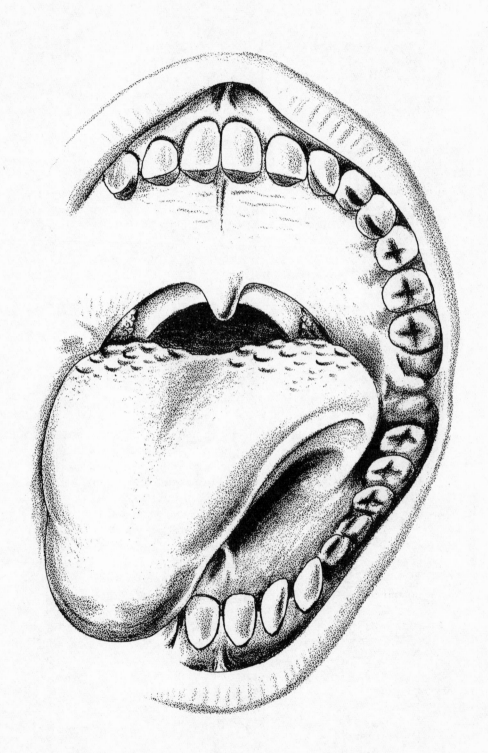

Figure 3–20.
Oral Cavity

focus on these structures and areas associated with speech and hearing activities would therefore be more appropriate.

The bones of the skull, both cranial and facial, provide protection and housing of structures important to the existence of the organism. The brain within the cranium, the auditory system within the temporal bones, the visual system and the olfactory mechanisms in their locales—all are part of the vital systems and organ-systems that maintain vital processes. The nose and its associated passageways present the first aspect of the respiratory tract. This tract is continued from the nasal passageways posteriorly and inferiorly via the nasopharynx, oropharynx, and finally into the laryngopharynx, discussed in the following chapter. The respiratory tract also can be served by the mouth because of its association with the pharynges. And, of course, the mouth also provides the important first phase of the digestive tract. It is at this point that food is ingested and prepared, with the masticatory apparatus, for its later transportation into the lower digestive tract, where it is further treated for the absorption and utilization of its nutritive elements.

Insofar as speech and hearing activities are concerned, a great many are dependent upon the structures of the oro-nasal region. For the moment, discussion of the central nervous system and its important function in speech and hearing can be postponed until a later time. Attention is then focused upon the auditory system housed in and about the two temporal bones. This system is so important that it too is considered in greater detail in Chapter 8. Thus, expressive speech activities take up the major role in this summary.

The acoustic events that are interpreted linguistically are the result of many fine, subtly different changes in the spaces of the oro-nasal region. These changes produce at least two kinds of phenomena: (1) the resonances or echo-like effects upon the tone produced in the larynx, and (2) the interferences that are made in the air stream as it escapes from the respiratory tract in the active phase of respiration: exhalation. Both of these activities are classified as articulatory, for they are the product of changes in structure position or relationship, which in turn causes changes in the size and shape of the chambers or in the air passageways.

For example, elevation of the soft palate, along with medial movement of the pharyngeal walls by appropriate muscular contraction, causes the velopharyngeal aperture to be closed or nearly so. This decreases the contribution of the nasopharynx and nose to the sound coming from the larynx and futher prohibits the passage of air to those spaces. Thus, the mouth becomes the resonance chamber, along with the larynx and the oro- and laryngopharynges, for the laryngeal tone. Further, the air traveling upward from the respiratory tract passes through the mouth alone. With movement of the tongue (elevation, retraction, protrusion, grooving, or other), the size and contour of the oral cavity are changeable to produce characteristic sounds, such as vowels. Consonants might be produced by interfering with or affecting those sounds so that there might be a friction component added (fricative), or an explosive element associated (plosive), or other of the types of sounds to which man has associated a linguistic purpose.

In Appendix II, "Physiologic Phonetics," a rather detailed presentation is made of the activities of the entire speech apparatus in producing the various speech sounds. Ample illustration of the summary statements made in the present section is given in detailed form in Appendix II.

ORO-NASAL REGION LANDMARK IDENTIFICATION

Directions: For the indicated illustrations, label the following landmarks.

FIGURES 3–1 AND 3–2
Occipital Bone
Parietal Bone
Temporal Bone
Sphenoid Bone
Frontal Bone
Maxilla Bone
Mandible Bone
Nasal Bone
Zygomatic Bone
Ethmoid Bone
Vomer Bone
Inferior Nasal Turbinate Bone

Molar Tooth
Premolar Tooth
Canine Tooth
Incisor Tooth

Frontal Process, Maxilla Bone
Alveolar Process, Maxilla Bone
Zygomatic Process, Maxilla Bone
Anterior Nasal Spine

FIGURE 3–3
Crista Galli
Cribriform (Horizontal) Plate
Perpendicular Plate
Middle Turbinate
Air Cells
Olfactory Groove

FIGURE 3–4
Body
Greater Wing
Lesser Wing
Pterygoid Process
Lateral Pterygoid Plate
Medial Pterygoid Plate
Hamulus
Sphenoid Sinus

FIGURE 3–5
Squamous Portion
Mastoid Portion
Petrous Portion
Styloid Portion
Tympanic Portion
Zygomatic Process
External Auditory Canal
Mastoid Process
Internal Auditory Canal

FIGURE 3–6
Alae
Septal Cartilage Border
Free Border
Inferior Border

FIGURE 3–7
Superior Border
Concha

FIGURE 3–8
Perpendicular Portion
Horizontal Portion
Orbital Process
Pyramidal Process
Sphenoidal Process
Nasal Crest
Posterior Nasal Spine

FIGURE 3–9
Alveolar Process
Frontal Process
Zygomatic Process
Palatine Process
Body
Maxillary Sinus
Nasal Passage
Anterior Nasal Spine
Canine Fossa

FIGURE 3–10
Incisive (Premaxillary) Bone
Palatine Process, Maxilla Bone
Horizontal Process, Palatine Bone
Posterior Nasal Spine
Transverse Suture
Longitudinal Suture
Incisive Fossa (Canal)
Maxillary-Premaxillary Suture
Canine Tooth
Lateral Incisor Tooth
Palatal Rugae
Hamulus (Medial Pterygoid Plate)

FIGURE 3–11
Body
Ramus
Angle
Coronoid Process
Condyloid Process
Oblique Line
Mental Protuberance
Mandibular Notch

FIGURE 3–12
Nasal Septal Cartilage
Perpendicular Plate, Ethmoid Bone
Nasal Crest, Sphenoid Bone
Sphenoid Sinus
Crista Galli
Sella Turcica
Vomer Bone
Anterior Nasal Spine
Posterior Nasal Spine
Palatine Process, Maxilla Bone
Horizontal Portion, Palatine Bone
Superior Nasal Crest
Greater Alar Cartilage
Nasal Bone
Frontal Sinus

FIGURE 3–13
Nasal Bone
Frontal Process, Maxilla Bone
Greater Alar Cartilage
Lateral Nasal Cartilages
Zygomatic Process, Maxilla Bone
Zygomatic Bone
Mandible Bone, Body
Mandible Bone, Ramus
Vermilion Border
Cupid's Bow
Philtrum
Quadratus Labii Superior Muscle
Canine Muscle
Zygomatic (Major) Muscle
Risorius Muscle
Buccinator Muscle
Platysma Muscle
Triangular Muscle
Quadratus Labii Inferior Muscle
Mental Muscle
Orbicularis Oris Muscle

FIGURE 3–14
Parietal Bone
Temporal Bone
Frontal Bone
Zygomatic Process, Temporal Bone
Zygomatic Bone
Temporal Muscle
Mandible, Body
Mandible, Condyloid Process
Mandible, Angle
Masseter Muscle
Internal Pterygoid Muscle
External Pterygoid Muscle

FIGURE 3–15
Vertebrae

Posterior Pharyngeal Wall
Eustachian Tube Orifice
Nasal Passages
Tongue
Oral Cavity
Bony Palate
Tensor (Veli) Palatine Muscle
Levator (Veli) Palatine Muscle
Glossopalatine Muscle
Palatopharyngeal Muscle
Palatine Tonsil
Superior Pharyngeal Constrictor Muscle
Velopharyngeal Sphincter Muscle
Hamulus, Medial Pterygoid Plate

FIGURE 3–16
Apex
Dorsum
Vallate Papillae
Sulcus
Valleculae
Glossoepiglottic Membrane
Epiglottis
Root (Pharyngeal Portion)
Foramen Cecum

FIGURE 3–17
Apex
Root
Lingual Frenum
Palatoglossus Muscle
Styloglossus Muscle
Hyoglossus Muscle
Genioglossus Muscle

FIGURE 3–18
Body
Greater Cornu
Lesser Cornu
Anterior (Ventral) Portion

FIGURE 3–19
Tooth
Vestibule
Mandible Bone
Papillae
Lingual Septum
Genioglossus Muscle
Transverse Lingual Muscle
Longitudinal Superior Lingual Muscle
Longitudinal Inferior Lingual Muscle
Geniohyoid Muscle
Mylohyoid Muscle
Hyoid Bone
Lower Lip

Mental Spines
Epiglottis

FIGURE 3–20
Labial Frenum
Upper Lip
Palatal Rugae
Maxillary Teeth
Palatal Raphe
Soft Palate

Uvula
Faucial Isthmus
Posterior Faucial Pillar
Anterior Faucial Pillar
Palatine Tonsil (Fossa)
Tongue Dorsum
Lingual Frenum
Mandibular Teeth
Lower Lip

chapter 4

THE PHARYNGEAL REGION

Although arbitrarily separated in this text from the oro-nasal region (discussed previously, in Chapter 3), the pharyngeal region is not so separated in the organism. The pharyngeal region is an important and vital part of the human vegetative system, and serves as the receiving receptacle in the swallowing act, as the continuation of the respiratory passage from the nose and mouth, and, of course, acts predominantly in speech as a major resonator of the laryngeal tone. Voluntary changes in its size and shape help to produce some of the meaningful changes in speech sounds. It is under both voluntary and involuntary control in its various acts.

CLINICAL NOTE

The speech clinician must be alerted to conditions of the three pharynges for sources of speech and hearing defects. Most speech pathologists are agreed that injuries, paralyses, and pathologic processes that affect the pharynx can have a causal relationship to a speech or hearing problem. To be sure, it is not in the province of the speech pathologist to examine and diagnose anatomic and physiologic defects in many instances; yet, it is of considerable importance that his clients have such examinations so that the speech clinician may have some impression of the physical status of the structures for appropriate therapy.

DIVISIONS OF THE PHARYNX

The pharynx, in general, is a musculomembranous tube having three distinct areas, each of which is in contact with, and may even be considered as a continuation of, three separated chambers; it is from these three chambers that the various pharynges (see Figure 4–1) derive their names: the *nasopharynx,* the *oropharynx,* and the *laryngopharynx.* These are the nose, the mouth, and the larynx, and the part of the pharynx closest to each is a continuation of the chamber so named.

The *nasopharynx* presents the widest portion of the pharynx at its most cephalad end. As already mentioned, this tube is a continuation of the nasal cavities through the choanae and is essentially a part of the respiratory rather than the digestive system. It also communicates with the middle ear of the temporal bone through the eustachian tube on its lateral walls. This opening to the auditory tube is a funnel-shaped orifice located below and in front of the pharyngeal recess (fossa of Rosenmuller) and horizontally posterior to the nasal choanae on either side. The cartilage or cushion (torus) of the tube is somewhat irregularly elevated, and provides attachment for the salpingopharyngeal fold. This fold contains the salpingopharyngeal muscle extending caudad into the pharyngeal musculature. As is the remainder of the pharynx, the nasopharynx is lined continuously with mucous membrane.

The *oropharynx* is that space that continues the pharyngeal tube inferiorly from the level of the soft palate to the level of the hyoid bone. Here it is arbitrarily said to terminate, and the space below is the third division of the pharynx. The oropharynx derives its name from the fact that it is a continuation of the oral cavity, and thus it is essentially a major space in the digestive system, although it serves the respiratory tract at the same time. The boundaries of the oropharynx are identified as the faucial isthmus, the oral cavity (mouth) anteriorly, the nasopharynx superiorly, the upper four or five cervical vertebrae (in children, the upper six) posteriorly, the laryngopharynx inferiorly, and the musculomembranous wall laterally. This lateral wall is an interrupted continuation of the oral cavity, presenting the two palatine arches (anterior and posterior) between which lies the faucial isthmus. The palatine tonsils are found between the two arches.

The *laryngopharynx* continues the pharyngeal tube inferiorly, narrowing to the smallest cross section of the pharynx, at the esophageal entrance. Its boundaries are generally located as the oropharynx superiorly, the esophagus inferiorly, the laryngeal cartilages and membranes anteriorly, the cervical vertebrae posteriorly, the horns of the hyoid bone, and the continuation of the musculomembranous oropharynx laterally. There is a superior connection with the epiglottis as well as an attachment with the cricoid cartilage at its most inferior point.

THE CONNECTIVE TISSUES

The pharynx has no dominant type of connective tissue; there are a few ligaments, considerable fascia and areolar tissue, and some cartilage connections in one area alone—the laryngopharynx. Superior to the pharynx are found the bones of the base of the skull; these are the body of the sphenoid and the basal part of the occipital bone. It is to these that the most cephalad and broad portions of the pharynx are attached. In addition, the anterior portion of this upper end is provided skeletal support by the bony tissues of the nasal cavities; the posterior portion is supported by the upper vertebrae, especially the atlas. Lower are found the soft palate, uvula, and pharyngeal isthmus that function as somewhat supporting structures. Laterally, the cartilage of the eustachian tube (torus tubarius) provides some support.

MUSCULATURE

In general, the muscles of the pharynges are designed to change the shape of the tube in the swallowing act, constricting the diameter in such a way as to squeeze the bolus of food down into the esophagus. In the act of swallowing, the muscles of the mouth and palate play an important role, but this role is difficult to separate from the role the same muscles play in various speech activities.

Five muscles are generally considered to be pharyngeal muscles: the *superior pharyngeal constrictor, the middle pharyngeal constrictor, the inferior pharyngeal constrictor,* the *stylopharyngeal,* and the difficult-to-find *salpingopharyngeal* muscle. (See Table 4–1 and Figure 4–2.) Another two muscles, the *glossopalatine* (palatoglossal) and the *pharyngopalatine* (palatopharyngeal), have been described earlier as being importantly related to the palate and tongue respectively. And, two more muscles, the *velopharyngeal sphincter* and the *cricopharyngeal*—which attract the attention of speech pathologists for several reasons—bring the total to seven muscles in this region.

The *superior pharyngeal constrictor* muscle has its origins in several locations, from a superior to an inferior direction. Fibers originate from the lower border of the medial pterygoid plate of the sphenoid bone, from the pterygo-

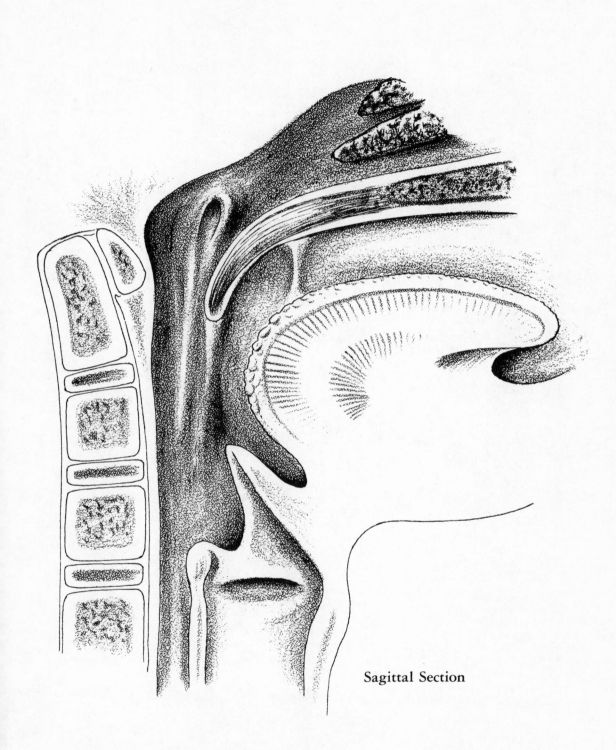

Sagittal Section

Figure 4–1.
Pharynges

TABLE 4.1 MUSCLES OF THE PHARYNX

MUSCLE	ORIGIN	INSERTION	ACTION	NERVE
Pharyngeal Muscles:				
Superior Constrictor	Lower posterior border of medial pterygoid plate; pterygomandibular ligament and raphe; mylohyoid ridge of mandible; mucous membrane of oral cavity; sides of tongue	Posterior median raphe of pharynx	Contracts pharynx; aids movement of food bolus toward esophagus	Cranial X (Pharyngeal Plexus)
Middle Constrictor	Both cornua of hyoid bone; stylohyoid ligament	Posterior median raphe of pharynx	Contracts pharynx; aids movement of food bolus toward esophagus	Cranial X (Pharyngeal Plexus)
Inferior Constrictor	Inferior side of cricoid cartilage; oblique line of thyroid cartilage	Posterior median raphe of pharynx	Contracts pharynx; aids movement of food bolus	Cranial X (Pharyngeal Plexus)
Velopharyngeal Sphincter	Midline of soft palate	Posterior median raphe of pharynx	Protrusion and elevation of portion of pharyngeal wall; aids in forcing soft palate posteriorly	Cranial X (Pharyngeal Plexus)
Cricopharyngeal	Sides of cricoid cartilage	Posterior median raphe of pharynx	Contracts pharynx	Cranial X (Pharyngeal Plexus)
Pharyngeal Levator Muscles:				
Stylopharyngeal	Base of styloid process of temporal bone	Mucous membrane of pharynx and thyroid cartilage	Elevates and widens pharynx	Cranial IX
Salpingopharyngeal	Lower edge of eustachian cartilage	Mucous membrane of pharynx	Elevates pharynx; distorts the torus tubarius	Cranial X (Pharyngeal Plexus)

mandibular ligament and raphe, from the mylohyoid ridge of the mandible, and from the mucous membrane of the oral cavity. These origins are all anterior to the body of the muscle, to its insertion and to the cavity of the pharynx. The muscle fibers arch nearly horizontally backward and form a thin quadrilateral muscle around the sides of the nasopharynx and part of the oropharynx. They insert into the fibrous posterior median raphe, where they meet with similar fibers from the opposite side. At the superior border are found the pharyngeal opening to the eustachian tube, the levator veli palatine muscle, and the pharyngeal aponeurosis. The action of the superior pharyngeal constrictor muscle is to narrow the lumen of the pharynx by constriction and thus aid in the movement of the bolus of food inferiorly. Its nerve supply comes from the pharyngeal plexus of the vagus (Cranial X) nerve.

The *middle pharyngeal constrictor* muscle is fan-shaped, with its narrow portion antero-laterally, which partially overlaps the superior constrictor muscle. It originates from the whole border of the greater cornu of the hyoid bone, from the lesser cornu of the same structure, and from the stylohyoid ligament. The muscle fibers fan out from this origin, the lower ones passing beneath the inferior pharyngeal constrictor, the middle ones passing nearly horizontally back, and the superior fibers passing upward and external to the superior pharyngeal constrictor. These fibers, from all parts, insert at the midline posteriorly, into the fibrous raphe. When contracted, the middle pharyngeal constrictor continues the squeezing action of the pharynx, forcing the bolus of food farther inferiorly toward the esophagus. Its innervation is the same as the previous muscle.

The *inferior pharyngeal constrictor* muscle is perhaps the thickest and widest of the constrictor group, with a somewhat narrow origin but a rather extensive insertion. Its fibers originate along the sides of the laryngeal cartilages, the cricoid inferiorly, and the thyroid at its oblique line. Its most inferior fibers pass nearly horizontally back; its upper fibers ascend around the sides of the pharynx. Both groups of fibers insert along with the same fibers from the opposite side into the fibrous posterior median raphe of the pharynx. Its action, when contracted, is to continue the previously described squeezing effect upon the bolus of food in deglutition, forcing it inferiorly into the esophagus. Again, the pharyngeal plexus furnishes the nerve supply to this muscle.

Two highly variable muscles are also listed by some authorities as important pharyngeal muscles. Although all authorities do not agree, their perhaps doubtful presence seems to explain much in both normal and abnormal functioning of the pharyngeal region. The first is the sphincter of Whillis, or the *velopharyngeal sphincter* muscle. This is actually a part of the superior constrictor muscle, but instead of having its origin along the structures previously mentioned, it is found along the midline of the soft palate, about midway on its anterior-posterior axis. These fibers pass as a definite muscle bundle horizontally back around the sides of the pharynx to insert into the posterior median raphe of the pharynx. Upon contraction, two effects are seen: (1) the posterior wall of the pharynx protrudes as an elevated horizontal fold, which may actually produce what is labeled Passavant's pad or cushion; and (2) the tissues of the soft palate are pulled posteriorly, corrugating those tissues on the nasal surface. This action occurs during deglutition and also during velopharyngeal closure in certain speech sound productions. Undoubtedly, it is an important muscle for speech as well as for effective separation between nasal and oral pharynges.

The second ancillary muscle of the constrictor group is the *cricopharyngeal* muscle. In basic structure, it is the most caudal portion of the inferior constrictor. Its bilateral origin is along the sides of the cricoid cartilage, along with the origin of the remainder of the inferior constrictor. Its fibers pass horizontally back around the sides of the most inferior portion of the laryngopharynx, to insert into the posterior midline raphe. This muscle is of considerable importance in

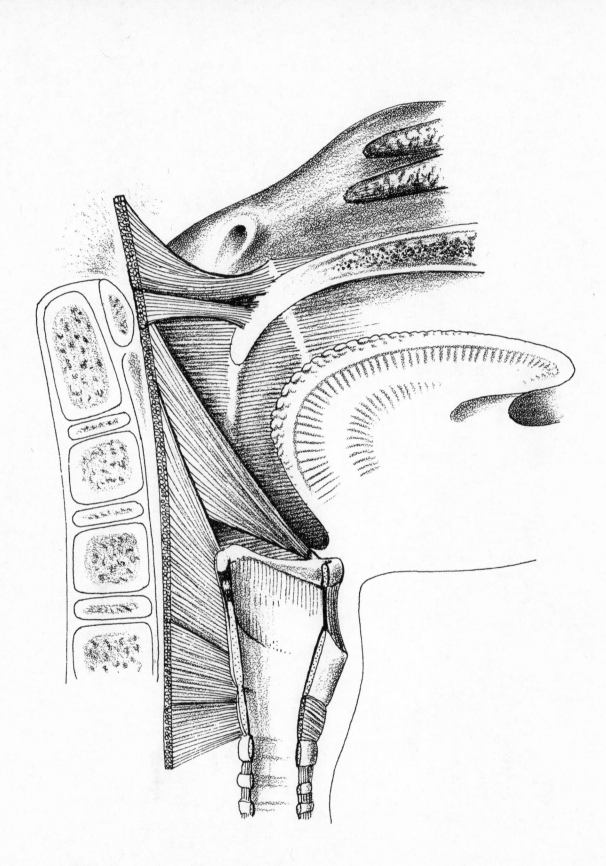

Figure 4–2.
Pharyngeal Constrictor Muscles

certain pathologic and surgical events. Both the cricopharyngeal and the velopharyngeal sphincter muscles receive neural innervation from the pharyngeal plexus (Cranial X).

CLINICAL NOTE

The usefulness of the muscles of the pharynx is evident when the vegetative functions are considered; speech, too, requires good operation of these muscles. In some pathologies, speech defects are outstanding characteristics, and speech therapy is frequently the major rehabilitative procedure. The patient with a repaired cleft palate, for example, is one who needs pharyngeal muscle study and training; the study includes evaluation of the action of these muscles. Loss of the insertion of some muscles, such as the velopharyngeal sphincter, may preclude good velopharyngeal closure. Another case is the person who has had a laryngectomy for laryngeal cancer; the surgeon usually tends to retain the cricopharyngeal muscle so that this may be used by the speech therapist in the development of adequate esophageal speech.

The Pharyngeal Levator Muscles

The pharyngeal levator muscles (see Figure 4–3) are the *stylopharyngeal* muscle and the *salpingopharyngeal* muscle.

The *stylopharyngeal* muscle is a slender group of fibers which, when considered bilaterally, have broadly divergent origins and which pass to a much more medial insertion in the pharyngeal wall. Its origin is at the base of the styloid process of the temporal bone, with its fibers passing downward and medially, spreading out as they pass between the superior and medial pharyngeal constrictor muscles. The insertion of this muscle is considered to be within the mucous membrane lining of the pharynx, blending with the other soft tissues of the pharynx, and in the thyroid cartilage, along with fibers from the palatopharyngeal muscle. From its obvious orientation, it can be seen that its action is to elevate the entire pharynx and to widen it superiorly, an action which occurs during deglutition to receive the bolus of food within the pharynx. Nerve supply is derived from the glossopharyngeal (Cranial IX) nerve.

The *salpingopharyngeal* muscle is similar to the stylopharyngeal muscle, having a reasonably fixed superior end with fibers extending into the soft tissues of the pharynx. These fibers originate along the lower border of the cartilage of the eustachian tube and pass directly downward, within the salpingopharyngeal fold, to insert into the walls of the pharynx, along with other muscle fibers. Its action is twofold: (1) to elevate the pharynx in deglutition, and (2) to effect distortion upon the torus tubarius in ventilation of the middle ear. Innervation is provided by the pharyngeal plexus.

In considering the general actions of the muscles of the pharynges, the effect of these actions in swallowing is the first vegetative function to be considered. The actions in speech production are refinements of, but remain essentially similar to, those basic acts. It is apparent that synergic action of the constrictors is required to effect the squeezing function in a smoothly continuous act from superior to inferior, forcing the bolus of food from oropharynx into esophagus. At that latter point, a contiguous and continuous squeezing action of the smooth-muscle tissues of the alimentary canal carry on the function of what is known as *peristaltic action*. This action is the sequential squeezing, or narrowing, of the musculomembranous tube from pharynx throughout the entire alimentary canal. Along with the muscles of the soft palate, the constrictors—and especially the velopharyngeal sphincter muscle—contract during the first stage of swallowing (and during production of many speech sounds) to effect velopharyngeal closure, separating the nasal from the oral pharynges. This closure need not be complete or tight to be effective. The separation between the two pharynges prevents the invasion by food and other foreign matter into the nasopharynx and nasal cavities. It is also of considerable importance in such acts as vowel sound production, blowing balloons, whistling, and like acts peculiar to man.

CLINICAL NOTE
The oral aspect of the swallowing act, or deglutition, is the product of an extremely complicated series of muscular contractions. These muscles and muscle groups contract in controlled sequences that are directed in part by the inherent demands of the primitive act of swallowing, as well as by the effects of learned neuromuscular patterns. Structural differences also contribute their effects to deglutition. The role of the speech therapist is to evaluate the contribution of these differences in light of a speech aberration and to program appropriate therapeutic procedures that consider these differences.

In the swallowing act itself, the muscles of the cheek, lips, and mandible close the mouth to prevent extrusion of food through the mouth. The tongue is elevated; at the same time the pharynges are elevated to receive the food. The tongue thrusts the food posteriorly into the pharynx through the faucial isthmus by progressive elevation of its dorsum. The isthmus closes behind the food as the tongue descends. Receipt of the bolus causes the pharynx to return to its lower beginning position with the food; the superior, then the middle, and, subsequently, the inferior pharyngeal constrictor muscles contract in peristalsis to force the food into the esophagus. The laryngeal isthmus is closed and somewhat covered by the epiglottis to protect itself from invasion by foreign materials. Once the food has entered the esophagus, the constrictors relax and await receipt of the next food mass.

Nervous Tissues of the Pharynx

Playing an important role in nervous stimulation of the muscles of the pharynx is a network of nervous tissue called the *pharyngeal plexus*. It is an extraspinal nerve center, which is supplied mainly through the vagus (Cranial X) nerve, and further supplies other muscle tissues in the head and neck regions. Certainly, the three pharyngeal constrictors—the superior, the middle, and the inferior—receive motor impulses through the pharyngeal plexus. The same nerve source also supplies the salpingopharyngeal muscle. However, the stylopharyngeal muscle receives its innervation from the glossopharyngeal (Cranial IX) nerve, as do several other structures of this important area.

Some variation in nerve supply is thought to occur. This variation is especially true when one is considering the inferior constrictor muscle, some fibers of which actually may be innervated through the external laryngeal and the recurrent laryngeal nerves. This is understandable when the intimate relationship between laryngopharynx and larynx is considered.

The student should be aware of the sensory nerve supply to the pharyngeal and oral regions, although this text does not pretend to cover that subject exhaustively. It is well known that the sensations of taste, along with temperature (hot and cold) as well as others, are operating in this region. In the mouth, the anterior two-thirds of the tongue is supplied for taste sensation by the facial (Cranial VII) nerve through the chorda tympani nerve. The posterior third of the tongue as well as the pharynx and other locations of taste buds are served by sensory fibers from the glossopharyngeal (Cranial IX) nerve. Although most of the taste buds are found on the surface of the tongue (in its epithelium) some of these organs are found on the soft palate and on the epiglottis as well. Few are actually found on the walls of the pharynx.

For more details of both motor and sensory functions in the pharyngeal region, reference should be made to specialized texts. Certainly, some knowledge

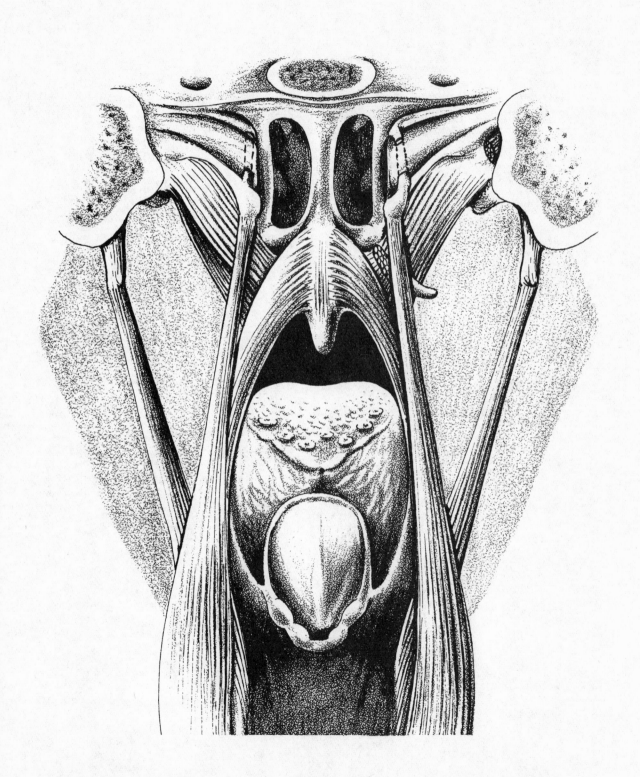

Figure 4–3.
Pharyngeal Levator Muscles

of these functions should be acquired by the speech pathologist for more thorough understanding of both normal and pathologic actions in both speech and vegetative operations.

SUMMARY OF FUNCTIONS OF THE PHARYNGEAL REGION

For life-sustaining activities, the control of the actions of the pharynges is largely reflexive. As swallowing takes place, velopharyngeal closure is an involuntary accompaniment. In breathing, the velopharyngeal aperture must be patent, or open, so that air might pass from the nose and nasopharynx through the pharynges and into the lower respiratory tract. Of course, the air destined for the lungs might enter the body through the mouth and thence into the pharynges and lower respiratory tract. Both nasal and oral entranceways are used to some extent by most persons at some times during their lives.

The presence of environmental air in the nasopharynx is of considerable importance for other purposes, as well. It will be remembered that the pharyngeal terminus of the eustachian tube is in the lateral pharyngeal wall. It is this tube that delivers environmental air into the middle ear, maintaining a balance of air pressure on both sides of the tympanic membrane. Although the opening to the eustachian tube is not always patent, it generally is easily opened by the fortuitous arrangement of palatal and pharyngeal muscles to the cartilaginous tube. First, the tensor (veli) palatine muscle has a goodly portion of its fibers attached to this structure. Because of this attachment and because of the attachment at the other end to the posterior border of the bony palate, it is thought by some that this is really a eustachian tube muscle, rather than a palatal one. This muscle, along with salpingopharyngeal, where it is of sufficient size and strength to do so, contracts during swallowing, yawning, and other such activities, to exert a twisting pull on the cartilage; this is sufficient to cause the tube to become patent, thus providing for the important air exchange.

The role of the pharynges in dealing with environmental air is obviously to channel the air from the nose downward to the lower respiratory tract: from nose through nasopharynx (or from mouth through oropharynx), downward to the lowermost pharynx, where it enters the aditus ad laryngis, the larynx, the trachea, and on. In respiratory activities, the pharynges are generally patent; associated structures such as the velum and epiglottis have an effect on the direction of the air flow.

In speaking activities, control of the pharynges might be combined reflexive and voluntary. At least it is clear that man can control movements of the structures to some extent; in fast-moving continuous speech, however, it appears that the habitual patterning must be coordinated so rapidly that detailed control over each structure and movement is unlikely. Perhaps some sort of servomechanism with a well-developed feedback system is responsible for the changes.

The pharynges are part of the resonance system of the vocal tract. This means that the sound delivered to them from the tone-producing apparatus (the larynx) is changed by being in the pharynges; this is similar to the commonly observed phenomenon when a sound is delivered in the open air, then into a partly closed space such as a bottle or a box, and then into a different-sized or -shaped bottle or box. The size, shape, and status of the pharyngeal walls are importantly related to the nature of the voice. Changes in any of those characteristics—size, shape, or status—change the sound. This change of sound is deliberate in some instances, but in other instances it occurs with changes in health, condition, or with age.

In the case of changes that occur with age, status changes that are due to muscle, fat, or mucous membrane changes are thought to create the voice characteristics of the older person. Other changes, in size and shape, are largely due to the velopharyngeal apparatus. Here the pharynges can be separated at the level of the palate or might be made continuous. The result of such manipulations is that the speech sounds are produced in a characteristic and acceptable fashion, or might become "hypernasal" in character and thus be unacceptable and defective. Certain speech sounds are normally nasal in character in English, but others should not be. Details of muscular action underlying velopharyngeal closure in speech are found in Appendix II.

PHARYNGEAL REGION LANDMARK IDENTIFICATION

Directions: For the indicated illustrations, label the following landmarks.

FIGURE 4–1
Nasal Passages
Eustachian Tube Orifice
Vertebrae
Posterior Pharyngeal Wall
Nasopharynx (Epipharynx)
Oropharynx
Laryngopharynx (Hypopharynx)
Bony Palate
Soft Palate
Uvula
Oral Cavity
Tongue
Vallecula
Epiglottis
Larynx
Esophagus

FIGURE 4–2
Nasal Passage
Bony Palate
Soft Palate
Vertebrae
Posterior Pharyngeal Wall

Superior Pharyngeal Constrictor Muscle
Velopharyngeal Sphincter Muscle
Pterygomandibular Raphe
Buccinator Muscle
Oral Cavity
Tongue
Medial Pharyngeal Constrictor Muscle
Hyoid Bone
Inferior Pharyngeal Constrictor Muscle
Cricopharyngeal Muscle
Thyroid Cartilage
Esophagus

FIGURE 4–3
Eustachian Tube Cartilage
Salpingopharyngeal Muscle
Styloid Process, Temporal Bone
Stylopharyngeal Muscle
Soft Palate
Palatal Raphe
Palatopharyngeal Muscle
Oral Cavity
Tongue, Root (Pharyngeal Portion)
Larynx

chapter 5

THE LARYNGEAL REGION

Although it is obvious that man is different from other animals, the reason for this difference is less obvious. Differentiation and specialization in function of the cerebral cortex and the larynx may be considered major factors in underscoring this difference. The cerebral cortex, however, cannot be fairly treated in a text of limited scope such as this. The larynx, on the other hand, becomes spotlighted in a text devoted to the task of explaining the speaking mechanisms. The larynx serves in the processes of respiration and phonation. Both are so importantly interrelated as to make differentiation difficult, if not impossible. However, the larynx can be described by certain characteristic structural properties.

The laryngeal is another of the regions or passages that serve only the respiratory tract. The larynx (see Figure 5–1 and Figure 5–2) is an expansion of the tubular respiratory system of air canals; it is so expanded to provide for the internal structures that produce a flexible valve. This valve is comprised of a pair of membranous "sliding doors" that lie across the larynx and are connected to the walls in front and back. The two vocal folds, or "sliding doors," are operated by action of the laryngeal walls and by the hinged end of the valve. Opening and closing the valve are extremely rapid, vibratory and complex actions. All movement in the larynx, including partial or complete closure of the glottis (the opening between the two vocal folds), is effected by specific muscular attachments. The analogy of sliding doors is an oversimplification in the phonatory act, but may be somewhat accurate in describing the closure in respiration. The vocal folds, then, are mobile extrusions from the lateral walls of the larynx, are lined with mucous membrane, and enclose a vocal ligament medially and vocal muscles more laterally.

The primary function of the larynx is to serve as a protective valve for the respiratory tract it surmounts. The enlarged cavity of the larynx is the entrance into the respiratory tract itself, and thus serves through its valve to protect this tract from invasion by foreign matter (anyone who has inspired a bit of food and engaged in a violent coughing spell could offer sufficient proof of this). The laryngeal cavity is divided roughly into two smaller cavities by the vocal folds. The upper one, known as the *vestibule,* connects with the laryngopharynx above and with the *atrium,* or lower cavity, below. The mucous membrane lining of the larynx is continuous with that of the pharynges and the trachea, or windpipe, below.

The top of the larynx is formed by a triangular opening—the *aditus*—which is rimmed by thick folds of tissue running from front to back, and which close in very violent actions, such as coughing. The front or anterior end of these folds is attached to the leaf-shaped and flexible epiglottis, a cartilage that serves to close the aditus further in actions such as swallowing. The epiglottis swings down over the aditus, thus covering it, and provides for the movement of food particles into the laryngopharynx and esophagus. The posterior end of the aditus is supported by the peaks of the two posterior cartilages of the larynx, the *arytenoids*. These folds are termed the *aryepiglottic* folds.

On either wall of the vestibule, just above the vocal folds, is another set of folds known as the *vestibular* (ventricular, or false vocal) *folds*. These folds are relatively large protrusions into the vestibule, but are not normally active in either respiration or phonation. Between the false vocal folds and the true vocal folds on either side is an opening in the wall of the larynx, ending at various depths within the wall tissue; this opening is the ventricle of Morgagni, which, although almost vestigial in man, houses mucous glands producing lubricating fluids for the folds beneath.

The lower part of the larynx, the atrium, is cone-shaped; its walls are called the elastic cone. It continues the space from the glottis inferiorly into the trachea. Its lower limit is arbitrarily defined as the lowest part of the lowest cartilage: the cricoid.

THE CONNECTIVE TISSUES

The larynx is supported by one major bone and formed by five major cartilages. There are at least four, and perhaps as many as six, minor cartilages that act as supporting tissues but that vary from individual to individual, not only in size but in actual existence. (See Figure 5–2.)

The single bone is the *hyoid*, a horseshoe-shaped bone providing basic support for various muscles of the tongue and for the majority of the laryngeal tissues. (See discussion of the hyoid bone in Chapter 3, under the section "The Facial Skeleton," and Figure 3–18.) It is supported in space itself by muscular and ligamentous tissues running superiorly to the mandible and the skull. The hyoid bone is oriented with its open end directed posteriorly, and its large body extends anteriorly. Extending backward from the body on either side is the greater horn of the hyoid. At about the point of juncture between the body and the greater horn is a smaller upward projecting lesser horn. These parts—the body, greater horn, and lesser horn—serve as points of attachment for muscles and ligaments of the larynx as well as for other organs.

The largest and most prominent of the laryngeal cartilages is the *thyroid* cartilage. This is actually a two-walled cartilage, the thin sheets (lamina) meeting at the anterior aspect of the larynx and neck, forming the laryngeal prominence or the "Adam's apple." If you were to place your extended fingertips of both hands together at an angle so that only the middle and ring fingers were touching, you would find a very rough analogy to the thyroid cartilage. If you elevated the thumbs high, you might have a reasonably good representation of the long superior horns, and the extended little fingers would produce slightly distorted (because of the inability to orient them directly downward), inferior thyroid horns, or cornua. Between the two palms of the hands would be the vocal folds, running from the ring fingertips straight back into the open part of the "V" formed by the rear of the palms. Tipping the thumbs outward slightly would produce the slight funnel-shape that is characteristic of the larynx.

Inside the walls of the thyroid cartilage, extending from the angle formed by the two lamina, are housed the vocal folds (both true and false), as well as the other intrinsic tissues of the larynx. Toward the posterior borders of the thyroid cartilage, two thin projections pass upward and downward to connect with other structures; these are the superior and inferior thyroid horns (cornua). The superior horn is in contact through ligaments with the greater horn of the hyoid bone, above, and the inferior thyroid horn is in contact through a true, diarthrodial joint with the cricoid cartilage, below. The lamina of the thyroid cartilage has an oblique

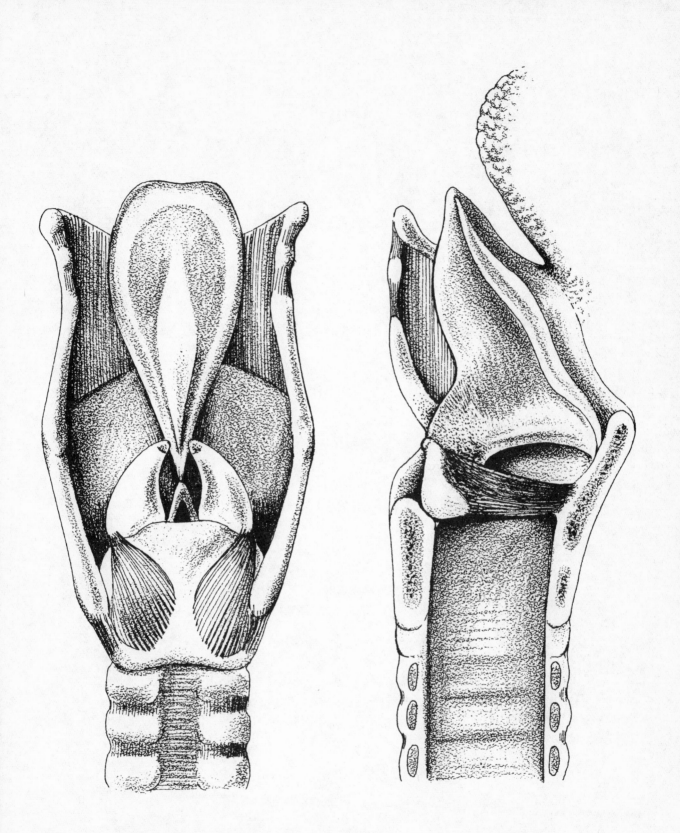

Posterior View   Sagittal View

Figure   5-1.
Gross Larynx

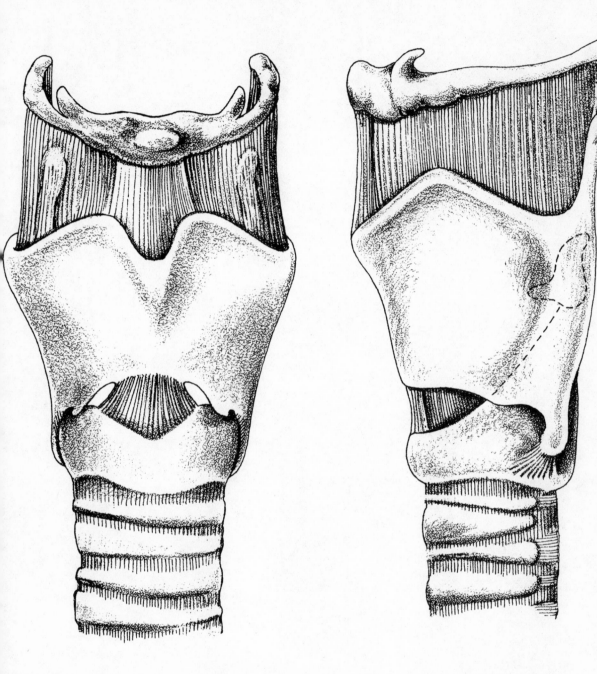

Anterior View   Lateral View

Figure   5–2.
Skeletal Larynx

line, a ridge of slight prominence extending from near the superior cornu down across the lamina toward the anterior medial aspect; this oblique line separates the points of attachment of muscles running to the larynx from above and below. The superior thyroid notch is that space just above the angle of the thyroid cartilage and just below the hyoid bone; it can be palpated by finger rather easily by finding the prominence and moving slightly above it to the soft space there.

The next largest cartilage of the larynx is the *cricoid,* a circular cartilage encircling the larynx immediately beneath the thyroid cartilage. It has its narrowest part (the arch) in the front, and it expands upward posteriorly into a tall and broad lamina, or signet. This posterior lamina stands high in the space between the open ends of the thyroid cartilage. The superior surface of the lamina of the cricoid is broad and somewhat concave, and supports the paired arytenoid cartilages, which further fill the posterior space between the two lamina of the thyroid cartilage. The cricoid cartilage is attached to the thyroid through ligaments, and to the first of the cartilaginous rings of the trachea below by the same means. The muscles attached to this cartilage pass from its sides and lamina to the thyroid and arytenoid cartilages, and have a definite effect upon the vocal folds. The inferior horn of the thyroid cartilage articulates with the cricoid, so that movement results in either a downward arcing of the thyroid prominence or a downward arcing of the lamina of the cricoid. Because the vocal folds are attached to the angle of the thyroid as well as to the arytenoid cartilages (sitting on the cricoid lamina), this arc has the effect of separating even farther the two ends of the vocal folds, thus lengthening and perhaps tensing them.

The paired *arytenoid* cartilages are located on, and articulate posteriorly with, the lamina of the cricoid cartilage in the larynx. These are small pyramids somewhat irregular in their angles and sides. There are four surfaces and three important angles. The arytenoids are so located that there are broad surfaces facing backward and toward the midline of the larynx, indicating that there must be an angle oriented anteriorly and another oriented laterally, and a surface that faces antero-laterally. The forward-projecting angle is called the vocal process, for to it is attached the vocal fold. The laterally projecting angle is the muscular process, which serves as the point of attachment for several important muscles that act to move the pyramidal arytenoid. The antero-lateral surface serves as the attachment point for muscles and ligaments running anteriorly from the arytenoid to the internal angle of the thyroid.

The apex of the arytenoid cartilage is thin and bent medially, somewhat backward. From its summit runs the thickened fold, mentioned earlier, which connects with the epiglottis, and thus is the *aryepiglottic* fold. Running across or near the summit are muscle fibers from below and connecting the apex with the epiglottis. These muscle and membranous tissues assist in vigorous closing of the aditus in swallowing and coughing. The medial surface of the arytenoid is lined with the mucous membrane, and forms the intercartilaginous portion of the glottis. In the closing of the glottis, the medial surfaces approximate each other and thus effect closure of just that part of the glottis. This approximation is made possible by the articulation of the arytenoid, as it is placed upon the superior surface of the cricoid cartilage lamina. Traditionally the inferior surface of the arytenoid (the base) is thought to slide and also to rotate in its articulation; some authorities feel that perhaps only the sliding motion is performed. This sliding motion is the result of muscles interconnecting the arytenoids; they are attached to the posterior surface of the cartilages.

The forward-projecting angle, the vocal process, of the arytenoid cartilages is of considerable importance in laryngeal structure and function. To this process are attached mucous-membrane lining, the vocal ligament, and the muscle of the vocal fold; these pass directly forward and slightly caudad to be attached into the angle of the thyroid cartilage internally. Movement of the vocal process will cause changes in the vocal fold, as will movement of the thyroid cartilage that affects the anterior attachment of the fold (assuming that the arytenoids remain fixed). The reverse is also true: Movement of the cricoid, and thus of the arytenoids sitting on the cricoid lamina, causes a change in the vocal folds (assuming that the thyroid cartilage remains fixed). Detailed studies of the nature of these changes may be found in various journals reporting X-ray and fluoroscopic, electromyographic, and acoustic techniques of analyzing the laryngeal changes during phonation and respiration, both normally and pathologically.

CLINICAL NOTE

Voice therapists are often called upon to serve persons having voice problems that result from cartilage defects. These defects may result from injury sustained by a blow or by a penetrating object, or from an abnormal growth, such as cancer or other neoplasm, which affects the operation of the larynx. Therapists are also called upon when the muscular tissues operating the structures of the larynx are injured or paralyzed. Illustrating this condition is the well-known form of paralysis, poliomyelitis, although other forms of paralysis equally affect the muscles causing defective vocalization.

Another of the cartilages of the larynx with which the speech therapist may be concerned is the *epiglottis.* The epiglottis is the relatively large, unpaired cartilage at the superior terminus of the larynx, having its broad end cephalad and its narrow, stemlike petiole attached at the angle of the thyroid, internally. This attachment is provided through the thyroepiglottic ligament. This thin and extremely flexible cartilage is further attached to the tongue through its lateral and median glossoepiglottic membranes, between which are found the vallecula, or spaces, beyond the posterior border of the tongue. The epiglottis is further attached from its anterior surface to the hyoid bone through the hyoepiglottic ligament, a ligamentous membrane running to the body of the hyoid. The epiglottic cartilage itself is described as being concave-convex, having a rather undulating appearance as well as action, and as having many indentations throughout its surface for the accommodation of mucous glands. Other muscular and membranous connections with the laryngeal cartilages have been discussed earlier.

The first of the minor cartilages of the larynx are the *corniculate* cartilages. These paired cartilages cap the arytenoids, serving to continue the length of the apexes of the latter. In some individuals, these corniculate cartilages are actually fused with the larger structures and are indefinable as separate. Another pair of minor cartilages are the *cuneiform* cartilages; these are an extremely variable pair of cartilages, found in the aryepiglottic fold, serving to stiffen and support that fold. In some persons, these cartilages are reasonably large and flat, extending downward from the fold into the quadrangular membrane below; in other persons, they are small cartilages found almost exclusively within the aryepiglottic fold alone. A third minor cartilage, not always present in humans, is the *triticeal* (wheat kernel) cartilage, which is found within the ligament or membrane connecting the superior horn of the thyroid cartilage with the greater horn of the hyoid bone (the hyothyroid ligament). A fourth minor cartilage is the *sesamoid,* infrequently found in man on the lateral borders of the arytenoid cartilages and connected with the corniculates by elastic ligaments.

The structures of the various cartilages vary in composition. The thyroid, cricoid, and arytenoid cartilages are made up of hyaline tissue, the epiglottis, corniculate, cuneiform, and the apexes of the arytenoids are made up of elastic tissue. The hyaline tissues tend to ossify with age, commencing in early adulthood, and by age 65 these cartilages may be entirely ossified. (Clinical attention must be directed to this change, which partly accounts for vocal differences between the young and the aged.)

The *ligaments* of the larynx serve important supporting functions to the cartilages and to the actions of the soft tissues in both respiration and phonation. There are two types of ligaments: (1) the extrinsic, which connect the hyoid bone with the thyroid and epiglottic cartilages, and the tracheal rings with the cricoid cartilage, and (2) the intrinsic, which interconnect the laryngeal cartilages.

Of the extrinsic ligaments, the uppermost is the hyoepiglottic, internally connecting the body of the hyoid bone with the anterior surface of the epiglottis. Running from the end of the greater cornu of the hyoid bone down to the tip of the superior thyroid cornu is the *hyothyroid* ligament. Extending from this ligament is the *hyothyroid* membrane, which runs from the inferior border of the hyoid bone to the superior border of the thyroid cartilage. At the anterior midline, this membrane thickens to become the *middle hyothyroid* ligament; because of the term "middle," the earlier mentioned ligament is frequently distinguished from its fellow by the term "lateral hyothyroid ligament." The last of the extrinsic ligaments is the *cricotracheal* ligament, which connects the ring of the cricoid with the ring of the first tracheal cartilages.

The intrinsic ligaments of the larynx connect the movable smaller cartilages of the larynx. The *middle cricothyroid* ligament is found anteriorly at the midline, fanning up to the thyroid cartilage from the arch of the cricoid. It is continued laterally by the *cricothyroid* membrane, which is the major structure of the elastic cone of the atrium of the larynx. The middle of the posterior surface of the arytenoid cartilage is attached to the lamina of the cricoid below by the *posterior cricoarytenoid* ligament. And, the epiglottis is attached to the thyroid cartilage by a thin ligament running from the stem to the angle of the thyroid, just above the attachment of the ventricular ligaments: the *thyroepiglottic* ligament.

Other ligaments of the larynx include those of the vocal folds, which are discussed later.

MUSCULATURE

The classical procedure of dividing the laryngeal muscles into two groups, extrinsic and intrinsic, is followed here. From a topographical point of view, visualization and understanding of these tissues are much simpler when they are studied as separate groups of muscles. By definition, the muscles of the extrinsic group are those attached to the cartilages of the larynx from nonlaryngeal structures. In general, these latter are the thorax, the mandible, and the skull. In viewing the origins in this way, it is not difficult to realize the vertical "sling-like" arrangement provided by such muscles, nor to understand that contraction of certain groups produce the position of the larynx in the throat, up, down, backward, or forward—or combinations of these. In all such actions, gravity is an important antagonist, along with the forces produced by other noncontractile tissues attached to the laryngeal cartilages.

Extrinsic Muscles

The extrinsic muscles are further divided into those that are above the hyoid (the suprahyoids) and those that are below the hyoid (infrahyoids). These muscles effect the position of the hyoid bone, which is basically the foundation structure of the larynx; movement of the hyoid is translated almost directly into movement of the laryngeal structures. Thus, the suprahyoid muscle group consists of muscles passing from the mandible and skull downward to insert somewhere upon the hyoid bone. These muscles are the *stylohyoid, digastric, mylohyoid,* and *geniohyoid.* (See Table 5–1.) Also related are the palatopharyngeal, stylopharyngeal, and the two lower constrictor muscles of the pharynx because of their inconstant but common fiber insertions upon the hyoid as well as upon the thyroid cartilage. The hyoglossus muscle is also a suprahyoid muscle, which was discussed earlier, in Chapter 3, as an extrinsic tongue muscle.

TABLE 5.1   EXTRINSIC MUSCLES OF THE LARYNX

MUSCLE	ORIGIN	INSERTION	ACTION	NERVE
Suprahyoid Muscles:				
Stylohyoid	Styloid process of the temporal bone	Body of the hyoid bone	Elevates and draws hyoid bone backward	Cranial VII
Digastric	Anterior belly arises from internal aspect of mandible close to midline; posterior belly arises on medial side of mastoid process of temporal bone	Intermediate tendon and the hyoid bone	Elevates hyoid; depresses mandible	Cranial V (Anterior belly) Cranial VII (Posterior belly)
Mylohyoid	Mylohyoid ridge of the mandible	Hyoid bone and median raphe	Raises and projects hyoid bone and tongue	Cranial V
Geniohyoid	Internal surface of mandible at the inferior mental spine	Anterior surface of the hyoid bone	Draws tongue and hyoid bone forward	Cranial XII
Infrahyoid Muscles:				
Sternohyoid	Medial extremity of the clavicle; superior and posterior portion of the sternum; sterno-clavicular ligament	Body of the hyoid bone, inferior surface	Depresses hyoid bone	Cranial XII
Sternothyroid	Superior and posterior portion of sternum and first costal cartilage	Oblique line of thyroid cartilage	Depresses thyroid cartilage	Cranial XII
Thyrohyoid	Oblique line of the thyroid cartilage	Body and greater cornu of hyoid bone	Depresses hyoid bone, or elevates larynx	Cranial XII
Omohyoid	Superior margin of scapula	Inferior border of the body of the hyoid bone	Depresses and retracts hyoid bone	Cranial XII

THE SUPRAHYOIDS

The four suprahyoid muscles listed serve to form the supporting fibers for a hammocklike arrangement, with the hyoid bone acting as the hammock itself. (See Figure 5–3.) Thus, the hyoid bone might be pulled upward by anterior and posterior contraction of all fiber groups or it might be pulled upward and backward, or upward and forward, by contraction of one or the other end of the supporting muscle groups. There are also provisions for some lateral movement because of the unique arrangement of some of the suprahyoid muscle fibers.

The *stylohyoid* muscle supports its name in its origin and insertion; it originates at the base of the skull at the styloid process. Its fibers pass downward and forward to insert into the body of the hyoid bone at the point of attachment of the greater cornu. Just before this attachment, the muscle is penetrated by the tendon of the digastric muscle. The nerve supplying the stylohyoid is a branch of the facial (Cranial VII) nerve. In action, this muscle retracts and elevates the hyoid bone, with similar effects upon the larynx in general.

The *digastric* muscle is a slinglike muscle with two bellies at either end, each with its own origin but having a common insertion at the middle. The anterior belly originates on the internal aspect of the mandible, close to the midline (symphysis menti); its fibers pass downward and backward toward the hyoid bone, ending in an intermediate tendon located just superior to the hyoid. The posterior belly originates on the medial side of the mastoid process of the temporal bone at the mastoid notch; its fibers pass downward and forward to terminate in the intermediate tendon. This tendon connects the two bellies of the digastric muscle, and is invested with a fibrous loop that continues inferiorly to the hyoid and attaches to its body and part of the greater cornu. Action elevates the hyoid bone or depresses the mandible. The nerve supply to the two bellies is thought to differ; the anterior belly receives its innervation from the trigeminal (Cranial V) nerve and the posterior belly from the facial nerve.

The *mylohyoid* muscle is a diaphragmatic muscle sheet forming the floor of the mouth, upon which rests the tongue; it is oriented between the two halves of the mandible, laterally, and attaches to the hyoid bone centrally. Its origin is generally given as the mylohyoid line of the internal aspect of the mandible, running from the symphysis to the level of the last molar tooth. Its most posterior fibers pass medially and downward to insert into the body of the hyoid bone, and the fibers anterior to this meet those fibers from the opposite side at the midline raphe, a thickened line of fibrous tissue extending from the symphysis menti to the hyoid bone. Its action is to elevate the hyoid and thus the laryngeal structures in general as well as the tongue. Its nerve supply is from the trigeminal nerve.

The *geniohyoid* muscle is a paired muscle, both members lying close to the midline immediately beneath the mandible, originating from the internal surface of the mandible at the inferior mental spine at the symphysis menti. The muscle bundle is fairly compact and thin, running posteriorly and slightly downward to insert into the anterior surface of the body of the hyoid bone slightly away from its midline. The geniohyoid muscle acts to draw forward the hyoid bone and the tongue. This muscle is innervated by the hypoglossal (Cranial XII) nerve, with fibers supplied from the first cervical nerve.

Group actions of the suprahyoid muscles require some consideration at this point. Both the tongue and the hyoid bone are recipients of the energies of these muscles; this is especially true in the process of deglutition. Movement of the bolus of food toward the pharynx and protection of the laryngeal entrance are effected by suprahyoid muscles. During the first stages of deglutition, the tongue foundation is moved upward by action of the digastric (anterior bellies), the mylohyoid, and the geniohyoid muscles. At the same time, the hyoid bone is likewise drawn anteriorly. Earlier stages of mastication and deglutition had pulled the hyoid bone directly cephalad, forcing the tongue upward ahead of it. As the bolus of food enters the pharynx, stylohyoid and posterior belly of the digastric contract to pull the hyoid bone posterior and upward; this contraction assists in closing the oropharyngeal isthmus as well as occluding the entrance to the larynx against food particles. Relaxation of these muscles, along with contraction of the infrahyoid muscles, returns the hyoid bone, and consequently the larynx, to its original position.

THE INFRAHYOIDS

Below the hyoid bone, running to the larynx and to the thorax, is the infrahyoid muscle group. These four muscles form a large part of the anterior portion of the neck, immediately alongside the larynx and the trachea. They are the *sternohyoid, sternothyroid, thyrohyoid,* and *omohyoid* muscles. (See Table 5.1 and Figure 5–4.)

The *sternohyoid* muscle has its origin in the most superior surface of the thorax, at the clavicle (posterior surface of the medial end), the sternoclavicular ligament, and the internal surface of the sternum near the midline. From this insertion, the thin band of muscle passes upward and slightly medially, finally running in close approximation to its opposite fellow, to insert into the hyoid bone on its inferior surface. Sternohyoid muscle action depresses the hyoid bone, especially in the recovery from the first stages of deglutition. Its nerve supply comes from the hypoglossal (Cranial XII) nerve.

The *sternothyroid* muscle is close to the midline of the neck as is the sternohyoid muscle, and originates at the internal surface of the sternum and from the costal cartilage of the first rib. It is a shorter and wider muscle band than is the sternohyoid muscle, and it runs upward and somewhat laterally to insert into the thyroid cartilage of the larynx at its oblique line. Its action is to depress the thyroid cartilage. It receives its nerve supply from the hypoglossal (Cranial XII) nerve.

The *thyrohyoid* muscle is a continuation of the sternothyroid muscle, traveling from the thyroid cartilage to the hyoid bone. Its origin is from the oblique line of the thyroid cartilage. It inserts into the body and lower border of the greater cornu of the hyoid bone. The action of this muscle is to depress the hyoid bone if the larynx is fixed, or to elevate the larynx if the hyoid bone is fixed. The nerve supply to the thyrohyoid muscle comes from the hypoglossal nerve.

The *omohyoid* muscle is a two-bellied, two-directional muscle with a relatively fixed central tendon; its course is from the scapula in the shoulder region to the hyoid bone. Specifically, its origin is at the superior margin of the scapula. From here, the inferior belly of the omohyoid muscle continues as a flat and narrow band across the lower part of the neck, passing behind the sternocleidomastoid muscle. At this point, it forms a tendon that is ensheathed by a fibrous expansion; this fibrous material is firmly attached to the clavicle as well as to the deep cervical fascia. The omohyoid muscle then changes its direction, rising nearly vertically to insert into the lower border of the body of the hyoid bone, just lateral to the insertion of the sternohyoid muscle, which it parallels. Its action is to depress the hyoid bone, to retract it, or to pull it to one side or the other. It receives its nerve supply from the hypoglossal (Cranial XII) nerve.

Group actions of the infrahyoid muscles appear to be restricted to returning the hyoid, and thus the larynx, to their normal positions following swallowing. The suprahyoids already have elevated the hyoid and drawn it forward, then dorsally, in early stages of deglutition. After the bolus has passed the laryngeal entrance, the infrahyoids contract to return the structures. It is also believed that the omohyoids contract during deep inspiration to stiffen the cervical tissues; this is thought to prevent constriction of the neck blood vessels during the inspiratory action.

Intrinsic Muscles

The intrinsic muscles of the larynx are generally felt to be responsible for the valvular action of the vocal folds in various biologic functions of the organism.

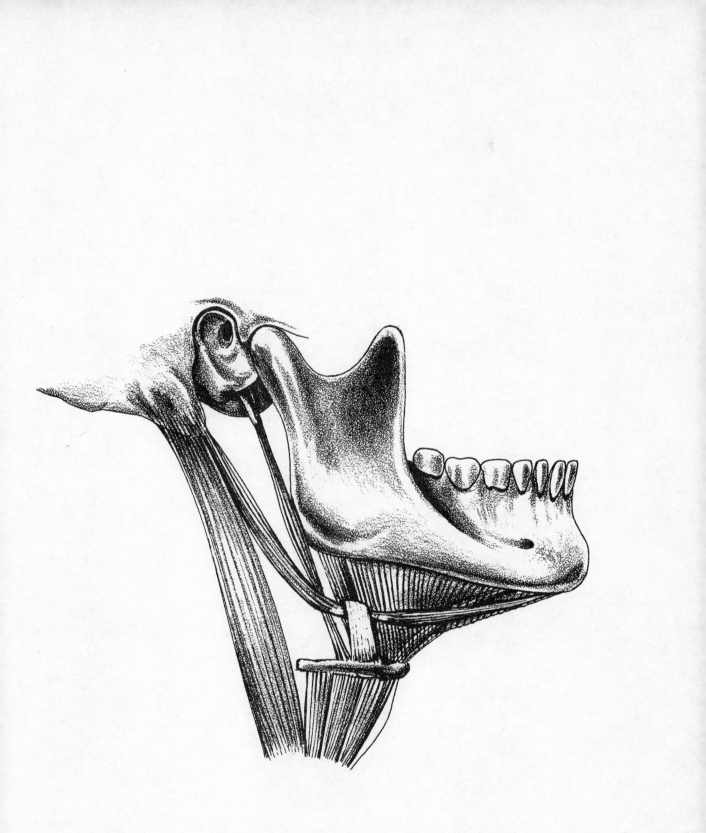

Figure 5-3.
Suprahyoid Muscles

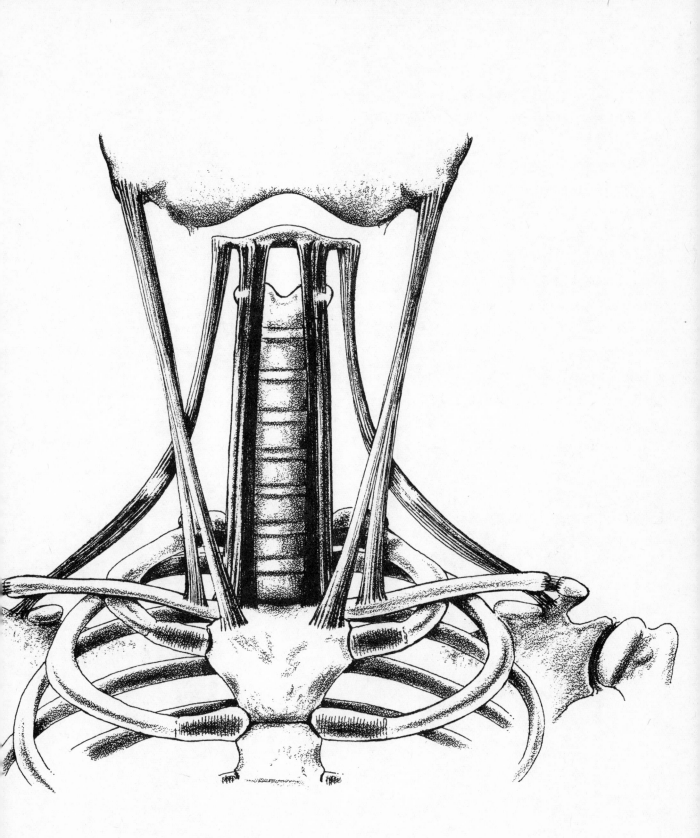

Figure 5–4.
Infrahyoid Muscles

Among, or perhaps added to, these functions are the phonatory abilities of normal vocal folds. It is true that the extrinsic muscles of the larynx—the suprahyoids and infrahyoids —contribute to the phonatory acts to some extent, and certainly, when deviant or defective, contribute to deviant or defective phonation, but the major consideration in the production of vocal sound is the role of the intrinsic musculature upon the structures producing the sound.

Five muscles constitute the group that provides for internal adjustments of the larynx during phonatory and other biological functions. Some authorities prefer to view the smaller divisions of these muscles as being separate, and thus name them individually and separately. Future research will determine the accuracy of this distinction when the structures of the muscles are more closely aligned with their functions, individually and combined. The muscles generally considered are the *cricothyroid, lateral cricoarytenoid, posterior cricoarytenoid, interarytenid,* and the *thyroarytenoid.* (See Table 5.2 and Figure 5–5.)

The *cricothyroid* muscle is found on the outer surface of the larynx in two parts: one oblique and one erect. Both originate anteriorly at the arch of the cricoid cartilage. The erect portion of this muscle arises in a nearly vertical direction to insert into the caudal border of the thyroid cartilage lamina. The oblique portion, being somewhat separated from the erect part, passes horizontally to the anterior border of the inferior horn of the thyroid cartilage and the inner surface of the cartilage. The actions of the two parts are somewhat differentiated because of their different insertions. The erect part contracts to elevate the arch of the cricoid cartilage; this results in a depression of the lamina of the cricoid. At the same time, the oblique portion causes the inferior horn of the thyroid cartilage to be rotated forward around an axis with its center near the tip of the horns; this serves to depress and extend, in an arclike fashion, the angle of the thyroid cartilage. These two acts—the lowering of the lamina of the cricoid cartilage and the angle of the thyroid cartilage—serve to lengthen the distance between the angle and the vocal processes of the arytenoids internally; the ultimate result is seen as a lengthening and a tensing of the vocal folds. This muscle differs from the others of the group in its nerve supply, which is derived from the external branch of the superior laryngeal nerve.

The *lateral cricoarytenoid* muscle on either side connects the cricoid with the arytenoid cartilages. Its origin is the upper border of the arch of the cricoid cartilage, and its fibers pass upward and backward. They insert into the anterior surface of the muscular process. In many instances, approximately 50 percent, differentiation of this muscle from the thyroarytenoid muscle is difficult or even impossible. The lateral cricoarytenoid muscle is a vocal fold adductor; upon contraction, it pulls the muscular processes of the arytenoid cartilages anteriorly, and the vocal processes move medially to approximate, and slightly tense, the vocal folds. The nerve supply comes from the anterior branch of the inferior laryngeal nerve.

The *posterior cricoarytenoid* muscle, the "safety" muscle of the larynx, runs from the external surface of the cricoid lamina to the posterior surface of the muscular process. Its origin is oriented vertically alongside the midline of the cricoid lamina, so that the uppermost fibers of this muscle run nearly horizontally and the lower fibers nearly vertically. They insert onto the dorsal surface and tip of the muscular process of the arytenoid cartilage. The action of the posterior cricoarytenoid muscle is to abduct the vocal folds by retracting the muscular processes, causing a rotating movement of the arytenoid cartilage. This muscle is the only abductor of the larynx, and thus the name "safety" muscle is derived. It is the antagonist of the lateral cricoarytenoid muscle. Nerve supply is from the posterior branch of the inferior laryngeal nerve.

The *interarytenoid* muscle (arytenoid) is a posterior midline muscle consisting of two portions, one of which is not paired. (See Figure 5–6.) These two

TABLE 5.2   INTRINSIC MUSCLES OF THE LARYNX

MUSCLE	ORIGIN	INSERTION	ACTION	NERVE
Cricothyroid	Anterior and lateral surfaces of arch of cricoid cartilage	Caudal border of the thyroid cartilage; anterior surface of lower cornu of thyroid cartilage	Draws thyroid down and forward; elevates cricoid arch; lengthens, tenses vocal folds	Cranial X (Superior laryngeal nerve)
Cricoarytenoids Lateral	Superior borders of cricoid cartilage	Anterior surface of muscular process	Draws arytenoids forward; aids in rotating arytenoids; tenses and adducts vocal folds	Cranial X (Inferior laryngeal nerve)
Posterior	Posterior surface of cricoid cartilage	Muscular process of arytenoid cartilage	Rotates arytenoid, abducting vocal processes	Cranial X (Inferior laryngeal nerve)
Interarytenoids Transverse	Posterior surface of arytenoid cartilage	Posterior surface of opposite arytenoid	Draws together arytenoid cartilages; adducts vocals folds	Cranial X (Inferior laryngeal nerve)
Oblique	Base of one arytenoid cartilage at muscular process	Apex of the opposite arytenoid	Draws arytenoid cartilages together	Cranial X (Inferior laryngeal nerve)
Thyroarytenoid	Internal and inferior surface of the angle of the thyroid cartilage	Vocal process and anterior lateral surface of the base of the arytenoid cartilages	Draws arytenoids forward; shortens and relaxes vocal folds	Cranial X (Inferior laryngeal nerve)
Vocalis (consisting of the deep fibers of thyroarytenoid)	Inferior surface of the angle of the thyroid cartilage	Vocal process of the arytenoid cartilage and vocal ligament	Differentially tenses vocal folds	Cranial X (Inferior laryngeal nerve)

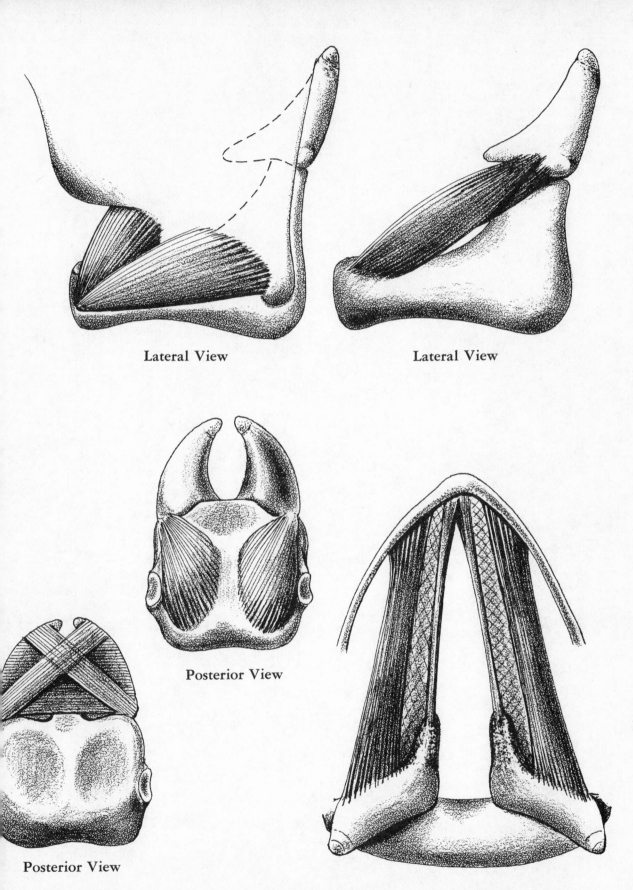

Lateral View

Lateral View

Posterior View

Posterior View

Superior View

Figure   5–5.
Intrinsic Laryngeal Muscles

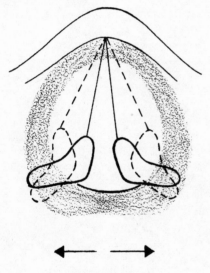

Abduction

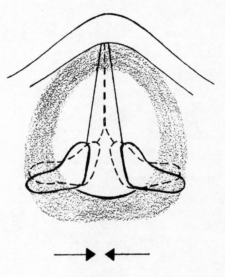

Adduction

Figure 5–6.
Arytenoid Cartilage Articulation

are the transverse portion and the oblique portion. The transverse part is unpaired, and runs from the posterior concave surface of one arytenoid cartilage to the same region of the opposite cartilage. The oblique and outermost portion originates dorsally near the tip of the muscular process of each arytenoid cartilage. Its fibers rise toward the apex of the opposite arytenoid, crossing the fibers of the other of the pair at the midline. At the apex, some fibers insert and terminate. Others continue on around the apex, a few join the thyroarytenoid muscle, and some run into the aryepiglottic fold to become the aryepiglottic muscle. The action of this muscle is to close the laryngeal opening by approximating the two artenoid cartilages; at the same time, the laryngeal vestibule is narrowed and the vocal folds may be approximated. The nerve supply of both parts of the interarytenoid muscle is the anterior branch of the inferior laryngeal nerve.

The *thyroarytenoid* muscle forms a large part of the vocal fold and the lateral walls bounding the fold. It arises internally from the lower portion of the angle of the thyroid cartilage, and its fibers pass posteriorly as a narrow, thin band of triangular structure. The broad horizontal part of the triangle forms a part of the lateral wall of the larynx and of the ventricular fold. The narrow medial band of fibers runs parallel to the vocal ligament, with approximately the same anterior and posterior attachments. The thyroarytenoid muscle, then, inserts into the vocal process and the antero-lateral surface of the arytenoid cartilage. This muscle contracts to move the arytenoid cartilage anteriorly thus shortening and relaxing the vocal fold. The nerve supplying this muscle is the anterior branch of the inferior laryngeal nerve.

The *vocalis* muscle is generally considered to be a part of the thyroarytenoid muscle. It has fibers coming from the thyroarytenoid muscle, exiting from the main muscle along the length of it, to terminate into the vocal ligament. This is true from both ends of the ligament, with both the angle of the thyroid cartilage and the vocal process of the arytenoid cartilage considered as points of origin and the vocal ligament as the insertion. Thus, fibers coming from these two points run both anteriorly and posteriorly, and leave the main bundle of muscle fibers to insert all along the length of the ligament, crossing other such fibers coming from the opposite end. The action may be rather complex and certainly is not well known. However, upon contraction of this muscle, the arytenoid cartilage will be pulled anteriorly, relaxing and shortening the vocal fold. Also considered as a part of its action is a differential contraction in such a way as to provide for differential tensing of the vocal fold; as a result of this, pitch differences during phonation might be accounted for. Earlier investigators had considered this an important function of this muscle and termed the fibers so identified as the "pitch fibers" of the thyroarytenoid muscle. The nerve supply is thought to be identical with that of the main muscle, the anterior branch of the inferior laryngeal nerve.

The functions of the preceding muscles are listed and described in a simple fashion; recent studies of the actions of the vocal fold, and of the prime movers of the fold, indicate that simple adduction or simple tensing is rarely the best description of what occurs. For example, some researchers have demonstrated that the contraction of individual muscle groups to produce either rotation or gliding of the arytenoids to effect changes in the vocal folds is not as simplified as previously described. These investigators point out, for example, that the normal resting position of the arytenoids is "over the crest" of the lamina of the cricoid, dorsally, and that muscular contraction causes the arytenoids to "mount" this crest; the effect is that the vocal processes of the arytenoids *seem* to approximate by rotation, then to approximate by gliding of the bodies of the arytenoids.

THE NERVOUS TISSUES

The musculature of the larynx receives its nervous innervation through the pyramidal cortex and is under fine pyramidal control. As Krieg states it:

> Speech is a purely cortical function and requires a high degree of organization. The pyramidal cortex only *effects* the movements of the muscles of the larynx, tongue and mouth; the control is vested in a higher center, which in turn is subject to other control . . . When the laryngeal area of the cortex is stimulated the subject vocalizes but does not articulate.[1]

The nerve pathway from the cortex is the common pyramidal pathway. The ultimate end of this pathway is in the lower portion of the pons, although some authorities feel it is to be the upper portion of the medulla oblongata. Here is found the *nucleus ambiguus,* the center and source of the fibers serving the laryngeal musculature. (See Figure 5–7.)

The nucleus ambiguus is a long slender column of nerve cells which give rise to the special visceral efferent fibers of Ranson that run through the glossopharyngeal, vagus, and accessory nerves. They are the nerves that ultimately supply those muscles mentioned by Krieg: those of the larynx, tongue, and mouth, and of the pharynx in general.

It can be seen that the primary cranial nerve supplying the laryngeal region is the tenth, or vagus. Two branches of this nerve are of import to the muscles of the larynx. In a short distance from its exit from the protective cranial vault, the vagus nerve gives off a small branch called the superior laryngeal nerve; this nerve runs along the side of the larynx to innervate the cricothyroid muscle, and only that muscle. It will be remembered that this muscle tenses the vocal ligament and fold during phonation. Later in the course of the vagus nerve, it gives off a larger branch; this branch travels caudally below major blood vessels in the neck-shoulder region (arch of the aorta on the left side and subclavian artery on the right) and reverses its direction; hence its name: the recurrent laryngeal nerve. As it rises, it enters the laryngeal musculature and thereupon becomes the inferior laryngeal nerve. It is this nerve (the recurrent and/or the inferior laryngeal nerve) that ultimately supplies all of the remaining intrinsic muscles of the larynx.

CLINICAL NOTE

Of considerable interest to the clinician are neural lesions producing phonatory defects, for these lesions are frequently irreversible, and treatment is complex and difficult. Among the types of dysphonias which may be produced are those developing in the region of the nucleus ambiguus; this type of lesion is similar to those of paralytic poliomyelitis and other destructive influences of the bulbar type. Phonation then may be destroyed or seriously disturbed in such cases, and voice therapy becomes a major procedure in the rehabilitation process. Another type of defect infrequently encountered by the speech pathologist is a lesion or disturbance of the peripheral nerve; such pathologies as thyroid gland problems or surgery, accident, tumor growth and pressures of other kinds produced by edemas or foreign matter may well produce phonatory defects. The extent of the lesion determines the extent of the phonatory defect, for it is entirely possible that only a small portion of the muscles will be affected and the vocal sound may be only disturbed and not absent.

[1]W. J. Krieg, *Functional Neuroanatomy* (2nd ed.), Philadelphia: Blakiston, 1955, p. 249.

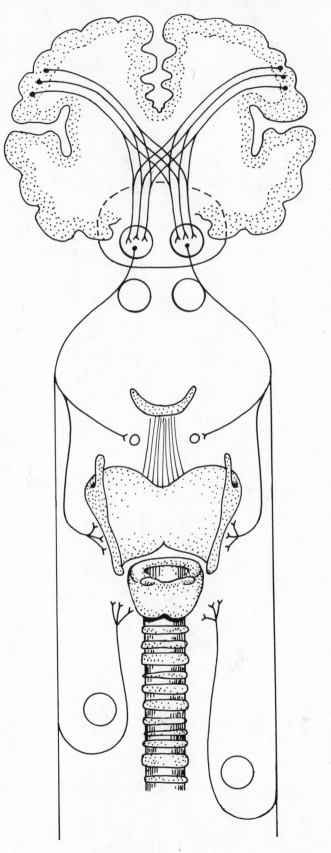

Figure   5–7.
Nerve Supply to Intrinsic Laryngeal Muscles

The muscles of phonation in the larynx must be closely related with those of swallowing. It is found that both the glossopharyngeal and the vagus nerves contribute to the pharyngeal plexus. The pharyngeal plexus, in turn, is largely responsible for nerve supply to the muscles of the pharynx and mouth, except for the tensor veli palatine. In very close approximation to glossopharyngeal, then, is the vagus nerve; it also supplies the pharyngeal plexus as well as gives off the two distinct nerves mentioned earlier; superior laryngeal and recurrent laryngeal nerves serving the laryngeal musculature. The constrictors of the pharynx, lying as they do in close proximity to the cartilages of the larynx and even finding origin in those cartilages, are likely closely related to the muscles of the larynx through the common neural origins that are found in the nucleus ambiguus.

The extrinsic (strap) muscles of the larynx (see Table 5.1) receive a somewhat complex neural innervation. Although the table indicates, for example, that Cranial Nerve XII serves the infrahyoid musculature, it is more likely that several nerves provide that innervation. Agreement does not seem to exist on the exact structure of the nerves in this region, for contributions to these muscles are said to come from Cranial Nerve X, Cranial Nerve XI, Cranial Nerve XII, as well as from the top two or three cervical nerves of the spinal cord. What seems to occur is that these cranial nerves act as sources of some fibers that contribute to a long looping nerve network, sometimes called the *ansa hypoglossi;* from this network come the various nerve fibers that serve to stimulate the musculature of the infrahyoid group. The suprahyoid group, on the other hand, do not present quite as complicated a picture, although there is considerable variation in the innervation of this group. This innervation can be seen to be related to embryonic developmental associations as well as functional relationships. Cranial Nerve VII (facial) serves both stylohyoid and the posterior belly of digastric muscles, both deriving from similar actions. Cranial Nerve V, on the other hand, innervates both the anterior belly of digastric as well as the mylohyoid, both being superior and anterior to the larynx in origin and both contributing to somewhat similar effects upon the laryngeal region. Hypoglossal Nerve (Cranial XII) serves the geniohyoid as it does genioglossus, which is so closely related to it in location and perhaps in some actions.

SUMMARY OF FUNCTIONS OF THE LARYNGEAL REGION

For the life and health of the organism, the larynx is an important apparatus. It serves as a valve that can close under certain circumstances to protect the lower respiratory tract. First, it closes to prohibit the entrance of foreign materials into the trachea, bronchi, and lungs. Second, should such materials enter the larynx and be stopped there, the valve can release suddenly to allow a blast of air (as in a cough) to remove the foreign material from the scene. The blast of air itself is the result of the valving with a consequent increase of air pressure developing below the closed glottis. Entrapping the air below the glottis allows the respiratory system (thoracic musculature and diaphragm) to stabilize, provides for fixation of the thoracic cage itself, and thereby offers a fulcrum for the muscles of the arms or chest or back to function more efficiently in performing work, such as lifting heavy objects or in eliminating the contents of the abdomen.

Man's speaking abilities are largely dependent upon there being some controllable sound source. The vocal folds within the larynx provide this apparatus. The intrinsic laryngeal muscles adjust the cartilages, so that the margins of the folds interrupt or interfere with the breath stream. Air pressure from below the glottis sets up a vibratory pattern in the vocal folds; this vibration creates the laryngeal tone, which is thereafter modified by the spaces (vestibule, pharynges, mouth, nose) above. Subtle changes in the mass, length, and tension, as well as medial compression of the two folds, allow for the changes possible in the vocal tone: pitch and intensity. Lengthening the vocal folds by cricothyroid muscle, for example, also tenses and decreases the mass; this creates a mechanism for elevating the pitch.

Control of the abduction-adduction abilities of the folds must be refined so that the laryngeal tone might be "turned on" and "turned off" at appropriate moments, that is, for speech sounds that are voiced or unvoiced. Further refinement is necessary for pitch changes, as in singing, or in prosodic speech aspects, as in inflectional changes. Loudness changes require the refined control of the larynx as well as a similarly refined control of the entire lower respiratory system; loudness is largely a function of changes in the subglottal air pressure. This subglottal air pressure provides the energy for the vibrating system; it is the source of power.

There are, then, two basic essentials to the production of tone by the larynx: (1) the creation of the air pressure to energize the vibratory apparatus, and (2) the adjustment of the paired vocal folds in relationship to that air pressure so that the tone might be established. These two events are dependent upon the central nervous system control available as well as the integrity of the muscular system, the cartilaginous framework, and the patency of the airway in both directions, among other things. For further information pertaining to the vocalization of speech sounds, reference should be made to Appendix II.

LARYNGEAL REGION LANDMARK IDENTIFICATION

Directions: For the indicated illustrations, label the following landmarks.

FIGURE 5–1
Epiglottis
Hyoid Bone
Thyroid Cartilage
Cricothroid Membrane
Cricoid Cartilage (Lamina)
Arytenoid Cartilage (Apex)
Arytenoid Cartilage (Body)
Arytenoid Cartilage (Muscular Process)
Aryepiglottic Fold
Triticeal Cartilage
Corniculate Cartilage
Hyothyroid Membrane
Thyroid Cartilage, Superior Cornu
Thyroid Cartilage, Inferior Cornu
Tracheal Rings
Aditus Ad Laryngis
Ventricular (False Vocal) Fold
Vocal Fold
Ventricle (of Morgagni)

FIGURE 5–2
Hyoid Bone, Body
Hyoid Bone, Greater Cornu
Hyoid Bone, Lesser Cornu
Hyothyroid Membrane
Middle Hyothyroid Ligament
Thyroid Cartilage, Superior Cornu
Thyroid Notch
Thyroid Prominence (Angle)
Thyroid Cartilage, Oblique Line
Thyroid Cartilage, Inferior Cornu
Cricoid Cartilage, Arch
Cricothyroid Ligament
Tracheal Rings
Arytenoid Cartilage
Posterior Hyothyroid Ligament
Triticeal Cartilage

FIGURE 5–3
Hyoid Bone
Mastoid Process, Temporal Bone
Styloid Process, Temporal Bone
Mandible Bone
Digastric Muscle, Posterior Belly
Digastric Muscle, Anterior Belly
Digastric Muscle, Tendonous Loop
Mylohyoid Muscle
Geniohyoid Muscle
Stylohyoid Muscle

FIGURE 5–4
Hyoid Bone
Thyroid Cartilage
Sternum Bone
Clavicle Bone
Sternohyoid Muscle
Sternothyroid Muscle
Thyrohyoid Muscle
Omohyoid Muscle
Sterno(cleido)mastoid Muscle

FIGURE 5–5
Thyroid Cartilage
Cricoid Cartilage
Thyroid Cartilage, Inferior Cornu
Cricothyroid Muscle
Arytenoid Cartilage
Cricoid Cartilage, Arch
Lateral Cricoarytenoid Muscle
Arytenoid Cartilage, Muscular Process
Corniculate Cartilage
Cricoid Cartilage, Lamina
Posterior Cricoarytenoid Muscle
(Inter)Arytenoid Muscle, Horizontal Portion
(Inter)Arytenoid Muscle, Oblique Portion
Thyroid Cartilage, Angle
Arytenoid Cartilage, Body
Thyroarytenoid (Vocal) Ligament
Glottis
Vocalis Muscle
Thyroarytenoid Muscle
Anterior Commissure
Intercartilaginous Glottis
Intermembranous Glottis

FIGURE 5–6
Identify primary landmarks.
Identify muscles associated with actions.
Identify nerve supply

FIGURE 5–7
Cerebral Cortex, Prefrontal Convolution
Decussation of Pyramid
Medulla Level
Nucleus Ambiguus
Vagus Nerve
Arch of the Aorta
Subclavian Artery
Recurrent Laryngeal Nerve
Inferior Laryngeal Nerve
Superior Laryngeal Nerve
Larynx

chapter 6

THE THORACIC REGION

The thoracic region houses a large part of the respiratory tract that furnishes the energizing force for phonation. This tract includes the trachea, bronchi, and the lung structures themselves. It lies within a bony and muscular cage that is highly flexible. The tract and the lungs are located superiorly to abdominal viscera, which exert important pressure upon the lungs.

The bony and cartilaginous structures involved in the thorax serve to protect the respiratory tract within; even more, they serve to effect the changes in that tract which ultimately result in the passage of air into and out of the body from its surrounding atmosphere. Voice production is associated with the outward flowing of this air.

CONNECTIVE TISSUES

There are numerous bones of interest in the thoracic region. At the dorsal aspect of the thorax are found the vertebrae, which join to form the backbone or spine, through which passes the spinal cord of the central nervous system. From the vertebrae, passing around the sides of the chest and oriented ventrally thereafter, are the flat ribs, which are interconnected by muscles and attached by cartilages ventrally to the sternum. Surmounting the entire structure are the clavicle and the scapula of the shoulder region, protecting the thorax superiorly.

Vertebrae

The typical vertebra is formed by a body and three processes. (See Figures 6–1 and 6–2.) These are attached to each other through the lamina. The body is the largest portion of the vertebra and is nearly cylindrical. It has a large spongy bone centrum with the usual compact bone cortex. It is oriented ventrally in the spine; that is, it is facing toward the belly wall. From its more dorsal extremity project the two lamina that form the arches of the vertebrae, which, along with the body, enclose the central canal and house the spinal cord. The two lamina are fused posteriorly and extend farther as a single spinous process at the midline. Projecting somewhat laterally from the lamina, on either side, are the paired transverse processes, of importance to articulation of the rib. On the transverse processes and body are the articulating facets—two inferior and two superior—for movement of the head and neck of the ribs.

The typical spinal column is a flexible structure composed of the various groupings of vertebrae. The superior cervical vertebrae are seven in number; the first supporting the cranium is the atlas, and the second is the axis. Below the seven cervical vertebrae are the twelve thoracic bones that receive the twelve ribs, and therefore serve as parts of the respiratory system. Beneath the thoracic vertebrae and continuing the spinal column caudad are the five lumbar vertebrae. Subsequent to these are the five united sacral and, finally, the four or five fused coccygeal vertebrae. (See Figure 6–3.)

Clavicle

The clavicle is the collar bone, forming a large part of the anterior portion of the shoulder girdle. It is classified as a long bone, being somewhat like an italic letter *f* in its shape. It is located immediately superior to the first rib, articulating ventrally with the manubrium of the sternum. From this point it extends laterally, then curves backward to the acromion process of the scapula.

This bone is importantly related to the upper extremity as well as to the thorax and head and neck regions. Thus, muscles that originate or insert along its length may well have some relationship to respiration. This is true of such muscles as pectoralis major, sternocleidomastoid, and even portions of the strap muscles: sternothyroid and sternohyoid.

Ribs

The costae, or ribs, are flat bones twisted in two planes to provide for the highly mobile yet protective thoracic cage surrounding the lungs. (See Figure 6–4.) There are usually twelve such ribs, although supernumerary ribs in the cervical region are not uncommon. They articulate dorsally with the body and transverse process of the corresponding thoracic vertebrae. Somewhat lateral to the articulating head of the rib is the straight neck, with its articulating tubercle, which moves upon the transverse process of the vertebrae immediately above.

Beyond its neck, the rib passes toward the lateral portion of the back of the human body until it makes a rather abrupt change in direction at the angle of the rib. Here it turns to curve anteriorly and then medially toward the ventral midline of the thorax. At the angle, too, occurs the twist of the rib which allows for an outward movement of the rib when it is elevated. The rib terminates in its own costal cartilage. In the case of the upper seven ribs, this costal cartilage continues independently to articulate with the sternum at an articulation facet provided. The next three ribs have their costal cartilages attached to those of the rib above. The last two ribs are unattached, and are the so-called "floating" ribs. Those lower five are sometimes called "false" ribs because of their lack of direct medial attachment to the sternum.

Muscle sheets interconnect the ribs, and there are muscles serving to attach the ribs to the vertebrae as well as to the sternum; such muscles are found internally as well as externally on the thorax. Another group of muscles are extra-thoracic, serving to attach the ribs as a group to structures above the thorax—such as the arms, neck, and cranium—as well as to structures below the thorax, such as the pelvis. These groupings might well assist the student in classifying the muscles as they are studied according to their functions and their effects upon the ribs.

Sternum

At the midline of the thorax is found the sternum, a segmented bone that serves to fix the ventral ends of the costal cartilages as well as to protect the contents of the thorax. The sternum is composed of three, easily identified, portions: the uppermost is the manubrium, the large middle portion is the body, and the highly variable inferior portion is the xiphoid process.

The manubrium sterni is an irregular octagon, and its free and concave cephalad side is termed the jugular, or sternal, notch. Its most lateral side is also concave for articulation of the first costal cartilage. Between the jugular notch and the costal cartilage is the slanting surface that receives the clavicle. The single caudal surface articulates with the body of the sternum at the sternal angle.

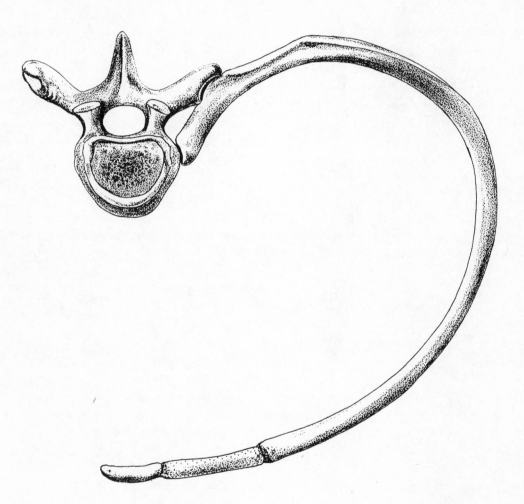

Figure 6–1.
Vertebrosternal Rib

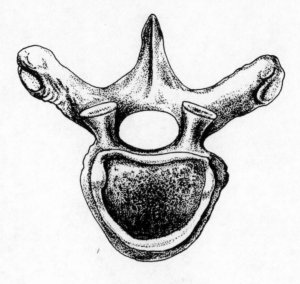

Superior View

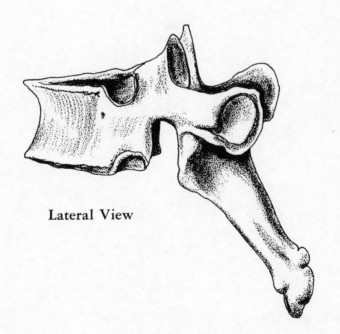

Lateral View

Figure 6–2.
Thoracic Vertebra

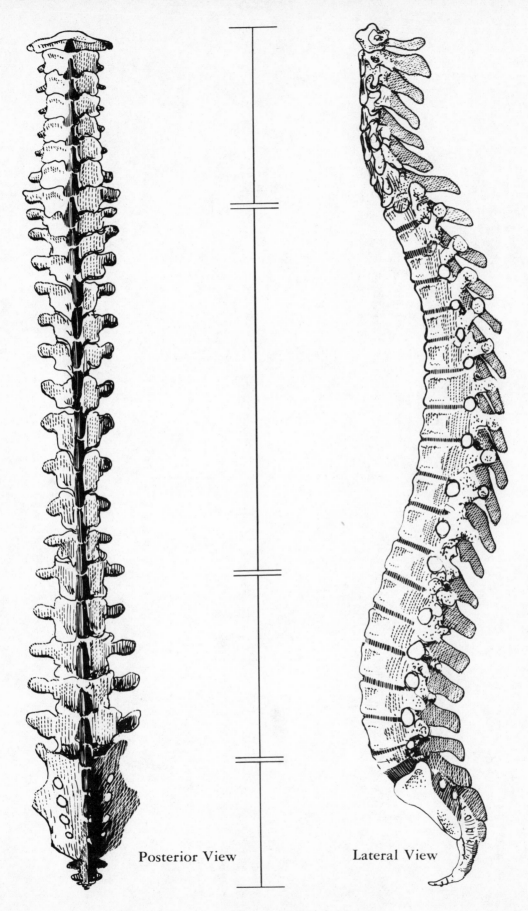

Posterior View   Lateral View

Figure 6–3.
Vertebral Column

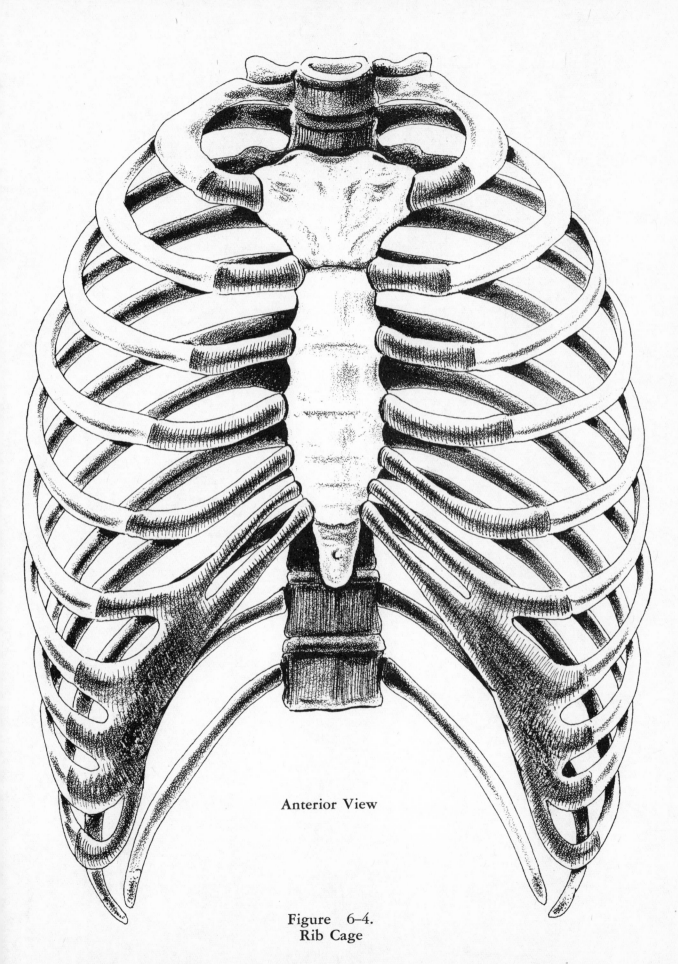

Anterior View

Figure 6–4.
Rib Cage

The body (corpus, gladiolus) frequently demonstrates obvious segmentation, with concavities designed for articulation with the costal cartilages. At the sternal angle itself, the second rib has its facet. Ribs three, four, five, and six are generally located inferiorly along the sides of the body until rib seven is reached, with its facet usually intermediate between the body and the xiphoid (or ensiform) process.

The xiphoid process is highly variable from individual to individual, although in general it is a long and thin cartilaginous process that usually ossifies in older age. It serves as attachment for the ligamentous linea alba of the abdomen as well as for the rectus abdominis muscle.

Ilium

The *ilium* is one of the three divisions of the hip bone, and it forms a large part of the pelvic girdle. (See Figure 6–5.) The other two bones are the *ischium* and the *pubis.* Of least interest to this text is the ischium; the pubis has minor interest. The ilium presents more important relationships to the muscles of respiration. The ilium, especially its convexly curved superior surface, is easily identified as comprising the upper and outer sides of the hip region. It curves rapidly downward to fuse with the pubic bone. To the outermost edge, the crest, of this superior surface are attached the following muscles of respiration: external abdominal oblique, internal abdominal oblique, transverse abdominis, and quadratus lumborum. The other portions of the ilium do not bear directly upon the muscles of respiration.

THE RESPIRATORY TRACT

Within the thorax, the respiratory system occupies the most space. Basically, this system is comprised of the passages that carry air to and from the external environment. These passages start at the nose, the oral cavity, the pharynges, and the larynx. Subsequent to these, the passageway continues through the neck and into the thorax by the trachea and its many branchings.

The trachea is a tube of cartilaginous rings and of musculomembranous portions extending downward from the lowermost part of the cricoid cartilage of the larynx. (See Figure 6–6.) This is about at the level of the sixth cervical vertebra. The trachea descends nearly vertically downward until it bifurcates (divides into two smaller tubes) at about the level of the fifth thoracic vertebra. The tracheal rings vary in number from sixteen to twenty. These are hyaline rings of incomplete circular shape and of irregular width and thickness around the circumference of the trachea. The incomplete portion of all the rings is dorsal, where the musculomembranous part of the tube completes the hollow structure. This dorsal portion is close to the similarly descending esophagus.

The trachea is lined with mucous membrane tissue, as is the entire respiratory tract. External to this lining is the muscular tunic, composed of smooth (nonstriated) muscle tissue. This layer is capable of contracting, under appropriate stimulation, to narrow the lumen of the tracheal tract. From the point of bifurcation of the trachea, the two bronchi pass laterally to the lungs. Entering the lung through its hilus, the right bronchus subdivides into three intrapulmonary bronchi, and the left bronchus divides into two. Subsequent to the major divisions of the bronchi and accommodating five lobes of the lungs, the bronchi continue to subdivide, ultimately producing the final unit of lung structure, the pulmonary lobule.

This last component, the pulmonary lobule, is the basic unit of lung structure and function. The bronchi have subdivided (secondary and tertiary) into minute bronchioles with sparsely distributed cartilaginous plates. These bronchioles give rise to the *terminal bronchioles,* which further divide into *respiratory bronchioles;* these latter are so-called because of the presence of numerous alveoli found on them. The next division of the bronchial tree is the *alveolar duct,* which gives rise to the *alveolar,* or, *air sacs.* The walls of these sacs present the minute *alveoli.*

The alveolus shares a single-cell-layered wall with the vascular capillaries where the *exchange phase* of respiration takes place. This refers to the vital process of the exchange of oxygen in the environmental air within the alveoli with the carbon dioxide within the blood. The pulmonary arteries from the heart deliver the blood with carbon dioxide wastes into the pulmonary capillaries located in the walls of the alveoli. Diffusion of the gaseous materials from one medium to the other takes care of the important exchange. The waste materials enter the air of the alveoli and are returned to the environment by the exhalation of the air from the lungs. The now-oxygenated blood in the capillary beds pass from the lung tissue via the pulmonary veins to return to the heart. From the heart the blood is pumped to the tissues of the body, where the oxygen is shared with other body tissues (internal respiration); and the cycle continues.

Atmospheric air, with its all-important oxygen, is brought to the alveoli through the process of (pulmonary) ventilation. The contraction and relaxation of thoracic and abdominal muscles provide for the change of air pressure within the pulmonary lobules, and air flows into and out of the lungs as a result of the volume and pressure changes.

The basic structures of respiration are the lungs. In reality, these are the sum of the branchings of the respiratory tract, ultimately forming the multitudinous miniscule air sacs, which are enclosed to form the lungs themselves. In the larger view, the lungs are highly elastic, conical structures easily collapsible because of the large amount of air held within their alveoli.

Each lung has a base, an apex, and two surfaces. The base is large and concave, the right being larger and more concave than the left. The concavity accommodates the convexity of the diaphragm and the lobe of the liver beneath. As the diaphragm elevates or depresses, the base of the lung follows the movement. The apex of the lung is a small rounded projection, which usually extends into the root of the neck above the clavicle.

The two surfaces of each lung are the costal and the mediastinal surfaces. The former is quite extensive, being formed in part by the extent and shape of the rib cage; this surface is smooth and convex and sometimes demonstrates the position of the individual ribs by appropriate indentations. The mediastinal surface is concave and irregular and faces medially toward the mediastinum, the middle space of the thorax which contains the heart and its coverings as well as the major portions of the respiratory tract (trachea and bronchi). The surface facing this space is indented to accommodate the pericardium of the heart, and has a further depression—the hilus—through which penetrate the bronchi, the pulmonary blood vessels, and the nerves.

The difference in the number of lobes of each lung is due to the placement of the heart and the remainder of the mediastinal contents. The right lobes are named superior, middle, and inferior; the left lobes are called superior and inferior.

Covering each of the lungs is a serous membrane, the pleurae. There are two such layers. The most immediate is the pulmonary pleura, which covers the surface of the lungs and extends deep into the fissures between the lobes. The outermost layer is the parietal pleura, which invests the internal surface of the thorax and covers the diaphragm. Both pleurae are together as one at the hilus and root of the lung. Elsewhere there is a space between the two layers, the pleural cavity, which is actually a potential space. In life and health the two layers together provide for smooth movements of the lungs in respiration.

The dimensions of the lungs differ from individual to individual, and differences according to sex are commonly known. Generally, it is agreed that the

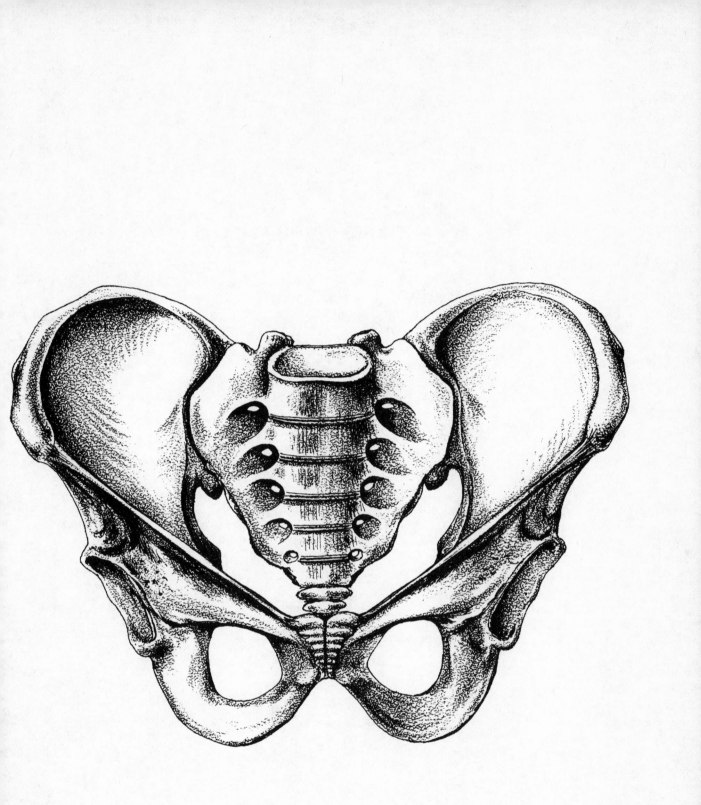

Figure 6–5.
Pelvic Region

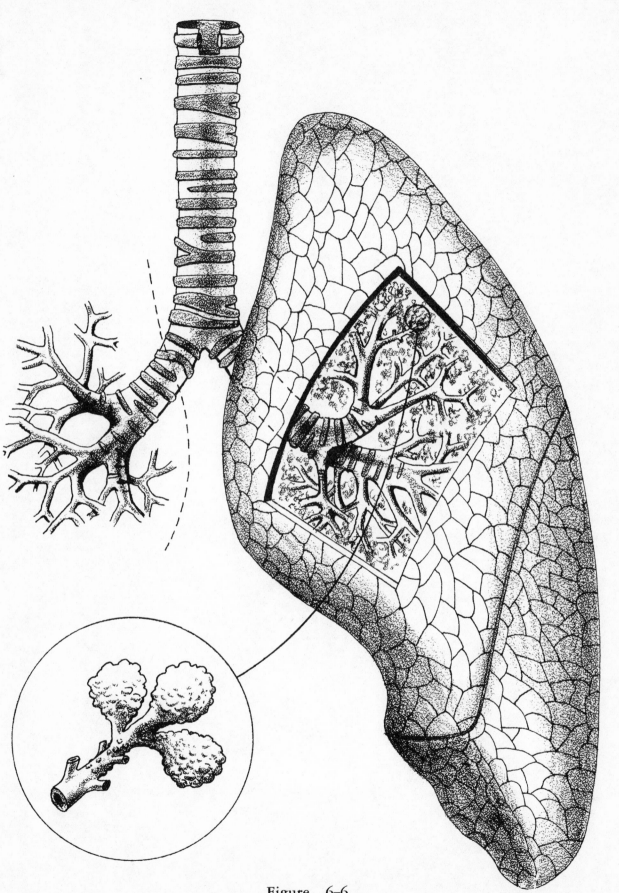

Figure 6–6.
Lower Respiratory Tract

total capacity of the lungs is about 6500 cc; this would include both the air and the tissues enclosing that air. However, an average male adult can inhale, after a deep exhalation, about 3700 cc, the vital capacity. A quiet inspiration averages about 500 cc, the tidal air. These figures represent averages useful for comparisons of extreme differences. Variation in lung utilization occurs also in a single individual, depending upon his environment, his physical condition, and his requirements for oxygen. The control of respiration is not an appropriate subject for this text, but certainly the phonatory act is dependent upon respiratory control, a fact that should not escape the interested student and clinician.

MUSCULATURE

Numerous muscles operate the thoracic region, most of which the student of speech pathology should know. These muscles may be grouped, in a rather arbitrary fashion, into a major and a minor grouping. Although other muscles of the thoracic group exist, the following muscles have been selected because of rather obvious and outstanding relationships to respiration and, consequently, to phonation. The major group is so labeled because of the direct relationship of these muscles to the act of breathing and to phonation. These include the *diaphragm,* the *external intercostals,* the *internal intercostals,* the *transverse thoracic, pectoralis major,* and *pectoralis minor.* (See Table 6.1.) The minor group consists of *levatores costarum, scalene, quadratus lumborum, serratus anterior, subcostal,* and the outstanding muscle of the neck region, *sternocleidomastoid.* A third group, discussed in detail later in this chapter, is the abdominal group, consisting of rectus abdominis, external oblique, internal oblique, and transverse abdominis muscles.

Major Group of Thoracic Muscles

The *diaphragm* is a muscle that deserves considerable attention. (See Figure 6–7.) It is not always classified as a thoracic muscle, although it has its major function directed at that cavity. This muscle has its origin around the entire internal circumference of the lower bony thorax, including the lumbar vertebrae and the lumbocostal fascia dorsally, the cartilages and bony portions of the lower six or seven ribs, and the xiphoid process ventrally. The muscle fibers fan medially forming two central tendons that support the lungs and heart. When at physiologic rest, the diaphragm is elevated and forms two semicircular domes upon which rest the bases of the lungs. Upon contraction, the domes are flattened because of the low origins of the muscle fibers; there is created a potential space between the diaphragm and the bases of the lungs. This space is filled with lung tissue as the atmospheric pressure outside the body forces air through the respiratory tract into the decreased air-pressure volume of the lungs. Nervous stimulation is derived from the phrenic nerve from cervical nerves 3, 4, and 5.

Respiration is only partly performed or effected by the diaphragm. Although some individuals, particularly females and trained singers, are primarily diaphragmatic breathers, a large part of the respiratory act is the product of rib cage movement. This movement is accomplished through concerted and coordinated movements of the ribs via the muscular contractions of the remainder of the major muscle group.

The *external intercostal* muscles are found along the borders of the ribs, running to the next rib in an oblique direction. There are eleven pairs of such muscles, extending from the tubercles of the ribs dorsally around the thorax to the costal cartilages. These are superficially located, with their origins located on the outer lip of the lower border of a rib and their insertions on the outer lip of the upper border of the rib below. Generally it is agreed that the external intercostals contract to elevate the ribs, thus acting as thoracic cavity enlargers.

TABLE 6.1   **MUSCLES OF THE THORAX**

MUSCLE	ORIGIN	INSERTION	ACTION	NERVE
Diaphragm	Entire internal circumference of lower thorax; *anterior:* xiphoid cartilage; *lateral:* cartilages and bony portion of 6 or 7 lower ribs *posterior:* crura of upper lumbar vertebrae	Central Tendons	Chief muscle of respiration; elevates ribs and draws down upon the central tendon; increases the vertical dimension of the thorax	Phrenic (from C3, 4, 5)
External Intercostals (11)	Outer lip of lower border of each rib from tubercle to costal cartilages	Outer lip of the upper border of the rib below	Elevates ribs	Intercostal (from T 1 to 12)
Internal Intercostals (11)	Inner lip of lower border of each rib running from the angle of the rib to the side of the sternum	Inner edge of the upper border of rib and the costal cartilage below	Aids in the elevation of the ribs	Intercostal (from T 1 to 12)
Scalenes Anterior, Medial, and Posterior	All connected variously to cervical vertebrae 3–7 at transverse processes	Upper surface of ribs, or outer surface of rib 2	Elevates or fixates ribs	C 4–8
Transverse Thoracic	Internal surfaces of sternum and xiphoid process	Costal cartilages and bony end of ribs 2–6	Depresses the ribs	Intercostal (from T 2 to 6)
Quadratus Lumborum	Posterior portion of iliac crest; transverse processes of lumbar vertebrae 3, 4, 5; iliolumbar ligament	Lower border of rib 12; tendons of abdominal mm.	Draws down rib 12; aids in fixing the origin of diaphragm	T 12; L 1–4
Pectoralis Major	Head of humerus bone	Ventral end of clavicle, sternum, costal cartilages 2–6	Elevates ribs	Lower cervical and first thoracic
Pectoralis Minor	Coracoid process of scapula	Bony ends of ribs 2–5	Elevates ribs	C 7–8

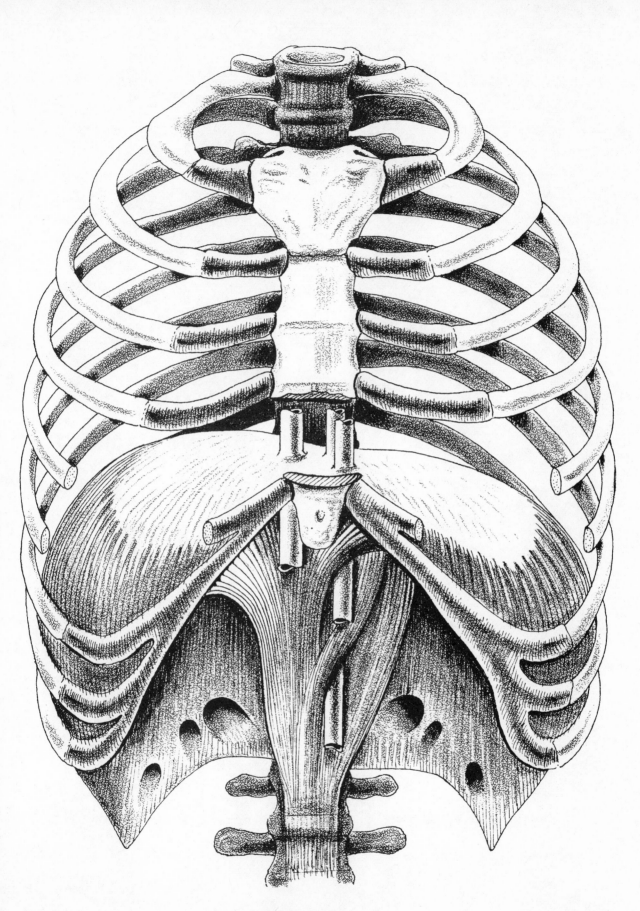

Figure   6–7.
Diaphragm Muscle in Place

This contraction and action is dependent upon the fixation of the first rib by the scalene muscles, of the lateral vertebral group. They are innervated by the intercostal nerves, supplied through thoracic nerves 1–12.

The *internal intercostal* muscles, also eleven in number, are found on the upper borders of the ribs, more internal than the external intercostal group. The fibers are also oblique, but their course is nearly at right angles to that of the external muscle, running from below, upward, and laterally from the front of the thorax and angling medially at the dorsal aspect of the thorax. These fibers start ventrally, near the sternum, so that they pass between the intercostal cartilages and continue along the ribs until they pass the angle. They originate on the upper border and inner surface of the rib, and on the costal cartilage, and they insert into the lower border and inner surface of the rib, and into costal cartilage, immediately above. These muscles are generally considered to be muscles of expiration in that they lower the ribs when contracted. There is some doubt as to the exact activity of the internal intercostals, but most authorities today seem to agree that, in general, they are antagonistic to the external intercostals. The nerve supply to the internal intercostal group is from the intercostal nerves, supplied through thoracic nerves numbered 1 through 12.

The lateral vertebral group is composed of three highly variable muscles, named the *scalene.* All originate upon the cervical vertebrae (cervical 3–7), at the transverse process. They pass downward and slightly laterally, deep to other muscles, especially to the sternocleidomastoid muscle. The *anterior scalene* muscle inserts into the first rib, just anterior to the tubercle; the *medial scalene* muscle inserts into nearly the same place, but somewhat more toward the midline of the thorax. The *posterior scalene* muscle is even deeper than the other two, and inserts onto the second rib, at about its tubercle. The action is said to elevate the ribs, although there is some doubt except when considering them as accessory muscles. It is fairly certain that they are fixators of the first and second rib for the inspiratory act. Cervical nerves 4–8 provide the innervation for these muscles.

The *transverse thoracic* muscle, another variable one, is generally found with its internal origin at the midline of the thorax, at the sternum and xiphoid process. Its fibers pass in bundles—some upward in a nearly vertical fashion, some upward obliquely, and some nearly horizontally—to insert into the costal cartilages and the bony ends of ribs two through six. Its action is said to depend upon the fixation of the twelfth rib by the quadratus lumborum muscle; it depresses the ribs, and thus is a muscle of expiration. Its nerve supply comes from the branches of the intercostal nerves, thus from thoracic nerves 2 to 6.

The *quadratus lumborum,* the fixator of the lower ribs, originates from the posterior portion of the crest of the ilium bone, the ligamentous and fibrous tissues of the posterior lumbar region, and the transverse processes of the lumbar vertebrae. Its fibers pass upward to insert into the tendons of the abdominal muscles as well as into the twelfth rib. Its action is mainly to bend the vertebral column, but it also assists in fixating the lowermost rib, and in depressing the rib cage in expiration. In inspiration, it fixates these lower ribs to provide purchase to the diaphragm muscle. Its nerve supply comes from the lumbar spinal nerves, 1–4, as well as from thoracic 12.

The larger muscles of the thorax are composed of *pectoralis major* and *pectoralis minor.* The *pectoralis major* is a large fan-shaped muscle with several divisions. The attachments are generally described as of thoracic origin; the insertion is on a single tubercule of the major bone of the upper arm, the humerus. (See Figure 6–8.) However, it is important here to consider this muscle as one of respiration, and therefore the usual origin and insertion are reversed. Thus, the origin of pectoralis major is here considered to be the head of the humerus, and the insertion is broad and fan-shaped, running from the ventral end of the clavicle, the sternum, and the costal cartilages of ribs two through six; the aponeurosis from external abdominal oblique muscle is also involved in this insertion. Its action, when the humerus is fixed, is to elevate the ribs and thus actively participate in enlarging the thorax in inspiration. Its nerve supply comes from the lowermost cervical and first thoracic spinal nerves.

The *pectoralis minor* is likewise a large thoracic muscle. It originates from the scapula at its coracoid process. Its fibers radiate downward beneath pectoralis major to the bony ends of ribs two through five. Its action, as here considered, is to elevate the ribs in inspiration. It is innervated by cervical nerves 7 and 8.

Minor Group of Thoracic Muscles

Among the so-called "minor" muscles listed earlier as being related to the respiratory acts are the *levatores costarum,* the *scalene, serratus anterior, subcostal,* and *sternocleidomastoid* muscles. *Levatore costarum* is actually a series of fan-shaped muscles that arise from the transverse processes of the vertebrae, from the cervical 7 to the thoracic 11. The fibers pass downward and slightly laterally to insert into the next inferior rib, from the head to the tubercle; lower in the thorax, some fibers pass to the second rib below. This muscle group receives its innervation from the intercostal nerves from thoracic 1 to 11. Its action is to elevate the ribs, and thus it becomes a muscle of inspiration because of the resulting enlargement of the thorax.

Superiorly in the thorax is the *serratus* muscle group, including *serratus posterior superior* and *inferior,* as well as *serratus anterior* muscle. The first two, *posterior superior* and *posterior inferior,* arise from the spines of the vertebrae; in the case of the superior group, this is the cervical vertebrae, and for the inferior group it is the lower thoracic and upper lumbar vertebrae. *Serratus posterior superior* fibers then pass downward and slightly laterally to insert into the upper borders of ribs two through five, dorsal to the angle. On the other hand, *serratus posterior inferior* fibers rise to fan out and insert into the inferior borders of the lower four ribs, nine through twelve. They oppose each other in actions as well, the upper group assisting in the elevation of the rib cage; thus it functions as an inspiratory group. The lower or inferior muscle depresses the lower ribs in expiration. This lower group also fixes the lowermost ribs in affording purchase for the contraction of the diaphragm, being antagonistic to the diaphragm, which is inspiratory in action upon contraction.

The *serratus anterior* muscle is a large series of bundles connecting the lower border of the scapula with the majority of the ribs, at least with the upper eight or nine. This muscle arises from the lower, or inferior, angle of the scapula and its bundles pass variously and anteriorly around the rib cage to insert into the ribs just anterior to the angle of ribs one through nine. Its nerve supply comes from the long thoracic nerve, which is developed from the lowermost cervical spinal nerves. Its action, as here considered in a rather restricted way, is to assist in elevation of the ribs, especially in forced inspiration.

The role of the remaining accessory muscles is not agreed upon. Among these may be listed subcostal, paralleling internal intercostals, and sternocleidomastoid muscle, the large muscle bundle running from sternum to mastoid process of the temporal bone across the sides of the neck. Both are listed as assisting in respiratory processes.

Abdominal Group

In studying the musculature of respiration, it is of importance to consider the abdominal group. (See Table 6.2.) These are four in number, and primarily operate upon the abdominal viscera; changes in position or density of the viscera change the pressure upon the thoracic cavity from below, and thus decrease the volume of the thorax.

The muscles to be considered in this category are *rectus abdominis, external oblique, internal oblique,* and *transverse abdominis* muscles. Together with

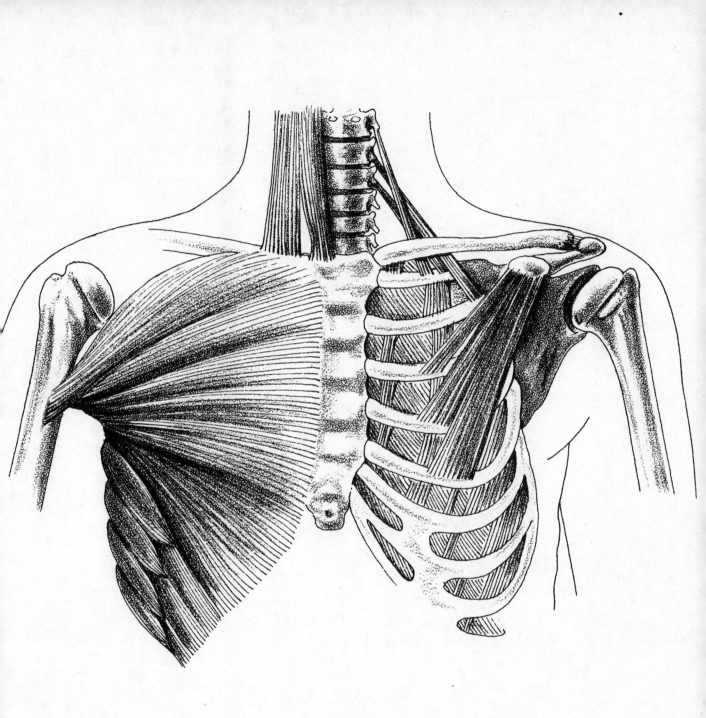

Figure 6–8.
Thoracic Surface Muscles of Respiration

TABLE 6.2   MUSCLES OF THE ABDOMINAL WALL

MUSCLE	ORIGIN	INSERTION	ACTION	NERVE
Rectus Abdominis	Crest and symphysis of pubis	Xiphoid process; costal cartilages 5, 6, 7	Supports and compresses viscera	Lower intercostals (T 7–11)
External Oblique	External borders of ribs 5–12	Crest of pubis; front half of iliac crest; linea alba; inguinal ligament	Supports and compresses viscera; depresses thorax	Lower intercostals (T 5–12; L 1)
Internal Oblique	Anterior half of iliac crest; lumbar fascia; inguinal ligament	Linea alba; cartilages of ribs 8, 9, 10; abdominal aponeurosis	Supports and compresses viscera	Lower intercostals (T 9–12; L 1)
Transverse Abdominis	Inguinal ligament; iliac crest; lower borders of ribs 6–12; lumbar fascia	Xiphoid process; linea alba; crest of pubis	Supports and compresses viscera	Lower intercostals (T 7–12)

the tendonous aponeuroses of the belly wall, these form the major portion of that wall. (See Figure 6–9.) Characteristic of the wall are the adhesive portions of the tendons, in some areas forming indistinct lines extending in a superior-inferior direction. At the midline of the ventral belly wall is the *linea alba,* a thickened tendonous portion that extends from above, at the xiphoid process, to below, at the symphysis pubis of the pelvic girdle. Somewhat lateral to this and beyond even the erect muscle of the abdominal wall is the *semilunar line* (linea semilunaris), again, a thickened, tendonous, curved line extending superiorly from near the xiphoid process and running around and down laterally to the far lateral edges of the belly wall and returning to the midline to almost the symphysis pubis again.

The *rectus abdominis* muscle is a paired, near-midline muscle, extending from thorax to symphysis. It originates along the crest and the symphysis of the pubis; it inserts at the xiphoid process and the costal cartilages of ribs five, six, and seven. It passes directly and inferiorly alongside the midline of the belly as a thick regular bundle that has three characteristic tendonous inscriptions, crossing at right angles along its length. This muscle contracts to compress the abdominal viscera, during the act of respiration, and thus is a major muscle of expiration. It is also largely responsible for flexing the vertebral column, when the thorax is fixed erect through its spinal musculature. Nerve supply comes from the lowermost intercostal nerves (thoracic 7–11).

External oblique is a muscle of the lateral abdominal wall that is continued ventrally by its aponeurosis. It originates on the external borders of the lower eight ribs as well as from the aponeurosis of the belly wall. Its fibers pass downward and forward to insert on the crest of the pubis, the anterior portion of the iliac crest, the linea alba, and part of the inguinal ligament. Its action, as far as respiration may be concerned, is to depress the thorax and compress the abdominal viscera; thus it becomes a muscle of expiration. It, too, acts upon the trunk, to flex and rotate it. Its nerve supply comes from the last intercostal nerves (T 5–12 and L 1).

The *internal oblique* is a muscle that originates in the lower dorsal regions of the abdomen, particularly from the iliac crest, the inguinal ligament, and the lumbodorsal fascia. Its fibers spread medially and superiorly until they end; the more dorsal fibers end on the lower three ribs, and the lower-originating muscle fibers pass nearby horizontally toward the midline to terminate in the linea alba, the abdominal aponeurosis, and the cartilages of ribs eight, nine, and ten. This tendonous sheath splits as it approaches the rectus abdominis muscle, part of the tendon passing beneath and part passing outer to the rectus. Internal oblique acts along with external oblique to compress the abdominal viscera in the expiratory process. It has other activities, such as flexing and rotating the spinal column, and flexing and rotating the pelvis. Its nerve supply comes from the last intercostal nerves, from T 9–12 as well as L 1.

The *transverse abdominis* is the innermost of the layered abdominal muscles. It arises from a rather broad origin, from the iliac crest and the inguinal ligament inferiorly, along the lumbodorsal fascia, and the innermost portions of the lower six ribs. This origin blends with part of the costal origin of the diaphragm muscle. The fibers of transversus pass nearly horizontally forward until they terminate as tendon in the linea alba at the midline of the abdomen, from the xiphoid process to the crest of the pubis. This muscle is innervated by the lower intercostal nerves, from thoracic 7–12. Its action is to support and compress the abdominal viscera, in the expiration of air, while aiding in flexion and rotation of the trunk, depending upon whether it is innervated bilaterally or unilaterally.

In review, one might point to the four abdominal muscles as being related to expiration of air, and thus they are important as sources of control for the column of air under pressure, which is the immediate energizer for the laryngeal valve, and phonation. The diaphragm muscle, too, is importantly related to expira-

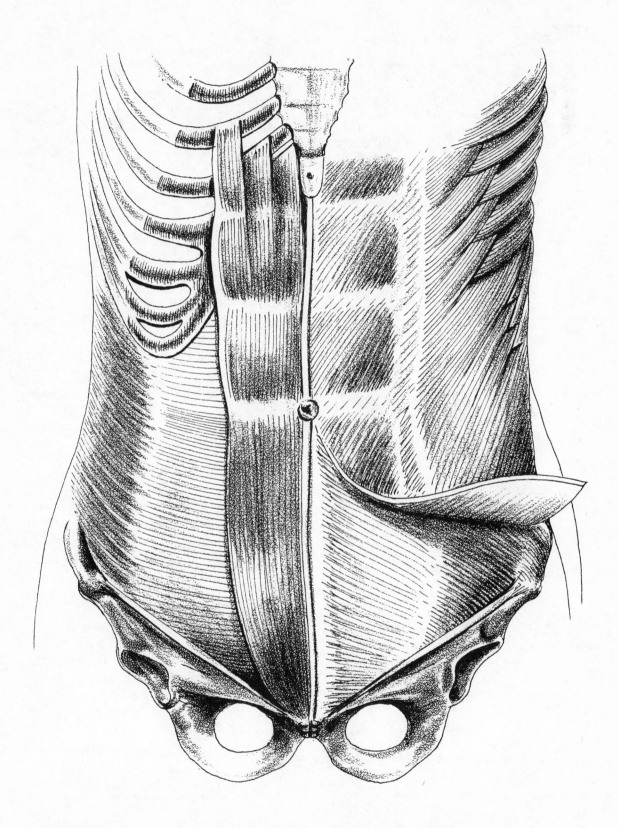

Figure 6–9.
Abdominal Muscles of Respiration

tion, although it is usually considered as inspiratory because of its effect when it contracts; upon controlled and differential relaxation of the diaphragm, finer control of the air column might be made possible.

CLINICAL NOTE

In considering possible pathologies producing speech and hearing problems, the thoracic region demonstrates both gross and specific defects. In the former, it has been noted that in individuals with reduced vital capacities, such as that seen in hypothyroidism or respiratory paralyses or in cases having had surgical excision of major portions of the lungs, reduced speaking loudness exists. Also, individuals with lesions of specific nerves that innervate important muscles, or those with damage to the trachea or bronchi, may well demonstrate decreased intensity or lack of ability to sustain or control phonation.

NERVOUS TISSUES

The nervous tissues of the thoracic region have been discussed in regard to each of the muscles and muscle groups involved with the respiratory acts. It can be seen, in summary, that these nerves are derived mainly from the spinal nerves. Each of the final innervating tissues receives contributions from segments of the autonomic nervous system, for this system is responsive to the needs of the body for more oxygen or for decreasing the concentration of carbon dioxide in the tissues. The internal respiratory control is a series of neurochemical centers in the blood vascular system which constantly measure the oxygen-carbon dioxide ratio. These centers ultimately stimulate the respiratory musculature into action when the biologic need is present. Cortical and voluntary control may be superimposed by the needs of the body for air under pressure for controlled phonation. The major centers of respiratory control are found in the medulla and pons; infections and injuries in those centers may cause respiratory difficulties, as in poliomyelitis.

SUMMARY OF FUNCTIONS OF THE THORACIC REGION

It should be clear that the respiratory tract, housed in the thoracic region, provides the necessary oxygen to the body tissues and removes certain of the waste products from the metabolic activities of those tissues. The respiratory tract is primarily a passive air conduit within a flexible framework. Enlargement of the framework increases the volume within the thoracic cage; this creates a decrease of air pressure within the respiratory tract. Environmental air being at a now greater air pressure level enters the respiratory tract until the air pressure within the thorax and lungs is the same as the air pressure outside the body. In so doing, of course, oxygen-laden air is brought to the lung tissues, where it is acted upon within the tiny alveoli and the oxygen diffused into the blood stream via the capillaries in the cell walls. At the same time, the wastes (carbon dioxide) in the blood are released into the air of the alveoli, and thence are released with the exhaled air from the lungs. This air is vital to life systems of the organism. The exhaled air under pressure provides the energizing force for the vibrating vocal folds to produce laryngeal tone.

The expansion of the rib cage to provide for the increased volume and associated decreased air pressure is the product of muscle contraction. There is some disagreement among authorities as to which muscles make the major contributions to thoracic movement, but it is fairly well known that the external intercostals are primary movers in the inspiratory cycle: thoracic enlargement. Of course, the diaphragm muscle is also actively contracting at the same time to enlarge the thorax in a vertical dimension. The internal intercostal muscles might also contribute to this phase, although some authorities feel that they are expiratory in function. Others add the contributions of the scalene muscle group, perhaps as auxiliary inspiratory muscles. From this point on, numbers of additional muscles that provide assistance to thoracic cage enlargement might be considered.

Decreasing the volume of the thoracic cage increases the air pressure within the lungs and thus forces it out of the respiratory tract. As mentioned above, this exhalation removes waste products from the alveoli. For speech purposes, this exhalation creates a column of air under pressure passing up the trachea to the larynx. At the larynx the valve apparatus there is capable of operating so that it might become a vibrating structure and create a sound. This subglottal air pressure, then, is the product of the mechanisms that will act upon the thoracic volume to decrease it.

Perhaps primary of all such forces, which can be termed passive, are elastic recoil of the cartilages and lung tissues, the effect of gravity, and the torque force produced when the ribs are elevated and their cartilages twisted. Next come the muscles of expiration, which return the ribs to their position of rest; some list the internal intercostals at this point, and others add such muscles as quadratus lumborum, the subcostals, and lastly the four abdominal muscles. These last create a pressure upon the abdominal viscera, forcing it up against the diaphragm to return it to its rest position, thus decreasing thoracic volume and expelling intrapulmonary air.

It must be added that not only the active participation of the muscles of expiration just listed provide for expelling of air, but the controlled relaxation of the muscles of inspiration also contribute to this important activity. It is possible that there is considerable individual variation in these functions. However, the end product in the study of the power source for laryngeal tone production is the development of subglottal air pressure that can be controlled.

THORACIC REGION LANDMARK IDENTIFICATION

Directions: For the indicated illustrations, label the following landmarks.

FIGURE 6–1
Rib, Head
Rib, Articulating Tubercle
Rib, Angle
Rib, Shaft
Rib, Costal End
Vertebra, Body
Vertebra, Transverse Process
Sternum
Costal Cartilage

FIGURE 6–2
Vertebra, Spinous Process
Vertebra, Superior Articulating Facet
Vertebra, Inferior Articulating Facet
Vertebral Canal
Vertebra, Transverse Process
Vertebra, Body
Vertebral Notch

FIGURE 6–3
Cervical Vertebrae (Number)
Thoracic Vertebrae (Number)
Lumbar Vertebrae (Number)
Sacral Vertebrae (Number)
Coccygeal Vertebrae (Number)
Spinous Processes
Bodies
Transverse Processes

FIGURE 6–4
Sternum Bone, Manubrium
Sternum Bone, Body
Sternum Bone, Xiphoid Process
Sternum Bone, Angle
Sternal Notch
Costal Cartilage
Ribs Numbered 1–12
Vertebrosternal Ribs
Vertebrochondral Ribs
Vertebral Ribs
Vertebrae
Ribs, Angle

FIGURE 6–5
Sacrum Bone
Ilium Bone
Ischium Bone
Pubis Bone
Symphysis Pubis
Iliac Crest
Inguinal Ligament

Obturator Foramen
Sacroiliac Joint

FIGURE 6–6
Trachea
Tracheal Bifurcation
Bronchus, Right
Bronchus, Left
Lung Apex
Lung, Base
Pulmonary Pleura
Terminal Bronchiole
Respiratory Bronchiole
Alveolar Duct
Alveolar Sac
Alveolus
Pulmonary Lobule

FIGURE 6–7
Ribs 8, 9, 10
Xiphoid Process
Diaphragm Muscle
Diaphragm Muscle, Central Tendon
Sternum Bone
Vertebrae

FIGURE 6–8
Clavicle Bone
Sternum Bone
Ribs 1–8
Humerus Bone, Head
Scapula Bone
Scalene Muscles (3)
Sterno(cleido)mastoid Muscle
Pectoralis Major Muscle
Pectoralis Minor Muscle
Internal Intercostal Muscles
External Intercostal Muscles

FIGURE 6–9
Sternum Bone, Xiphoid Process
Linea Alba
Linea Semilunaris
Ribs 5–10
Rectus Abdominis Muscle
External Abdominal Oblique Muscle
Internal Abdominal Oblique Muscle
Transverse Abdominal Muscle
Inguinal Ligament
Symphysis Pubis
Iliac Crest
Tendonous Inscriptions
Sacroiliac Joint

The ability of a person to hear depends upon the integrity of several different types of tissue in the ear: membranes of mucous and fibrous types, bones, ligaments, muscles, canals filled with fluid, and nerve fibers with various types of supporting tissues. In operation, these are all closely associated, so that the auditory stimulus is transferred from the environment through the various transducing devices until it reaches the brain and becomes a meaningful event to the receiving individual. The environmental air vibrates with its sound; this vibration is picked up by a taut membrane; the membrane passes the vibration on to a trio of closely articulated bones. These ossicles pass the vibration on through an opening in the petrous portion of the temporal bone. This window communicates with a series of fluid-filled canals; the vibratory pattern is transformed into waves in the fluid; and these wave disturbances are picked up by sensitive hairs and hair cells, which act as triggers to set up neural impulses. The neural impulses, in turn, travel along nerve fibers to nerve centers until they are received, and perceived, in the cerebral cortex.

The *auditory system* might be considered a four-part system. (See Figure 7–1.) The first three, in the order in which the stimulus is transmitted, make up a rather commonly described trio. This usually starts with the *external ear,* which consists of those structures surrounding and contributing to the airway leading into the other sections. The *middle ear* consists of the structures in which the mechanical conductors are found. The *inner ear* is composed of the petrous portion of the temporal bone, the cavities of that bone, and their nonneural components. The *neural ear,* the fourth section of this system, consists of the sensory end organ and the nerves that connect it to the cerebral cortex. Presenting the neurologic components as a fourth division is an unusual approach; it is so presented that it might be highlighted and elevated to a position it deserves, as evidenced by the considerable research aimed at better understanding it.

THE EXTERNAL AUDITORY STRUCTURES

The external auditory structures are those that form a channel for air to enter the sides of the skull. Through this air there pass vibrations, which are actually changes in the relationship between and among molecules of that air. The important tissues are cartilaginous and bony.

The *auricle,* or, *pinna,* of the external ear is the so-called "sound collector," composed of a thin plate of cartilage covered by integument, or skin. (See Figure 7–2.) It has numerous ridges, indentations, and a somewhat pendulous lobule. The ridges and indentations are as individually characteristic as are any other parts of the human organism; they generally consist of the skin-covered cartilage that, in effect, funnels toward its centrally located entrance to the *external auditory canal.* The area immediately outside this entrance is the *cave.* Between it and another indentation, the *skiff,* is the limb (crus) of the *helix.* The helix itself is the folded rim of the auricle extending from between the two spaces mentioned, up and around the auricle until it blends below and behind with the *lobule.* From the upper midpoint of the lobule projects a slight cartilaginous elevation, the *anti-tragus.* Another, extended upward and around the conchal space, is termed the *antihelix.* Between it and the helix is the *scaphoid fossa* of the external ear. Projecting anteriorly from the integument of the face outward over the entrance of the external auditory meatus is the flaplike *tragus* (buck). Other landmarks to be found are the two *limbs of the antihelix,* the *intertragal notch, Darwin's tubercle,* the *anterior notch, posterior sulcus,* and the landmarks and muscles found on the posterior surface of the auricle. Detailed descriptions of these points are of academic interest at this point.

The *external auditory meatus* is the air-filled canal entering the side of the head from the auricle. A full two-thirds of this meatus is formed of bone from the folds of the tympanic portion of the temporal bone. The other outer third of the external auditory meatus is cartilage lined with skin that houses both *hair follicles* and *ceruminous glands.* Overall length of the meatus is about 25 mm (about 1 inch), although it follows an angled course for this short distance. The cutaneous lining of the osseus portion of the meatus is very thin, very tightly adherent to the bone beneath, and contains no hairs or glands. This lining becomes the lateral and very delicate layer of the *tympanic membrane.*

CLINICAL NOTE

The external auditory mechanism contains the environmental air, giving it access to the primary receptor-mechanism of the auditory system. In this way, it cannot be labeled as the conductor of sound as it sometimes is considered. It serves very little as an active participant in the hearing act; loss of the auricle itself produces a barely distinguishable auditory defect. Loss of the external meatus is more significant, for the primary receptor-mechanism is no longer provided access to the airborne acoustic vibrations. Such an auditory defect is highly variable, depending upon the type and extent of the canal defect. It is more commonly a congenital defect. Other defects result from impacted cerumen (wax), from blockage by foreign bodies, and from injuries and infections of the canal.

THE MIDDLE AUDITORY MECHANISM

The mechanical transmission of the acoustic stimuli, which ultimately will reach the individual as sound, is accomplished through a series of structures of membrane, bone, and their ligaments. (See Figure 7–3.) The first of the mechanical vibrators is the *tympanic membrane,* a three-layer, disclike structure that is exposed laterally to the external air. Further, it has as part of its own intrinsic structure a major portion of the first bone in the ossicular chain that further transmits the acoustic stimulus.

The *tympanic membrane,* is affixed into the *tympanic sulcus* of the tympanic portion of the temporal bone. As a result, the membrane is oriented in a sloping plane: downward, forward, and medially. It is also deeply concave near its midpoint; the deepest part of the concavity is the *umbo,* corresponding to the end of the *manubrium of the malleus bone.* Also, because of this bony attachment, the majority of the tympanic membrane is kept under tension and is thus labeled *pars tensa* (tense portion). There is a loose portion, known as *Shrapnell's membrane* (or *pars flaccida*), which extends from a V-shaped line across the upper portion of the tympanic membrane to the upper margin. The flaccid portion is not

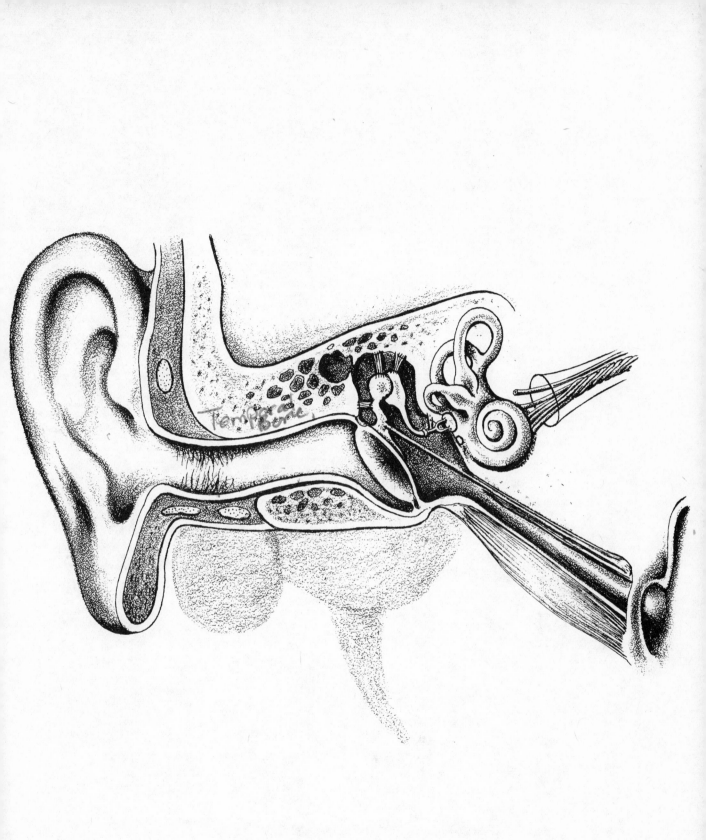

Figure   7–1.
Auditory Mechanism

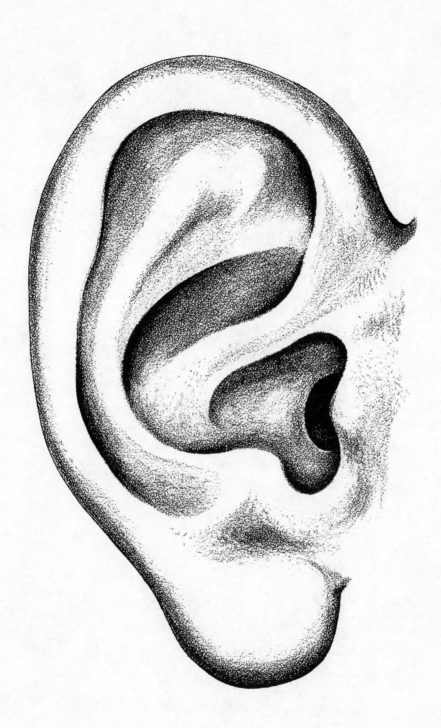

Figure   7–2.
Auricle

Figure 7–3.
Middle Ear

affixed firmly to the surrounding bone, for there is no tympanic sulcus in this upper region of the tympanic part of the bone. The small, but noticeable, fold of tissue making the line of demarcation between loose and tense portions is called the *anterior* and *posterior malleolar folds,* and the *chorda tympani nerve,* a portion of the facial (Cranial VII) nerve, is contained therein.

The outermost layer of the tympanic membrane is a continuation of the cutaneous lining of the external auditory meatus. The innermost and most medial layer is a continuation of the mucous-membrane lining of the middle ear. This is the same tissue-type that lines the respiratory tract, the mouth, nose, throat, as well as the sinuses. Even the mastoid air cells within the mastoid process of the temporal bone are lined with this same type of tissue: mucous membrane.

The middle, or inner layer of, tissue of the tympanic membrane is fibrous. This fibrous lamina is in intimate contact with the manubrium of the malleus, which in turn is covered by the mucous membrane layer. The middle layer is of utmost importance to audition, for it provides the thin resilient connective tissue important to vibration of the entire structure. The fibers of this layer are both circularly and radially arranged within the tense portion. In the flaccid portion, only elastic fibers are found, a matter of some importance when it is considered that the major function of the upper part of the tympanic membrane is to provide for air-pressure equalization, at least to a minimal degree, between the tympanum and the external environment.

The *tympanum* itself is an air-filled cavity that is walled by the lowermost portions of the temporal bone. It also communicates with the external environment, so that there remains a supply of environmental air at environmental air pressure within the tympanum of the normal and healthy individual. This interchange is made possible through the *auditory tube* (of Eustachius), which leaves the tympanum from its anterior inferior region to pass through the temporal bone at the junction of the squamous and petrous portions. It is continued beyond that point as a cartilaginous canal until it opens into the lateral walls of the nasopharynx, just above the level of the velum. At this point, the cartilage of the ostium becomes thicker and vertically oriented to form the torus tubarius. To this frame about the opening are attached at least two of the muscles of the nasopharynx and palate studied earlier: tensor (veli) palatine and salpingopharyngeal. These muscles distort the cartilaginous opening of the auditory tube during swallowing and other palatal and pharyngeal activities, thus providing for opening the tube and allowing for the air exchange as well as for the escape of the more fluid products of the mucous lining of the cavities. The auditory tube is generally horizontally oriented in infancy; but as the head grows, the tube takes a sloping angle until it is obliquely oriented downward, forward, and medially from the tympanum.

The tympanum is high in its vertical dimension, about 15 mm, or slightly over one-half inch; its antero-posterior dimension is about the same. Its lateral dimension is variable, but generally it is as small as 2 mm at the level of the tympanic membrane, or as large as 6 mm at its uppermost end. Thus, its widest point is less than a quarter of an inch from side to side. Although these figures are not standard because of the great variation in individuals, they do demonstrate the great difference between the width, height, and breadth of the tympanum. How wide this really is might be demonstrated by placing two five-cent pieces together; their combined thicknesses approximate the width of the tympanum.

The upper regions of the tympanum are continuous with a somewhat expanded area called the *attic,* or *epitympanic recess.* This is usually defined as that space above the level of the superior margin of the tympanic membrane. The roof over the tympanum is a very thin layer of the petrous portion of the temporal bone, called the *tegmen tympani.* At the upper and posterior area of the cavity is a space known as the *aditus,* which is actually an opening into the *tympanic antrum.* This last is a further enlargement of the posterior space. It communicates with the more posterior air cells of the mastoid process. All of these cavities are lined with mucous membrane, including the mastoid air cells.

The walls of the tympanum, close as they may be to each other, are labeled according to their relationships to other structures. For example, the posterior wall is the mastoid wall because it communicates with the mastoid air cells. The medial wall is the labyrinthine wall; the roof is the tegmental wall; the floor is the jugular wall because of its association with the jugular bulb beneath it; the anterior wall is the carotid wall because of the proximity of the internal carotid artery on its opposite side; the lateral wall, of course, is the membranous wall because of the presence of the tympanic membrane.

The superior portion of the middle ear is traversed by the ossicular chain. The overall distance covered by this chain is short: from 2 to 6 millimeters, as mentioned previously. The first of these ossicles is the *malleus* (hammer). A part of this ossicle has been described along with the tympanic membrane, for its larger process (the *manubrium*) may be considered to be part of the membranous wall. The malleus further demonstrates a head, neck, and two smaller processes—the anterior and the lateral. The large upper portion of the malleus, the head, is housed above the level of the tympanic membrane in the epitympanic recess. It is oval, presenting on its posterior surface a large articular facet for the second ossicle—the *incus.* The malleus head and manubrium are connected through the slightly constricted neck, immediately below which is a prominence to which the two processes are attached. The anterior process is a very tiny spicule that projects anteriorly. To this process is attached the anterior ligament, running to the fissure between the petrous and the tympanic portions of the temporal bone. (This anterior process is the residual of Meckel's cartilage, which is of some importance in the embryo to the developing ear.) The lateral process of the malleus also arises just below the neck and projects laterally against the tympanic membrane at about the level of the malleolar fold. From this process also extends the lateral ligament, attaching the malleus to the tympanic portion of the temporal bone at the tympanic fissure, or notch of Rivinus. A third ligament—the *superior (malleolar)*—supports the malleus and extends from the head of the malleus to the roof of the epitympanic recess.

With the manubrium imbedded within the layers of the tympanic membrane, it can be seen that vibratory actions of that membrane are continued onward via the manubrium. Movement of the manubrium causes movement of the head of the malleus; this movement is transmitted through the articulation at the diarthrodial joint with the second ossicle: the *incus (anvil).* Some protection may be available against extreme vibrations because of the presence of the *tensor tympani muscle* of the middle ear. It inserts into the manubrium of the malleus from its origin across the tympanum in its own semicanal above the eustachian, or auditory tube. Its reflex contraction, it is thought, protects the chain from disruption or destruction by tension placed upon the membrane and the malleus, so that vibration cannot be transmitted at large amplitude levels.

The second ossicle, the *incus,* is shaped somewhat like its namesake—an anvil; like the malleus, it projects the bulk of its body up into the epitympanic recess. It, too, has special landmarks and processes—in this case called crura, or processes. From the rather flattened and rounded body, with its anteriorly-facing articular surface for the malleus, the short crus extends posteriorly. This is attached to the mastoid wall of the tympanum, which is just below the entrance into the antrum, by the posterior incudal ligament. There may be a superior incudal ligament that connects the body of the incus to the tegmen tympani, although it often appears as a simple fold of mucous membrane. The long crus of the incus is oriented at right angles to the short crus, being directed downward and medialward toward the labyrinthine wall. At its extremity, it thins, then expands into a rounded knob called the lenticular process (of Sylvius). This process articulates with the *stapes (stirrup),* the last of the three ossicles. Here, too, is found a true joint.

The *stapes* presents, at the articular end, a head and neck from which diverge two crura; these are affixed into the two ends of an oval footplate. The neck extends slightly below a somewhat broad head and provides insertion for the *stapedius muscle.* The two crura are oriented with one rather straight crus directed anteriorly and a more curved second being directed more posteriorly. The oval footplate is received into the *oval window* (vestibular window) and attached thereto by the *annular ligament* around its circumference.

CLINICAL NOTE

Pathologies involving the tympanic membrane or the ossicles are common to the population having hearing losses, especially of the conductive type. Scarred and distorted tympanic membranes, from infections or other injuries, limit the sensitivity of this structure to vibratory stimuli. The articulation of the ossicles is also limited under certain conditions: otosclerosis (growth of spongy bone at the stapes footplate), adhesions fixating or interfering with articulation, middle ear fluids, and eustachian tube closure resulting in decreased air pressure and subsequent distortion of the tympanic membrane and ossicles. Tumor growth, such as cholesteatoma, mastoiditis, and other less common conditions, is also known to affect the auditory abilities of some individuals.

The two muscles of the middle ear have already been mentioned: the *stapedius* and the *tensor tympani.* (See Table 7.1.) The *stapedius* has its origin in a cavity on the mastoid wall of the tympanum; this cavity forms a small pyramidal eminence and presents a tiny hole at its apex. Through this aperture extends the minute tendon of the stapedius muscle, which then attaches to the posterior aspect of the neck of the stapes bone. Its action is reflexive, moving the stapes laterally and thus tensing or immobilizing the parts within the oval window; stapedius is probably a protective muscle in this action, especially against ossicular vibrations of great amplitude which might cause damage either at the articular joints or beyond the ossicles within the inner ear. It receives its nerve supply from a branch of the facial (Cranial VII) nerve.

The *tensor tympani* muscle is somewhat similar to the stapedius in that it, too, has its muscle fibers encased in a bony cavity with only its tendon passing to the point of attachment. The tensor tympani's origin is from alongside the eustachian tube and from its bony neighbors, especially the great wing of the sphenoid and the petrous portion of the temporal bone. The tendon of the muscle exits from this semicanal, makes a right angle turn, and passes laterally toward the tympanic membrane. It inserts into the upper part of the medial surface of the manubrium of the malleus. Its action is reflexive, as is that of the stapedius, moving the malleus medially and tensing the tympanic membrane as a protective device during stimulations of great amplitude. Its nerve supply derives from the otic ganglion from the mandibular division of the trigeminal (Cranial V) nerve.

In summary, the tympanum is an air space across which travels a chain of three articulated bones. These bones respond to the vibrations of the tympanic membrane, which in turn is sensitive to the acoustic vibrations in the external air. The ossicular chain is supported in space by various ligaments and is acted upon by two muscles. The tympanum surrounding the ossicles is in communication with the environment through the eustachian tube, the nasopharynx and nose, and with the air cells of the mastoid portion of the temporal bone. It is further in indirect contact with other regions, including the convolutions of the brain through the very thin tegmen tympani, as well as with the mechanism for equilibrium and the mechanism for auditory reception: the inner ear.

TABLE 7.1 **MUSCLES OF THE MIDDLE EAR**

NAME	ORIGIN	INSERTION	ACTION	NERVE
Stapedius	Pyramidal eminence	Posterior surface of the neck of the stapes	Moves stapes laterally; immobilizes oval footplate	Cranial VII
Tensor Tympani	Edge of eustachian tube opening; greater wing of sphenoid; petrous portion of temporal bone	Manubrium of malleus	Tenses tympanic membrane; moves manubrium of malleus medially	Cranial V (Mandibular division)

THE INNER EAR

The inner ear presents a closed canal system of fluids. The pressures created by the footplate of the stapes bone, developed from the mechanical vibratory pattern of the ossicles, cause changes within these chambers of the inner ear. Certain of these hydraulic changes ultimately are stimulators of sensory nerve endings; these acoustic stimuli become auditory impulses that ultimately reach higher centers of the nervous system.

Traditionally, the inner ear is classified as those canals within the petrous portion of the temporal bone which house the vestibular mechanisms and the organ of hearing. There is definite and demonstrable connection between these structures and the chambers they occupy; however, there is little connection between their functions in the normal individual. In pathology, their connection becomes of importance, of course, and differential diagnostic procedures are often based upon this proximity and association.

The oval, or vestibular, window, into which the oval base of the stapes is placed, opens into the structure known as the *vestibule.* The vestibule is an entrance chamber leading into various other chambers. In this particular vestibule, fluid-filled (perilymph) chambers open into both the vestibular apparatus and the auditory (cochlea) mechanism. The vestibular mechanism is a complex arrangement of chambers whose primary function is to house the sensory end organs responsive to positional changes of the head; thus, it is the end organ for equilibrium.

A large part of the equilibrium mechanism is housed in two membranous capsules within the vestibule: the *saccule* and the *utricle.* These capsules are fluid-filled. This fluid is the endolymph (otic fluid). From the saccule and utricle extend three other membranous canals, housed within somewhat larger bony spaces. The three canals are nearly circular in their orientation, returning to re-enter the vestibule through enlarged areas, called ampullae. Each of these semi-circular canals is oriented at right angles to each of the others, and each membranous portion contains sensory end organs of equilibrium. Thus, the canals are so placed that movement of the head in any direction will move the contents of one or more of the semicircular canals and stimulate the sensory fibers therein.

Yet another chamber exits from the vestibule of the inner ear. This opening is into the *cochlea,* the spiral chamber that houses the sensory end organ for audition. The entrance from the vestibule continues as a canal of the cochlea, which is appropriately called the *vestibular canal (scala).* This, too, is fluid-filled (perilymph). Paralleling the vestibular canal is the membranous canal of the cochlea—the *scala media,* or *cochlear duct;* this duct is filled with endolymph, as is the remainder of the membranous labyrinth of the inner ear.

The vestibular canal of the cochlea spirals about two and a half times until it reaches the apex of the cochlea. There, it changes its direction and returns to the base of the cochlea, again spiraling two and a half times. Where the canal reverses itself, the space is called the helicotrema; from that point, the canal is called the *tympanic canal,* or *scala.* It terminates in a window occluded by the secondary tympanic membrane. This round window (tympanic window) is found just below the promontory of the labyrinthine wall of the middle ear. The promontory itself is a bulge accommodating the base of the cochlea and is easily identified on the middle ear wall.

To recapitulate, the cochlea is composed of a bony canal system of perilymph. This system starts at the vestibule of the inner ear, travels in a spiral fashion through two and a half turns, reverses its direction to return to the base, and terminates in a mobile window. The two canals share the cochlea with an interposed third canal, the scala media, which continues the membranous canal system of the inner ear. This membranous canal is filled with endolymph; it is in communication with the membranous canals of the vestibular apparatus through the ductus reuniens.

The middle canal—the *scala media,* or *cochlear duct*—is of considerable importance to hearing, for within it is the spiraling prominence extending along its length known as the *organ of Corti.* The organ of Corti provides a terminus for the sensory end organ for audition. It is affixed to the base membrane of the cochlear duct; this *basilar membrane* is also a boundary wall between the cochlear duct and the tympanic canal. The roof over the cochlear duct separating it from the vestibular canal is the *vestibular* or *Reissner's membrane.*

The two boundary membranes, the basilar and the vestibular, form two of the walls of the endolymph-filled cochlear duct. The third and outermost wall is the bony housing for the cochlea itself; this wall contains the *spiral ligament,* supporting the cochlear duct, along with the *spiral stria,* which is vascular and is the nutritional supplier of the cochlea.

The perspective of the cochlea, and its contents, can be seen when one looks at a cross section of that structure. (See Figure 7–4.) Here, one can see that the greatest portion of the cochlea is perilymphatic. The smaller membranous portion is the cochlear duct and is located on the outer portion of the cochlear canal system, spiraling around two and a half times and ending at the apex as a closed canal. The strong basilar membrane supports the sensory end organ, even forming a part of that organ.

The basilar membrane is held in place by the spiral ligament on the outer wall of the cochlea, and by the osseus spiral lamina extending from the inner wall of the cochlea. This membrane is composed of cells and multitudinous fibers that are critical to the characteristic vibratory motions of the entire structure. There are specialized cells (e.g., Claudius, Hensen) found on the upper surface of the basilar membrane, especially toward the outer portion of the membrane. Toward the inner portion are found several rows of elongated supporting cells, cupped at the top to hold the rows of outer hair cells. Further inner structures, acting to give rigidity to the organ of Corti, are the two *pillars of Corti;* these calcium salt structures lean together to form the inner tunnel of Corti. At their top, they are continuous with the reticular membrane, a network of tissue through which pass the rows of hairs from the hair cells. Inward from the pillars are found more supporting cells and their hair cells above, again with hairs extending through the reticular membrane into the endolymph.

It is at this point that the basilar membrane is attached to the osseus spiral lamina and where also will be found a thickened tissue structure: the *spiral limbus.* From the superior margin of the limbus projecting into the endolymph of the cochlear duct is the gelatinous tectorial membrane. This extends outward over the reticular membrane and approximates the upward pointing hairs from the hair cells.

Attached to the walls of the hair cells are the terminal buttons or loops of the auditory nerve fibers. These fibers distribute themselves to several hair cells as they branch. The fibers from the outer hair cells pass inward across the inner tunnel, join with those fibers of the inner hair cells, and enter the osseus spiral lamina.

A much simplified description of the activity occurring at the organ of Corti would emphasize the wave of disturbance set up in the fluid system started by the rocking of the oval footplate of the stapes into the perilymph of the vestibule. This acoustic phenomenon is distributed to the perilymph of the vestibular canal, where it disturbs the vestibular membrane at critical points. This, in turn, sets up a wave of disturbance in the endolymph of the cochlear duct. The tectorial membrane is distorted, causing a displacement of the hairs of the hair cells. When this last occurs, there is a cell wall distortion, which is of sufficient

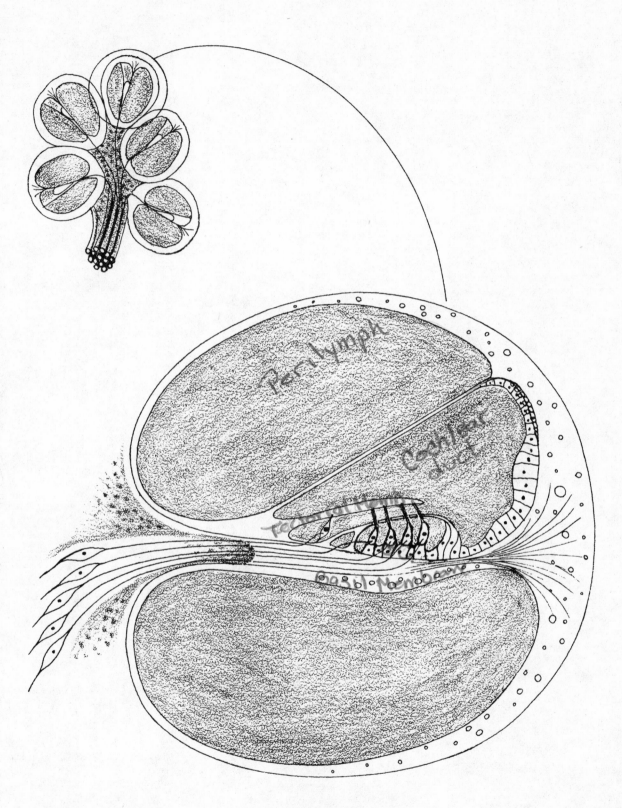

Cross-sectional View

Figure   7–4.
Cochlea

influence to cause the nerve impulse to be set up in the auditory nerve fiber there attached. The actual firing of the end organ or receptor is probably due to electrochemical changes occurring at the surface of the cell membrane.

> CLINICAL NOTE
> The condition of the sensory nerves, the status of the supporting cells and of the tectorial membrane, the nature of the endolymph—all play roles in the act of hearing. Certain pathologies affect each of these regions and structures, so that auditory deficits occur. For example, intense or loud noise may disturb the hair cells and the tectorial membrane, pathologies of the sensory nervous system might develop, the endolymph content might change, as in endolymphatic hydrops. In each, hearing losses are known to occur; the organism's reactions to these deficits dictate the degree of handicap.

THE NEURAL EAR

This neural system is the fourth transmission system of the auditory process. (See Figure 7–5.) From the beginnings of this system on the hair cells of the organ of Corti, the tiny neurofibrils pass toward the core of the cochlea—*the modiolus*—which is oriented toward the brain. As the nerve fibers enter this core, their cell bodies are gathered together to form the spiral ganglion. From here, the nerve fibers pass through the modiolus to enter into the internal auditory meatus, along with the vestibular portion of the auditory (Cranial VIII) nerve. The fibers within the modiolus and those outside it that serve the hearing system are known as the cochlear nerve, or cochlear division.

The auditory nerve is composed of the cochlear and the vestibular divisions, which have a total of about 50,000 individual fibers. The breakdown is to the advantage of the auditory portion, there being about 30,000 fibers in that part, whereas the vestibular portion has about 20,000. In comparison with some other cranial nerves, these are considered rather small; the optic (visual) nerve, for example, contains over a million nerve fibers. These fibers in the auditory nerve are true bipolar neurons, with a peripheral process extending toward the sensory end organ and a central process, which has its myelin sheath, acting as an axis cylinder (axon) and communicating with the central nervous system.

The cochlear nerve enters the brain stem laterally at the level of the juncture of the medulla and the pons. It separates from the vestibular division at about this point. There is a further division of the cochlear nerve: one portion is directed toward the posterior aspect, and the other toward the anterior aspect of the brain stem. Here the nerve fibers terminate in the ventral and the dorsal cochlear nuclei. These fibers, from the cochlea to the cochlear nuclei, are the *first-order neurons* of the auditory system.

At the two nuclei, synaptic connections take place. From here, *second-order neurons* arise to carry the auditory impulse farther centrally. And from here, neural anatomists demonstrate some degree of disagreement as to the course taken by the various groups of neurons. The essence of the disagreement stems around the matter of crossing of neural groups; some anatomists feel that there is considerable crossing of nerve fibers from one side of the pathway to the other, whereas other anatomists feel that the crossings are minimal. All, however, are agreed that there are crossings. In these crossings, there is ultimately bilateral representation in the cerebral cortex of each ear. Otherwise, the following description of the central connections is, in general, adequate, although details of it may be questioned.

The *second-order neurons* from the dorsal cochlear nucleus generally cross to the opposite side of the brainstem through the trapezoid body, with some fibers terminating at the nucleus of the trapezoid body of the opposite side. Fibers of the second order from the ventral cochlear nucleus cross in the trapezoid body also and, likewise, some of their number may terminate within the nucleus of the trapezoid body of the opposite side. From both the ventral and dorsal cochlear nuclei, fibers may start their pathway homolaterally (same side) to the brain.

This path to the brain rostrally is the *lateral lemniscus,* a grouping of second-order auditory fibers in the main. Somewhere along this pathway, a group of auditory nerve fibers pass directly to the nucleus of the facial nerve (Cranial VII). This connection is a simple explanation of the palpebroacoustic reflex (startle response) to acoustic stimuli of unexpected commencement and of considerable intensity. The lateral lemniscus also provides a site for termination for some fibers in its own nucleus, en route centrally; at the nucleus of the lateral lemniscus, it is known that some of the nerve fibers again cross to the opposite side before continuing their pathway to the cerebral cortex.

The next major way station of the auditory pathway is the inferior colliculus, at the mesencephalon. Here, too, some auditory fibers terminate to synapse with others; these others may continue toward the same side of the cortex, or they may decussate (cross) to the opposite side. It is generally agreed that the inferior colliculus serves as a center for reflexes in response to sound.

From the inferior colliculus the auditory fibers pass to the medial geniculate body, an important auditory center. From here the nerve fibers extend through the region known as the auditory radiations, where there is some fanning-out of the fibers. The fibers then terminate in the temporal lobe of the cerebral cortex, in the two transverse temporal gyri. As indicated earlier, each ear is actually bilaterally represented in this region of the cortex.

As many present-day authorities state it, the various parts of the cerebral cortex are intimately connected and interconnected by association fibers, and the entire body—the cortex—operates as a unit. This is true of the auditory system, although some specific areas of auditory function have been identified. The auditory reception area, of course, is that just described in the anterior portion of the temporal lobes on either side of the brain. The auditory area, however, is enlarged considerably by auditory regions functioning for more complex purposes. Blending with the reception area anteriorly, generally agreed as being Brodmann's areas 41 and 42, are more posterior and superior auditory areas of the cortex. These are supposed to carry on the functions of recognition, association, and recall. This is especially true of the uppermost portion of the temporal lobe of the cerebral cortex, where Wernicke's area is found. One other important area is located in the most anterior projection of the superior temporal lobe, where there is thought to be a center for musical recognition and memory.

CLINICAL NOTE

Clinically, these areas become of great importance to the functioning of the individual. No longer is it wise to treat a lesion or injury of the cortical area as a localized injury. As an illustration, such a lesion could not be labeled an auditory defect because of the great number of interconnections with other areas. The term "aphasia" is as specific as some dare to use. This suggests an inability or disability on the part of the injured individual to recall, associate, or sometimes even to recognize auditory stimuli that have passed through an otherwise intact auditory system to that point. Several types of terminology are used to point this up: Wernicke's aphasia is an auditory receptive defect, receptive aphasia is more or less the same thing, and sometimes paraphasia is considered to be essentially an auditory defect in that the person is unable to monitor his own language behavior satisfactorily. Such injuries are found fairly commonly among the population having aphasia. The proximity of the auditory area in the cerebral cortex to the various motor areas is such that an injury to one region

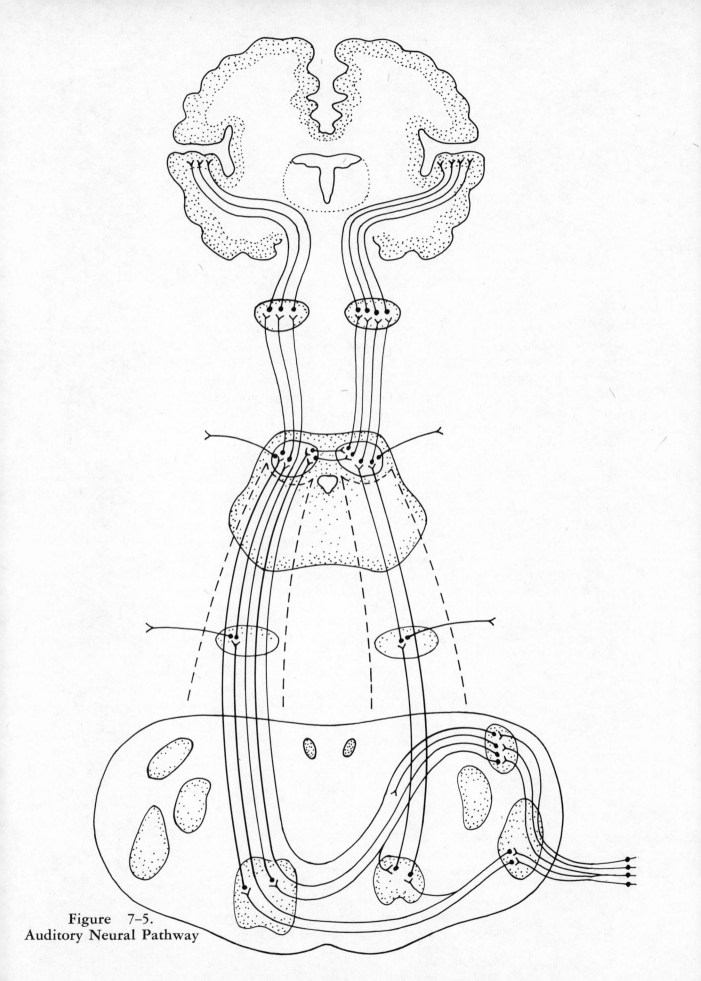

Figure 7–5.
Auditory Neural Pathway

might well produce damage in the other, and of course produces an operating organism different from his fellows in a number of ways.

In summary, the auditory or hearing mechanism is composed of four components: the air system, consisting of the auricle and the external auditory canal; the mechanical system, consisting of the tympanic membrane, the three ossicles, and the footplate of the last bone of the chain; the hydraulic system, consisting of the perilymphatic fluids of the inner ear as well as the endolymphatic channels of the membranous capsules; and the neural system, composed of the sensory end organ (organ of Corti), the various nerve fiber groups, nuclei, pathways, and cortical terminations and associations. The clinical field of audiology comprehends all of these regions and these systems. Modern audiometry and audiometrists are especially interested in the functioning of the nervous system in audition, in the normal as well as the defective person. Recent advances in audiometry have assisted in the differentiation of retrocochlear from cochlear lesions of the auditory system as well as further describing the auditory defects in other areas.

SUMMARY OF FUNCTIONS OF THE EAR

The ear serves to receive sound from the environment and to transform that sound into activities that will ultimately take a representation of the sound to the cerebral cortex. The actual sound itself, the vibrating molecules of air, for example, do not strike the end organ for hearing directly. They must initiate a vibrating pattern in a taut membrane, the tympanic membrane, which then transforms those vibrations into movements of itself and thence of the first of the three ossicles. In doing this, the sound has passed from the external ear, in immediate and direct contact with the environmental air and the airborne sound, to the middle ear.

Within the middle ear, the ossicles transmit the sound and amplify it at the same time. The air-filled middle ear acts as a balanced air-pressure system, so that the tympanic membrane will be influenced only by sound vibrations and not by other forces. It is, of course, protected from loud sounds by the reflexly stimulated tensor tympani muscle. In passing from the malleus to the incus and then to the stapes, the sound is actually a vibratory behavior of this chain of bones interconnected by true joints. The last tiny bone—the stapes—also has a protective device—the stapedius muscle—which also is thought to be reflexly controlled on the occasion of an extremely intense sound.

The vibrating stapes passes its influence into the inner ear via the oval window. Upon entering, the sound is passed into a fluid medium, remaining a pattern of vibration, however. From this first contact in the inner ear—the vestibule—the sound enters the spiral cochlea through the vestibular canal. The fluid through which the sound is passing is perilymph. The membranous canal that takes up the vibration is filled with endolymph. In this membranous canal in the cochlea—the cochlear duct—is found the structure that actually houses the sensory end organ for audition: the spiral organ of Corti. This fairly complex structure extends the several turns of the cochlea and supports the sensing devices: the hair cells. Thus, vibratory movement (which is sound) has passed into this inner ear through fluids from one canal system to another to finally affect the "triggering" device so delicately balanced within. When the vibration reaches sufficient intensity, the trigger is pulled and the nerve impulse is now established.

The unique capability of nervous tissue to be irritable and to transmit from one place to another the indication of the stimulus causing the irritation (here sound vibration) causes emphasis to be placed on a different type of transmission system. This is especially true because of the kinds and numbers of interconnections made by the nerve fibers as they carry the sound as a nerve impulse toward the cerebral cortex. Certainly, it is known that the nerve fibers themselves come to an end and transmit the impulse to another nerve fiber that carries the impulse onward; thus, there are numbers of these synapses, or neural connection sites. These make possible a number of reflexes (such as the palpebroacoustic) and also establish a network of brain-bound fibers that cross and sometimes recross from one side of the nervous system to the other. Ultimately, the impulse is carried to the temporal lobe of the cerebral cortex, where it is perceived as sound, and meaning is attached to it.

Further discussion of the nature of sensory systems in general is provided in the next chapter. Understanding of how the auditory impulse is received in the cerebral cortex and how it becomes a part of a vast interrelated complex of nerve centers and pathways cannot be achieved from such a simplified presentation as is made here. It is hoped that further study will be made of the auditory system, especially, as well as the nervous system as a whole.

EAR LANDMARK IDENTIFICATIONS

Directions: For the indicated illustrations, label the following landmarks.

FIGURE 7–1
External Ear
Middle Ear
Inner Ear
Neural Ear
Auricle
External Auditory Canal
Cartilaginous External Canal
Bony External Canal
Tympanic Membrane
Mastoid Air Cells
Malleus Bone
Incus Bone
Stapes Bone
Middle Ear (Tympanum)
Eustachian Tube
Tensor Tympani Muscle,
Tensor Tympani Muscle Canal
Semicircular Canals
Cochlea
Facial Nerve
Auditory Nerve

FIGURE 7–2
Auricle
Helix
Antihelix
Scaphoid Fossa
Triangular Fossa
Crus of Helix
Concha (cave)
Concha (Skiff or Cymba)
Tragus
Antitragus
Intertragal Incisure
Lobule
External Auditory Canal
Darwin's Tubercle

FIGURE 7–3
External Auditory Canal
Tympanum
Tympanic Membrane
Mastoid Air Cells
Aditus Ad Antrum
Eustachian Tube
Malleus Bone, Head
Malleus Bone, Neck
Malleus Bone, Manubrium
Superior Malleolar Ligament
Malleus Bone, Anterior Process
Tensor Tympani Muscle, Tendon
Incudomalleolar Joint

Incus Bone, Body
Incus Bone, Long Process
Incus Bone, Lenticular Process
Incudostapedial Joint
Stapedius Muscle
Stapes Bone, Head
Stapes Bone, Neck
Stapes Bone, Crura
Stapes Bone, Footplate
Pyramidal Eminence
Shrapnell's Membrane
Pars Tensa, Tympanic Membrane
Malleolar Fold

FIGURE 7–4
Modiolus
Osseus Spiral Lamina
Spiral Ligament
Vestibular Canal
Perilymph
Vestibular Membrane
Endolymph
Cochlear Duct (Scala Media)
Vascular Stripe
Basilar Membrane
Tectorial Membrane
Limbus
Inner Hair Cells
Outer Hair Cells
Supporting Cells
Pillars of Corti
Tunnel of Corti
Nerve Fibers
Spiral Ganglion
Tympanic Canal

FIGURE 7–5
Spiral Ganglion
Nerve Fibers from Cochlea
Dorsal Cochlear Nucleus
Ventral Cochlear Nucleus
Superior Olivary Complex
Medulla Level
Pons Level
Trapezoid Body
Lateral Lemniscus
Nucleus of Lateral Lemniscus
Inferior Colliculus
Medial Geniculate Body
Auditory Radiations
Cerebral Cortex
Temporal Lobe
Superior Temporal Convolution

chapter 8

THE NERVOUS MECHANISM

An earlier definition indicates that there are structures in the organism whose purpose is to maintain the integrity and economy of that organism. These structures coordinate the functions of the various organs and systems by adjusting to internal and external events or stimuli. These form the nervous system. They receive stimuli from the environment, both within and without the body, transform these stimuli into nervous excitations, transmit these impulses to various nervous centers, which in turn retransmit them to other centers for action, reaction, or storage.

Through the activities of the nervous system, the organism lives. It becomes aware of odors, sounds, temperatures, pressures, light, pain, and other events and conditions. The organism then can move its legs or head or other portions of its structure; or it can elicit the production of glandular secretions, such as gastric juices or saliva; or it can recall past events or actions. The nervous system is capable of protecting the organism, without the organism's conscious and volitional effort, as in the action of the reflex. It is capable of producing complex activities, multiple actions, by coordinating and controlling the component parts of those actions. The nervous system feeds into a complex action the appropriate amounts of energy to maintain a reasonably balanced action, as, for example, when the processes of feeding, swallowing, breathing, and maintaining posture may occur juxtaposed, or overlapping, in time.

Structurally, the nervous system is composed of a great number of neurons. These neurons are supported and maintained through the special connective tissue of the nervous system: the neuroglia. The neurons of the body are all remarkably alike, although obvious differences among them occur, depending upon location within the system and the function they subserve. Several important locales of the nervous system are of outstanding importance in the study of the speech and hearing behavior of the individual.

CLINICAL NOTE

The integrity of the nervous system is constantly under suspicion in speech and hearing defects. The careful clinician always investigates for possible neural involvement in such cases as delayed speech, articulation errors, hypernasality or other resonance problems, auditory deficits, and phonatory defects. In brief, nearly every one of the major categories of speech and hearing deficiencies may have some etiologic basis within the nervous system underlying the control of the structures responsible for that particular function.

THE NEURON AND NEURON CHAIN

The *neuron* is the only tissue involved in the conduction of nerve impulses; it is genetically, structurally, and functionally the unit of the nervous system. It is composed of the nerve cell (cell body) and all of its processes. Although these units, the neurons, are anatomically separate in that there is no continuity of substance between or among neurons, there is a contact or relationship between and among neurons: the *synapse.*

Extensions from the cell body are called *axons* and *dendrites.* There is generally only one axon from each cell body; it can be of considerable length, up to 3 feet in some instances. The dendrites of a cell body are plural, each of them generally having numerous branchings. Although it is not a universal rule in the nervous system, the axon usually carries impulses away from the cell body, whereas the dendrite carries them toward the cell body.

So that the organism can receive stimuli and then react to it, there must be a series of at least two neurons in a chain: (1) the sensory neuron to be irritated by the stimulus, and (2) the motor neuron to cause a muscle (or gland) to be stimulated. There is a functional relationship between the two that is called a synapse. The axon of one cell is in contact with the dendrite or the cell body of another cell. The direction of flow of the nerve impulse is from axon to dendrite or cell body, not the reverse. There are several theories as to the nature of the synaptic transmission itself. One theory suggests that the neural impulse in the axon releases acetylcholine, which in turn stimulates the second neuron to pick up the impulse. Another theory points to an electrical charge differential between the two neurons, initiated by the axon of the first neuron. Certainly, there have been found both chemical and electrical activities in the synaptic regions, and the changes in either or both of these seem to be related to both the normal transmission and the abnormal functioning of the system.

The simplest illustration of the neuron chain is the classical *reflex arc.* (See Figure 8–1.) These neurons exist and operate at various levels of the nervous system, but the most common examples are found in the spinal system. Here only two neurons are necessary. The first, in order of activity, is the sensory neuron with its receptor end in the skin or wherever the end-organ for sensation might be. This *first-order neuron,* then, is stimulated by some irritant (exemplified ultimately as pain, cold, pressure, etc.), and the resulting neural impulse is carried toward the cell body.

The route taken by this wave of excitation—the nerve impulse—depends upon the type, location, and central connections of the nerve fiber itself. In general, though, it might be said that this nerve fiber, carrying the impulse, joins with other such fibers in the anatomic vicinity, perhaps serving essentially the same function. As the group of fibers grows, it becomes a "nerve." This nerve passes toward the vertebral column and the spinal cord within, entering the spinal cord via the "dorsal root."

Within the dorsal spinal root are found the cell bodies for the entering sensory neurons. Grouped, they form the spinal ganglion. Beyond this landmark, the nerve fiber enters the spinal cord to penetrate to the dorsal gray horn. Here there are various forms of termination of the sensory fibers. Most fibers divide into an ascending branch and a descending branch, each of which has numerous collateral branches.

In the simplest two-neuron reflex chain, or arc, the collaterals then pass to the ventral gray horn, where the synaptic connection with the cell body of the motor (efferent) neuron is made. It is sufficient to state that the wave of excitation from the sensory fiber is transferred to, or better yet, sets up another wave of excitation in, the *second-order neuron.* With the impulse now initiated in the

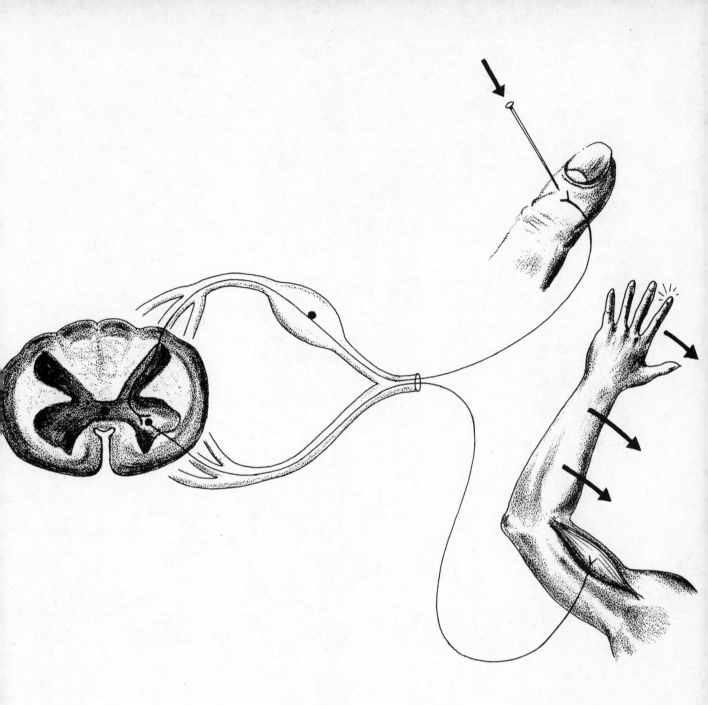

Figure 8–1.
Simple Reflex Arc

motor fiber, it travels from the spinal cord through the ventral root of the spinal nerve until it terminates in the neuromuscular bundle and causes the muscle to contract.

In the case of the more common type of reflex chain, where there are more than two neurons effecting the arc, a third neuron is interposed. This third neuron is the *association,* or *internuncial,* neuron. In this case the sensory fiber, having entered the spinal cord and its gray horn, synapses with this central neuron. Its cell body might well be in the dorsal gray horn, or nearby, and it sends connecting fibers to the appropriate effector neuron or elsewhere. It is this alternative routing of the central (internuncial) neuron that produces the extremely complicated and complex nerve pathways of the higher animals. Numerous authorities have pointed out that with greater numbers of connections among the central neurons, as is the case in man, there is created a greater number of possible alternatives in the organism's responses to stimuli. The opposite is true as well: there is much less chance for stereotyped behavior among the animals with higher developed central nervous systems.

The reflex is responsible for patterns of movement in a segmental way. Thus, we have flexion, or withdrawal, reflexes from irritative stimuli; there are extensor reflexes in which posture is maintained in a gravitational field. Other types of reflexes exist, of course. Through association fibers, reflexes become integrated as part of general body behavior, and in man, cognitive processes as well as physical, chemical, and electrical processes in reflex and other neurologic activity contribute heavily in that behavior pattern.

SPINAL NERVES

The spinal cord is a direct continuation of the medulla oblongata and in this way it is in functional communication with higher centers, up to the cerebral cortex. For understanding of the voluntary muscular system and of the reflex, it is important to examine and understand the structure of the spinal cord and its nerves.

A spinal nerve exits through the juncture of the vertebrae in the spinal column, actually at the intervertebral foramen. Distributed distally as a nerve trunk, it has derived from its more central origin, the spinal cord within the vertebral canal of the contiguous vertebrae. This central origin can be considered, in a rather oversimplified manner, to be dual: the most dorsal portion is the *sensory root,* which enters the spinal cord; the more ventral portion is the *motor root* and is leaving the spinal cord. Various other intercommunications occur with the autonomic nervous system, prior to the actual formation of the final spinal nerve.

The dorsal, or sensory, root presents a somewhat enlarged portion, after having separated from the spinal nerve at the foramen. This enlargement is the *ganglion,* composed of the cell bodies of all the sensory nerve fibers. From this point, centrally, the nerve root further subdivides into numerous rootlets, which ultimately form a continuous and evenly spaced line along the dorsal-lateral surface of the spinal cord. Where the rootlets enter the cord, the area is known as the *dorsal horn.* This region actually has a vertical dimension, and might be better termed the "dorsal column." Because it is a part of the gray matter of the central nervous system, this column would then be called the "dorsal gray column." It passes through the spinal cord, transmitting sensation in the cord, from its uppermost point, at about the level of the atlas vertebra, to its lowermost point, at about the level of the first lumbar vertebra.

Nerve fibers serving sensory functions travel to several regions of the nervous system. The connections ultimately communicate with subcortical and cortical centers, where the sensation is perceived and acted upon by subsequent interconnections. Also, there are connections with other major pathways, prior to reaching the highest centers, so that gross adjustment in the body may be accomplished without volitional involvement. And there is the previously mentioned possibility of rather rapid reflex activity at or about the level of the spinal nerve.

Motor nerve fibers originate in the ventral gray column of the spinal cord, in centers that are in contact with interconnecting fibers from the dorsal and the intermediate gray columns as well as fibers descending from higher centers through the white columns. These latter are the fiber tracts, such as the pyramidal and the extrapyramidal pathways. The motor fiber exits from the spinal cord as the ventral root, gives off some collaterals that connect with the autonomic ganglia in that vicinity, and then joins with the dorsal root to complete the spinal nerve of that segment of the cord.

Disruption of the motor nerve fiber eliminates innervation to that muscle fiber, and thus a paralysis develops. The depth or extent of the paralysis depends upon the number of nerve fibers inoperative. In extreme cases in which large numbers of nerve fibers are inoperative, the muscle receives no innervation and slowly atrophies. Generally, however, there is a constant, low level stimulation of muscle fibers by these motor nerve fibers. Thus, in every large muscle, some few of the muscle fibers are constantly in states of contraction due to the firing of some few of the nerve fibers. This constant state of low degree of contraction is termed muscle tonicity, or tonus. When large numbers of nerve fibers to a muscle fire, the muscle as a whole contracts, moving the limb or producing the skeletal movement for which that muscle is designed.

CLINICAL NOTE

In certain pathologic states neural innervation to skeleton muscles is disturbed. The paralysis could be flaccid or spastic. Speech therapists frequently are called upon to treat communicative problems stemming from such lesions—which, in the case of spinal nerves, is usually a flaccid paralysis and requires skill and understanding to retrain paralyzed muscles —or to develop adequate compensatory muscular activity.

CRANIAL NERVES

The brain and the brainstem provide a number of major nerves that serve the head and neck region in both a motor and a sensory role. These are the cranial nerves, which are labeled by both Roman numerals and names. The names are based upon function (e.g., optic, auditory), structure (trigeminal), or location (hypoglossal, vagus). The nerves are numbered according to their location or points of connection into the brain or brainstem. Thus, Cranial I (olfactory) is the highest and most anterior of the twelve, while Cranial XII (hypoglossal) is the lowermost, having its source from a point at approximately the juncture of the medulla and the spinal cord. It must be remembered that some cranial nerves are purely motor nerves (trochlear, abducens), and others are purely sensory (olfactory, optic), and still others are admixtures of both functions to various extents (facial, glossopharyngeal, vagus).

There may be occasions when information pertaining to one of the nerves not directly related to speech or hearing is importantly related to a speech or hearing problem. However, emphasis shall be laid upon an especial few of the cranial nerves. Attention is drawn to Cranials V (trigeminal), VII (facial), VIII (auditory), IX (glossopharyngeal), X (vagus), XI (accessory), and XII (hypoglossal). (See Figure 8–2.)

Cranial V is named trigeminal because of its threefold portions. Soon after leaving the brainstem at the side of the pons, it divides into three parts: the ophthalmic, the maxillary, and the mandibular. Both the ophthalmic and the maxillary divisions are mainly sensory in function, running to the brain from the eye and its environs—the forehead, nose, cheek, jaw, teeth, mouth, and other regions where sensation to the skin and mucosa is served. The mandibular division of

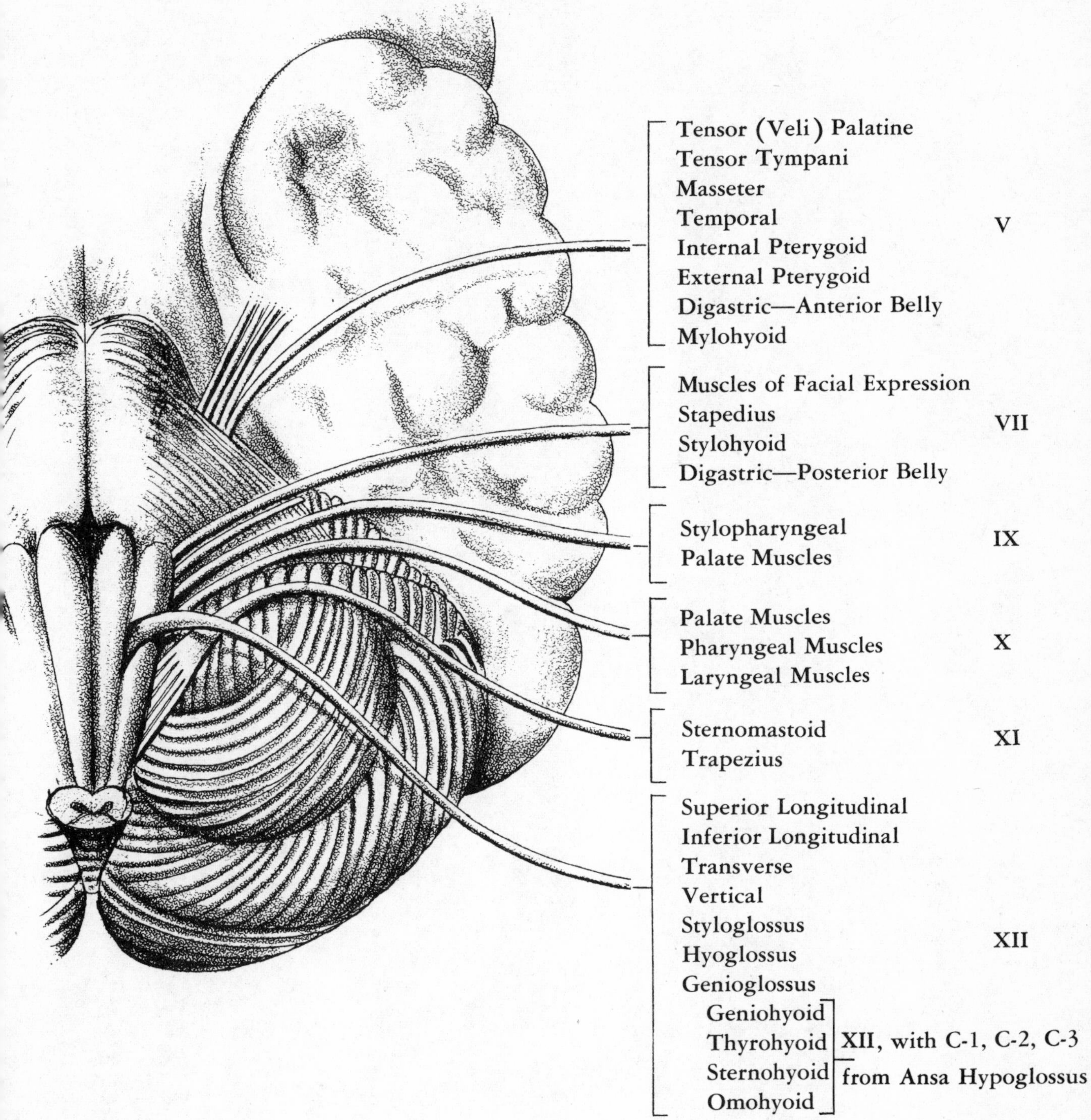

Figure 8–2.
Cranial Nerves Serving the Speech Musculature

Cranial V leaves the pons, exits from the skull through the foramen ovale, and becomes the masticator nerve, serving the muscles of mastication as well as some other oral structures. These same muscles are important to speech production.

Cranial VII (facial) serves the structures of the facial region in both motor and sensory functions. The motor division of VII leaves the central nervous system from the lower portion of the pons; it enters the internal auditory meatus, along with the cochlear and vestibular divisions of Cranial VIII, and leaves the skull at the stylomastoid foramen. It runs through the parotid gland and then divides into numerous branches to serve the facial region. Most of the muscles of facial expression, scalp, auricle, as well as buccinator, platysma, stapedius, stylohyoid, and the posterior belly of the digastric muscles receive innervation from this major nerve. The sensory areas subserved by Cranial VII are mainly those of taste in the anterior two-thirds of the tongue (through the chorda tympani nerve) and the soft palate. There is a neural relationship between this cranial nerve and the salivary glands, also.

Cranial VIII (auditory, acoustic) is primarily sensory in function, although its two divisions serve different sensations: audition and equilibrium. The cochlear division, serving the auditory function, has sensory fibers that originate at the spiral organ of Corti, pass through the spiral ganglion, thence into the internal auditory meatus and into the inferior peduncle, between the pons and the medulla. The vestibular division, serving orientation of the body in space, originates in the utricle, saccule, superior and lateral semicircular canals, and the ampulla of the posterior semicircular canal. Its fibers pass from the vestibular ganglion into the internal auditory meatus, along with those of the cochlear division, to enter the medulla en route to the cerebellum.

Cranial IX (glossopharyngeal) is both motor and sensory in function, serving the posterior portion of the tongue, mouth, and pharynges. It has its major central nervous system origins in the medulla, leaving that region through the petrous portion of the temporal bone. Its motor fibers run to the pharyngeal musculature; its sensory fibers run to the same general area, serving taste in the posterior third of the tongue and other sensations in the fauces, tonsils, pharynx, and the soft palate.

Cranial X (vagus), containing afferent and efferent fibers, originates at the medulla level and exits from the skull through the jugular foramen. At this point it is joined by the cranial portion of XI, which accompanies it throughout its passage. Vagus, the "wanderer," serves both motor and sensory functions to widely dispersed regions, from the auricle to the abdominal viscera. Its sensory fibers originate at the skin of the auricle, part of the external auditory canal, pharynx, larynx, and the viscera of the thorax and the abdomen. Its motor fibers serve the pharynx, base of the tongue, and larynx as well as the viscera of the thorax and abdomen through autonomic nervous system ganglia. An important division of this cranial nerve—the recurrent laryngeal nerve—and its terminus—the inferior laryngeal nerve—is of considerable interest when the operations of the larynx are studied. It must also be remembered that the superior laryngeal nerve, supplying the cricothyroid muscle, is also of vagus origin.

Cranial XI (accessory, or spinal accessory) is mainly a motor nerve, originating in the medulla and leaving the skull through the jugular foramen. Here, it is joined with a portion derived from the first five or six segments of the spinal cord. That portion originating in the medulla joins with Vagus to innervate some muscles in the pharynx, larynx, uvula, soft palate, and perhaps contributes to the recurrent laryngeal nerve. That portion of the spinal accessory that derives from the upper portion of the spinal cord is the efferent nerve to the large sternocleidomastoid and the trapezius muscles.

Cranial XII (hypoglossal) is also primarily a motor nerve. Its origin is also medullary and it leaves the skull as a single nerve after the joining together of a small group of nerve rootlets emerging from the medulla. It is motor to the intrinsic muscles of the tongue, the extrinsic muscles of the tongue, excepting palato-glossus (innervated by vagus), and to the strap muscles of the neck through a loop known as the ansa hypoglossi. This latter structure is complex in origin, deriving from the hypoglossal nerve as well as the cervical nerves of the spinal cord. It innervates such muscles as sternohyoid, sternothyroid, thyrohyoid, and omohyoid.

Other muscles of the regions just described are served by Cranials V (trigeminal) and VII (facial). For example, mylohyoid and the anterior belly of digastric muscles are innervated through trigeminal, and stylohyoid and the posterior belly of digastric muscles join the facial group to be served by Cranial VII.

CLINICAL NOTE

Lesions to cranial nerves produce many and varied symptoms and signs. Examples of these, among the nerves discussed, are facial paralysis when Cranial VII is involved, hearing defects when VIII is disturbed, resonance and articulation in the case of lesion of IX, respiration, breath support and phonation should X be injured, posture and general tonicity of neck regions in the case of involvement of XI, and articulation and resonance should XII be damaged.

THE MOTOR SYSTEM

Control of the activities of the body, especially the skeletal musculature, is provided through a central nervous system arrangement that originates in the cerebral cortex. The major center is along the precentral gyrus, the convolution that is just anterior to the central sulcus on either hemisphere. This is Area 4, which is closely associated with other such centers in the vicinity. Some of these (e.g., Area 6), supplement the work of the major center, but there are also certain centers that are inhibitory because they serve to initiate activities that are essentially antagonistic to those coming from the primary motor center. The balance between the motor impulses from the primary motor center and those coming from the centers for inhibition determines the efficiency of operation of the individual in his muscle activity. Imbalance produces varying degrees of inefficiency, from simple clumsiness and incoordination to complete disruption and failure of the system to operate at all.

The Pyramidal Pathway

The primary motor system has very large cells shaped like pyramids; they serve as the initiators of the impulse to the musculature. These pyramidal cells have many interconnections, some of which derive from other regions of the brain and central nervous system. Their axons travel downward in definite pathways, through various centers which in turn receive nerve fibers from the other major areas of the brain. (See Figure 8–3.) The effectiveness of the pathway is influenced by the contributions of these lower centers. Thus, for example, a motor impulse passing to a muscle of the arm with the intent of raising that arm high above the head would pass through a center that has interconnections with the cerebellum. These interconnections, then, would inform the coordinating centers of the cerebellum of the intended action, and appropriate postural changes of the body might result so that elevation of the arm would not throw the body off balance. At the same time, impulses from the cerebellum into the intermediate center would inform the descending motor fiber of the fact that the body is indeed off balance and thus would affect the strength of that impulse, perhaps cutting down on its intensity and thus slowing the arm-elevating action until the body had adjusted its balance to accommodate the new position of the arm.

Many such subcenters exist. Each has myriad interconnections with areas

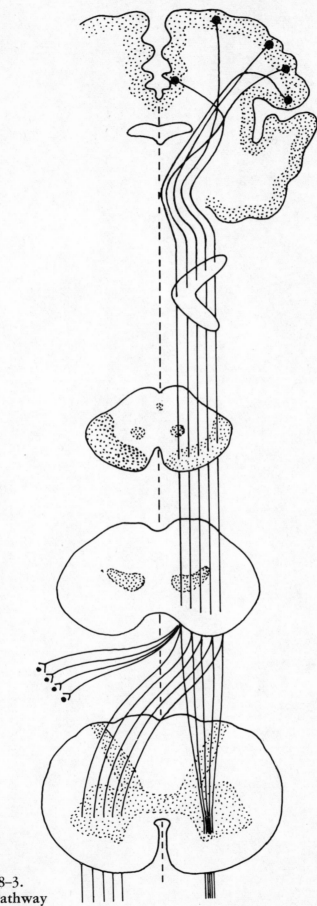

Figure 8–3.
Pyramidal Pathway

that have relatively specialized functions. There is constant feedback, in the normal organism, from each of these centers to others which would have some pertinence to the activities of the other. Certainly the extent of such interconnections is far from understood today, and future research will serve to demonstrate further the multiplicity of these contacts.

Passing down through the various subcortical regions of the brain, through the internal capsule, through the pons and through the medulla, the greater portion of the great motor pathway from each hemisphere then crosses to the other side of the brainstem. This crossing occurs at the lowermost boundary of the medulla and defines that boundary. Because the crossing of the fibers from both sides produces a bulge in the brainstem at that area, the region is known as the "pyramid," and the crossing is called the decussation of the pyramid. Nearly all motor fibers from the cerebral cortex decussate, although some one-fifth of them remain ipsilateral until they cross lower in the spinal cord.

The termination of the motor pathway is within the ventral gray column of the spinal cord. Its center of termination becomes a center of origin for the spinal nerve fibers that are en route to the muscle it serves.

CLINICAL NOTE

Lesions in the nervous system are often classified as upper or lower motor neuron lesions, depending upon the site of the lesion and the nervous tissue affected. Although a generalization is not possible, it does sometimes follow that a lower motor neuron lesion provides total paralysis of a flaccid type to the musculature served simply because it is the final line of innervation and is singular. Upper motor neuron lesions may also produce a flaccid paralysis for a similar reason, but also may produce some other type of defect—such as spastic paralysis or incoordination—because other neural routes to the musculature involved may be intact and continue to stimulate that region without the coordinated control necessary. Thus, a lesion to the recurrent laryngeal nerve on one side may well produce a flaccid paralysis of the vocal fold on that side, because that nerve is a lower motor neuron. However, a lesion to the brain stem or elsewhere in the central nervous system could disrupt nerve fibers going to the same laryngeal structures, but the paralysis or the defect could be other than flaccid.

Although many of the fibers originating in the cortex terminate in the spinal cord, it must be obvious that a large number also terminate at levels above the cord. For example, the muscles that are served by the cranial nerves receive some of their innervation from this pathway. Those neurons that serve the cranial nerves terminate in centers in the pons and medulla, and are called corticobulbar fibers; those that continue on caudad through the decussation, or otherwise, are corticospinal. Those that cross are found in the lateral corticospinal tract of the spinal cord, and those that remain ipsilateral (about 20 percent of the total) are found in the anterior or ventral cerebrospinal tract. These latter neurons generally serve the muscles of the trunk and are thought to decussate at the spinal level rather than the medullary level.

The Extrapyramidal Pathway

The corticospinal system just described is also known as the pyramidal pathway. It is the most direct system of muscle innervation from the cerebral cortex. There is, however, a secondary system that serves to do much the same thing, although it is generally thought to be more like a servomechanism that is self-controlled and directed. This is the extrapyramidal system. It comprises all structures or centers, other than those of the pyramidal system, that send motor impulses from the brain to the spinal cord. Frequently listed in this group of centers are the globus pallidus, the subthalamic nucleus of Luys, the substantia nigra, the nucleus ruber, and the inferior olivary nucleus. Of course, each of these centers is in direct contact with the cerebral cortex.

These centers act individually as division headquarters, being originators of impulses to the musculature. Together, they form a network that works very closely with the pyramidal tract and the cerebral cortex. The extrapyramidal pathway is considered the "old pathway." It is centered around the basal ganglia, deep in the cerebrum, some portions of which were in the list given above. Other portions of the basal ganglia include the corpus striatum, caudate nucleus, lentiform nucleus (putamen, globus pallidus). As such, this route is mainly a pathway for integration of motor activity. It is a relay system, with no direct pathway to the spinal cord, and it probably represents a phylogenetically previous system (thus the term "old pathway") that has now been short-circuited by the pyramidal system. Certainly, this is a complex system in operation, possibly because it is importantly related to higher integrated behavior patterns that may be and usually are modified by experience.

The extrapyramidal system, through the basal ganglia and other way stations, operates to smooth out motor activities of complex types. It can be utilized as an initiating system for volitional acts, although the pyramidal cortex is believed to be the primary center for volitional activities. In essence, it appears that the habitual and automatic activities of the body, such as those dealing with posture and reactive behavior in general, are mediated by the extrapyramidal system. It has been suggested that once the cerebral cortex has learned a motor skill to the point that it becomes automatic, it is then relegated to the basal ganglia and the extrapyramidal pathway for continued direction.

CLINICAL NOTE

Among the neuropathologies underlying speech disorders derived from lesion of the extrapyramidal system are Parkinsonianism, athetosis, chorea, and some forms of spasticity. Basically, the lesions occurring in various nuclei, centers, or pathways effect a release from stabilizing inhibitory mechanisms; from such lesions the various types of dysarthria, including cerebral palsy, result, although knowledge is far from complete in these pathologies.

Because of the many interconnections of the extrapyramidal system, clear-cut delineation of the pathologies possible is very difficult. It must be remembered that not only does the precentral motor area serve the efferent system in general, but there are other centers of initiation and inhibition which are located in the frontal lobe. Thus, some lesions may be paralytic or release in nature and another group may be irritative and excitatory, and the two groups are nearly impossible to differentiate. Here, again, localization of function is difficult if not impossible.

THE SENSORY SYSTEM

To protect and preserve the integrity of the organism, sensory systems have evolved which provide means for the animal to react to its environment. Specialized cells are responsive to specific environmental changes, both external and internal. As the highest developed animal, man has an extremely large variety of receptors for sensation: for example, touch, cold, smell, sound, and taste.

The receptors themselves are structurally different, depending upon the type of stimulus they are responsive to. Generally, there are two types. The exteroceptors include those sensory end organs that are cutaneous (for touch, heat, cold), those for chemical stimuli (taste and smell), and the distance receptors (vision and hearing). The interoceptors, on the other hand, are represented by the proprioceptors (which respond to changes in muscle and position conditions) and the special receptors associated with the viscera and blood vessels (serving such sensations as hunger and thirst).

The anatomic structure of the nerve ending provides for the specificity of sensitivity. For example, the skin has touch corpuscles that are responsive to heat and cold; it has free nerve endings which, being the most widely distributed receptors in the body, serve pain. These are the "near" receptors. The so-called "distant" senses of vision and audition have become associated with rather complex housings to facilitate their functioning. For example, the three divisions of the ear that provide for certain changes in the original stimulus through mechanical means before the auditory receptor, the nerve endings on the hair cells of the organ of Corti, are stimulated; the airborne vibrations in the environment do not in themselves set up the nerve impulse in the sensory system.

The interoceptors include those associated with muscles, tendons, and joints; some authorities have classified the vestibular function of the semicircular canals in the same group. Other interoceptors include those mentioned above: those in the viscera, blood vessels, and smooth muscle tissue. The proprioceptors are found in muscle spindles (specialized structures of sensory end organs), muscle tissue, and connective tissue within the fleshy substance of muscle. When the muscle changes in its tension, as by stretching, nerve impulses are established that give the central nervous system information concerning that condition and the position of body parts. This is not information that reaches consciousness, usually, but is acted upon by subconscious processes.

In reaching the central nervous system, the nerve fibers from the body enter the spinal cord via the dorsal root. Ultimately, the path decussates (crosses to the opposite side of the spinal cord) and rises rostrally in pathways. The pathways carry different modalities: pain, touch, proprioception in their own paths. These make up the "white matter" in the central nervous system and include such routes as the two spinothalamic tracts and the medial lemniscus. There are differences in the routes taken by these sensory fibers and those of the head.

The sensory fibers carrying sensation generally arrive at or near the thalamus. Within the thalamus are several centers or nuclei subserving the differing systems arriving. With important central connections throughout the central nervous system at the thalamus itself, it is often considered as the primary sensory center, where sensations might be considered as perceived. The thalamus is responsible for relaying sensory information to the cerebral cortex, although it has other connections elsewhere as well.

The sensations reaching the cerebral cortex from the general body (somatic sensory) reach the parietal cortex especially in the postcentral gyrus but spreading beyond somewhat. Other sensory receptor areas include that for vision in the olfactory lobe and audition in the temporal lobe. There are numerous association fibers interconnecting the various cortical areas, so that the import of two or more sensations can be fully realized and appreciated. And, of course, the great complexity of nerve fibers from the cerebral cortex throughout the body provides for appropriate responses to the recognition of the incoming sensory stimuli.

SUBCORTICAL AREAS

In passing from the cortex to lower centers, the nerve fibers communicate with various other areas and centers. Each of these has an effect upon the overall functioning of the nervous system as well as upon the individual nerve impulses transversing the system. Thus, the myriad interconnections among neurons serve the important process of maintaining the integrity of the organism as a whole. Some authorities have stated it a little more dramatically by indicating that an injury to any part, from the smallest nerve fiber to the largest cortical region, is an injury to the entire system.

Below the cortex and below the sensory radiations is the *thalamus.*

It has numerous connections with other brain regions, including the cerebellum as well as the pons. There are several trunk lines interconnecting these regions, such as the superior cerebellar peduncle, also known as the brachium conjunctiva, between the thalamus and the cerebellum. The relatively large *pons,* or *bridge,* is an enlarged portion of the hindbrain. It is termed the bridge partly because it serves as a point from which major trunk lines depart to other important centers. It also houses centers, nuclei, from which radiate various nerves serving the head and neck muscles. The pons also has interconnections to and from the cerebrum, cerebellum, and spinal cord.

A somewhat smaller region of the brainstem—sometimes considered the lowermost portion of that division and sometimes as the uppermost end of the spinal cord—is the *medulla oblongata.* The medulla is of particular importance to students of speech and hearing, for in this region are located nerve fibers and nerve centers for many of the basic functions subserving communication processes. For example, within the medulla are located the motor nuclei of the glossopharyngeal, vagus, cranial portion of the accessory, and the hypoglossal nerves. All are important members of the cranial nerve group. Also found in this region are the sensory nuclei of the glossopharyngeal and the vagus nerves as well as some of the vestibular centers; the cochlear (auditory) nuclei are located at the junction between the medulla and the pons.

In housing the nerves and the nuclei mentioned, the medulla then is importantly related to the functions of articulation of speech and of deglutition (swallowing); further, it is concerned with coughing, sneezing, salivation, sucking, and vomiting, as well as being motor innervator to other bodily activities more indirectly related to speech. Some of these are respiration, cardiovascular behavior, and digestive activities that have control centers in the medulla.

CLINICAL NOTE

Injuries of the subcortical regions sometimes result in problems with which the speech and hearing clinician will deal. For example, the slowly disappearing disease poliomyelitis often destroyed nerve centers in this region, causing paralysis of musculature important to speech. Thus, respiration, phonation, and articulation, among other functions, often were disturbed. In other instances, injuries or tumors to this region could result in auditory disorders. In such cases as cerebellopontine angle tumors, for example, definite auditory disabilities are known.

THE CEREBRUM

The central nervous system itself is composed of the brain and the spinal cord. It is differentiated from the peripheral nervous system and the autonomic nervous system. The cerebrum is the major portion of the brain. It fills the upper part of the cranium and consists of two equal portions, called hemispheres, which although united at the bottom are grossly separated at the midline by the longitudinal fissure. (See Figure 8–4.)

The cerebrum, or the forebrain, in terms of the phylogenetic development of this part of the nervous system, consists largely of the cerebral cortex, plus portions of the diencephalon. This latter division of the brain consists of the thalamus, the epithalamus, and the hypothalamus. These serve as final mediating centers and pathways for nerve impulses entering and leaving the cerebral cortex. The *thalamus,* it is believed, serves as a primary sensory-perception area, while the sensory areas of the cortex act to refine those impressions to a greater detail. The cortex of the cerebrum is the outer layer of gray matter covering the entire brain. Less than one-third of the *cerebral cortex* is actually exposed because of the many folds or convolutions of the gray matter of this region. Such important tissue is protected and separated from the bones of the skull by the three

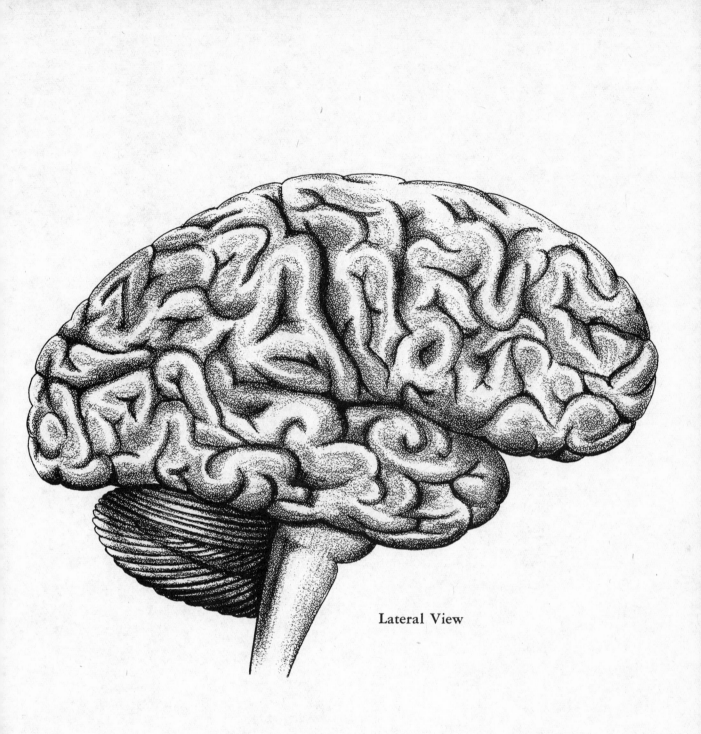

Lateral View

Figure 8–4.
Brain

investing membranes, or meninges: the pia mater, the dura mater, and the arachnoid.

The cerebral cortex subdivides into lobes, which receive their names from the bones about them. Thus, the most anterior portion of the cortex on either side is the *frontal lobe.* More posterior to this lobe on either side is the *parietal lobe.* At the farthest dorsal portion of the cerebrum is the *occipital lobe.* Below the frontal lobe on either hemisphere is the *temporal lobe.* The fissure of Sylvius separates this lobe from the frontal lobe. When this fissure is spread open, it reveals the Island (insula) of Reil beneath.

The upper border of the fissure of Sylvius is the lower margin of the frontal lobe. The majority of this border is called the *operculum.* Rising from the operculum, near its posterior portion, is another fissure, the *central sulcus* (fissure of Rolando). Behind this fissure is the parietal lobe, and before it is the frontal lobe. Running up and down on either border of the central sulcus are two convolutions, or gyri, called the *posterior central gyrus* and the *anterior central gyrus.* These particular convolutions are of considerable importance to the speech and hearing therapist in that the anterior gyrus seems to have located in it all of the initiating nerve cells for most voluntary motor actions, and the posterior gyrus seems to have an equivalent localization of the sensory or somasthetic aspects of the central nervous system. At the base of the central sulcus, encompassing a good deal of the operculum, is the generalized Broca's area, which has long been thought to be specifically related to the functions of speech and language.

CLINICAL NOTE

Injuries to the regions just described often result in symptoms and syndromes amenable to speech therapeutics. Among the pathologic types are aphasia—a language disorder due to injury to the cerebral cortex—and dysarthria—a motor speech dysfunction sometimes due to injury of the anterior central gyrus or communicating subcortical regions.

A large part of the frontal lobe is thought to subserve functions such as memory and personality, although it has not been clearly and precisely defined. The parietal lobe is essentially a general-body (somasthetic) sensory lobe. The occipital lobe seems to be related primarily to vision, its reception, perception, and memory. The temporal lobe serves audition.

Being the highest center of the central nervous system, the cerebrum has developed its complexity to its greatest extent in man in comparison to other forms of animal life. It is the center for voluntary control over functions that might well be under involuntary control in other animals. It is the center for the reception and perception of complex stimuli. It is the center for recording in memory banks of both the sensory and the motor experiences of the individual. And, of course, it is unique in man in that it is a center for the codification of these experiences in terms of linguistic or symbolic processes.

Radiating from and to the cerebral cortex are nerve fibers to and from subcortical areas, including the thalamus and immediately adjacent points, as well as fibers running to and from the lower portion of the brain and the spinal cord. Those coming to the cortex are essentially projection fibers from the sense organs. These have passed through the thalamus. This center is sometimes referred to as the basic seat of certain sensations as well as being the chief relay station for those impulses to the cortex. Running from the cortex are nerve fibers that ultimately stimulate activity of parts of the body—muscles and glands, for example. These are known as *efferent,* or *motor nerve, fibers;* the others are *afferent,* or *sensory, fibers.* Within the cortex itself are other nerve fibers, interconnecting the various lobes and convolutions. These are the association fibers. In some instances, association fibers are so closely packed together that the area in which this occurs is called an association area; Broca's area is just such an association area.

Through or alongside the thalamus pass most of the impulses transmitting sensations. Thus, touch, pressure, hot, cold, and other such sensations are mediated by this center. It is felt that such sensations as pain are actually recorded into consciousness within the thalamus itself. In the thalamic region are two prominent geniculate bodies—medial and lateral—that subserve the major senses of audition and vision. Audition utilizes the medial geniculate body, and vision is served by the lateral geniculate body. Of all the afferent impulses, only the sense of olfaction (smell) does not pass near or through the thalamus.

THE CEREBRAL CORTEX

It has been noted that the cerebral cortex has been arranged structurally into hemispheres, lobes, convolutions, and sulci, among others. Functional charting of the cortex, as differentiated from structural charting, has been performed by numerous authorities in an attempt to delineate regions to special activities: motor and sensory. Such charting was first done by Campbell in 1905, later repeated on a slightly different basis by Brodmann in 1909, and in 1925, revised in a less systematic manner by Economo and Koskinas. Brodmann's chart of the principal cortical areas is often used today to demonstrate generalities of function.

Brodmann organized the cortex into its lobes and further subdivided the functional areas into numbered locales. Immediately anterior to the central sulcus in the frontal lobe is Area 4, the motor area. Between it and the next major region anteriorly is a strip region, sometimes numbered 4S, which borders, or perhaps blends with, the precentral motor Area 6. Toward the front is Area 8, the frontal eye field, a special motor area. The prefrontal area of the cortex includes Areas 9, 10, 11, and 12; these are commonly known as the frontal association areas, about which little is known to date.

In the parietal lobe—the region between the central sulcus, Sylvian fissure, parietooccipital sulcus, and the midline—are several regions concerned with bodily sensation functions. Areas 3, 2, and 1 are in the postcentral area. These receive great numbers of projection fibers from the thalamus. Immediately posterior to these areas is the preparietal area known as 5a, a typical sensory cortical area. Next to this, is 5b, the superior parietal area that is also sensory. Area 7 encompasses most of the inferior parietal region. In these three latter areas, it is thought that auditory and visual association take place, especially around the region known as the supramarginal gyrus, which is at the posterior-inferior part of the parietal lobe.

The temporal lobe, found below the Sylvian fissure and bounded posteriorly by the parietal and occipital lobes, encompasses a large portion of the entire cerebral cortex. Its primary and most important function appears to be to serve audition. The transverse convolutions of Heschl receive the acoustic radiations from the medial geniculate body. According to Brodmann's numbering system, this region includes Areas 41 and 42, the primary acoustic areas.

The occipital lobe of the cerebral cortex is the visual center of the brain. It is composed of at least three areas, 17, 18, and 19, which are located beginning from the posterior pole of the lobe. Area 17 receives the optic radiations from the lateral geniculate bodies, and is called the primary visual cortex. Area 18, a ringlike organization of cells immediately anterior to Area 17, is like the area in the auditory region (temporal lobe, Areas 41–42), and is known as the visuo-psychic area. Like its auditory counterpart, it provides for understanding of the information received by the purely sensory receiving area. This understanding is based upon past experience. Area 18 is the preoccipital area, and actually lies partly within the parietal lobe. Its function is to further the understanding of the visuopsychic region by association of visual stimuli with other sensory experiences. It operates much like the supramarginal gyrus of Area 7 in its association function.

These few numbers represent those most commonly used in describing the cerebral cortex. Others exist, of course. Of singular interest to the student of speech pathology is the area referred to as the operculum, in the third frontal convolution, known as Broca's area. Brodmann, however, numbers this area in two parts: Areas 44 and 45. The whole region may be both motor and associational in function, but is definitely related to the body structures that are importantly related to the production of speech. Localization of function is a procedure of considerable question among neurophysiologists and speech pathologists and is not always in accord with the principles of the organismic point of view. However, the student must appreciate the fact that localization theory is based in part upon clinical evidence, both from accidental traumatic events and surgical intervention, in which localized stimulation is tied in closely with specific observable functions or actions.

CLINICAL NOTE

It is fairly well known that lesions or injuries of the cerebral cortex in Areas 44 and 45 produce what is commonly known as apraxia, a disturbance in speech. This is especially true when it occurs in the dominant hemisphere which, it is generally agreed, is that side of the cortex opposite the side of the body most efficiently used. Thus, a lesion in the left hemisphere in Broca's area in a right-handed individual might be responsible for this speech disorder. Interestingly, the same injury to a left-handed person is likely to produce a similar result.

THE AUTONOMIC NERVOUS SYSTEM

The autonomic nervous system contributes importantly to the total functioning of the nervous elements of the body. This system of nerves is efferent and directed toward the visceral organs of the body, serving the glands, the cardiovascular system, the peripheral involuntary muscles, the intrinsic muscles of the eyes, and muscles associated with hair follicles. Most of the activities carried on in these regions are reflex mechanisms. They are based upon sensory apparatus affiliated with the spinal nerves of the central nervous system and the central communicating regions of the spinal cord and the brainstem.

Certain nerve fibers of the central nervous system are destined to connect with the autonomic nervous system. Ultimately, they provide contact with a series of cell-body accumulations (ganglia) located outside the spinal cord but along its length on either side. Those nerve fibers within the spinal cord and brain stem are known as preganglionic fibers. Those that continue peripherally beyond the ganglia are postganglionic fibers.

The ganglia (and their postganglionic fibers) of the cranial nerves are like those that exit from the spinal cord in the sacral region in that they are not as numerous as those from body regions in between. These two widely separated portions of the autonomic nervous system, the cranial and the sacral, are known as the *parasympathetic division* of the autonomic nervous system. They serve to innervate the smooth muscles of the cranium and the pelvis and abdomen, respectively. The middle section of this nervous system is known as the *sympathetic division.* Its fibers are derived from the thoracic and the lumbar spinal nerves. From there and from the sympathetic ganglia, they are distributed to all parts of the body, including those that are also served by the parasympathetic division. Thus, there is some overlapping of neural innervation in these systems.

The autonomic nervous system, although basically a reflex system, is under higher center control. What cerebral cortex control may be present is directed through the hypothalamus. Other higher centers, still largely reflexive and without voluntary control under normal conditions, are found at lower levels, such as the medulla. In this latter example, there is a respiratory center as well as a vasomotor center. In the *respiratory system,* the carbon dioxide content of the blood is constantly monitored by chemoreceptors. When the balance of carbon dioxide reaches certain signal levels, the servomechanism is triggered and the respiratory pattern of the animal is changed to equalize that level. A similar system operates for the *vasomotor system,* dilating and constricting the lumen of blood vessels when the body needs demand such changes. Again, further changes of other functions of the body are provided by the autonomic nervous system, such as glandular and ocular, when the need arises. Of course, there are conditions in which some of these activities can be initiated voluntarily, or their patterns can be changed by cortical control. However, it remains true that the majority of the control is automatic and autonomic, to provide for rapid reaction to the body's needs. It is true that the common appellation to the entire system has been derived: the "fight or flight" system.

CLINICAL NOTE

It is generally believed that it is the autonomic nervous system that is responsible for the phenomenon known as the psychogalvanic skin response, or electrodermal responses. This event has been utilized in clinical audiometry in situations in which involuntary responses to auditory stimuli indicated the condition of the auditory systems. Basically, the client is conditioned to a pure tone followed by electric shock; the conditioning is demonstrated by changed electrical conductivity of the palm of the hand due to uncontrollable sweat production. The change in conductivity (or in some instances, resistance) is charted, and comparison with charts of known auditory-autonomic systems is made.

NERVOUS SYSTEM LANDMARK IDENTIFICATIONS

Directions: For the indicated illustrations, label the following landmarks.

FIGURE 8–1
Spinal Cord
Dorsal Aspect of Spinal Cord
Ventral Aspect of Spinal Cord
Dorsal Root
Ventral Root
Sensory Nerve Fiber
Motor Nerve Fiber
Gray Matter
White Matter
Synapse
Cell Body
Sensory End Organ
Motor Endplate
Spinal Nerve

FIGURE 8–2
Demonstration Figure

FIGURE 8–3
Cerebral Cortex
Internal Capsule
Cerebral Peduncle
Corticalspinal Tract

Pons
Medulla
Cranial Nerve Centers
Decussation
Spinal Cord
Contralateral Pyramidal Tract
Ipsilateral Pyramidal Tract

FIGURE 8–4
Cerebrum
Cerebral Cortex
Cerebellum
Central Sulcus
Frontal Lobe
Parietal Lobe
Occipital Lobe
Temporal Lobe
Pons
Medulla
Spinal Cord
Superior Temporal Convolution
Precentral Motor Cortex
Postcentral Sensory Cortex

Abduction: to draw away from the midline.

Acromion (ac-ROW-me-on): the point of the shoulder.

Adduction: to draw toward the midline.

Adipose (ADD-i-pos): usually related to various tissues that store fat cells.

Aditus (ADD-i-tuss): an entrance, usually related to the opening into the laryngeal area called *aditus laryngis,* to *aditus ad antrum,* or to *aditus* of mastoid air cells.

Afferent (AFF-erent): that which conducts toward the center, usually related to sensory nerves.

Ala (AY-lah): a structure that has winglike characteristics; the wings or laminae.

Alveolus (al-VEE-o-luss): a sac or socket of teeth, lungs, or glands.

Amorphous (ah-MORE-fuss): shapeless; without distinct form.

Ansa (AN-sah): any looplike structure of bone or nerve.

Anterior: toward the front or abdomen, in man.

Antrum (AN-trum): a hollow or cavity, usually applied to those cavities or sinuses located in the various bones.

Apex: the topmost part of a structure that is conical or pyramidal in shape.

Aponeurosis (apo-new-ROW-sis): a tendon that is usually flat, broad and sheet-like.

Appendix: any extension of a structure that acts as an appendage.

Approximation: any action that brings two or more structures into an adjoining position.

Areolar (ah-REE-o-lar): related usually to a meshlike organization of connective tissue that occupies various spaces in the body.

Articular: pertaining to surfaces or structures that meet to form a joint.

Astrocytes (AS-tro-sites): nerve cells or bone corpuscles that are star-shaped.

Atlas: term given to the first cervical vertebra.

Atrium (AY-tree-um): chamber or space in the heart, lungs, ear, and larynx.

Auricular (aw-RICK-you-lar): usually related to the center portion of the external auditory meatus, or to the external ear in general.

Autonomic: a self-controlling structure or system; usually related to a portion of the nervous system uncontrolled by the brain or spinal cord.

Axis: the name given to second cervical vertebra; also the pivot-point; the center.

Axon: the portion of the neuron that carries stimuli away from the cell body, usually the longest portion of the neuron.

Bicuspid: name applied to teeth that have two prominent cusps or heads.

Bifurcate (BY-fur-kate): to divide into two portions.

Brachial (BRAY-key-ull): usually applied to structures and tissues of the arm.

Bronchiole: name applied to each of the divisions resulting from the forking of the trachea.

Buccinator (BUCK-sin-ay-tore): a flat muscle located in the cheek, which helps to compress the cheeks.

Canine: name applied to the longer, pointed teeth used for holding and tearing (cuspid).

Capillary: the smallest vessel of the vascular system that aids in conducting blood from arteries to veins, and v. v.

Capitulum (kah-PIT-you-lum): a small, round protuberance on a bone surface.

Capsule: an encapsulating membrane acting as a container.

Cardiac: pertaining to the heart.

Carotid (kah-ROT-id): the arteries that run to the brain, or to the head in general.

Cartilage: a body tissue intermediary between bone and epithelium, which furnishes strength, shape, and flexibility.

Caudal (KAW-dull): toward the tail or lower end.

Caudate (KAW-date): possessing a tail.

Centrosome (SEN-tro-sohm): a concentration of cytoplasm that houses the agent responsible for sexual division of cells.

Cephalad (SEF-ahl-ahd): toward the head or upper end.

Cerebellum (ser-eh-BELL-um): the small portion of the brain located behind and below the cerebrum. Its major responsibility is coordination of bodily actions.

Cerebrum (SER-eh-brum): the largest portion of the brain. It is incompletely divided into two major hemispheres and contains many convolutions and fissures.

Cervical (SIR-vi-kull): related to the region of the cervix or neck; usually applied to bones and nerves.

Choana (ko-AY-nah): the nostril, naris, or posterior opening of the nasal cavity.

Cilia: small hairs located on cell borders and responsible for movement of food and wastes; also applied to the sensory nerve fibers located within the cochlea of the inner ear.

Collagenous (ko-LAJ-en-us): usually white tissue that has a high concentration of the protein collagen; also, usually applied to the white, fibrous connective tissue.

Concha (KONG-ka): the pit, hollow, or cavity of the external ear.

Condyle (KON-dial): a round protuberance usually located at bone ends, as on the mandible.

Corniculate (kore-NICK-you-let): cartilaginous nodules located on the arytenoid cartilages in the larynx.

Cornu (KORE-new): a structure shaped like a horn.

Coronal: crown; the anatomical plane that divides the body into front and back sections.

Corpus: any body.

Corpuscle: a small body; usually applied to specialized bodies located in nerves, epithelium, bone, blood, etc.

Cortex: any outer layer of substance; usually applied to the outer layer of the brain (cerebral cortex) or of bone.

Costal: that which pertains to the rib; usually applied to the cartilages that connect the ribs and the sternum.

Cranial: related to the head or upper end.

Cricoid (CRY-koid): signet-shaped; usually applied to the cricoid cartilage in the larynx that acts to support the thyroid and arytenoid cartilages.

Cuneiform (cue-KNEE-i-form): a wedge-shaped structure; cartilages located near the arytenoid cartilages of the larynx.

Cutaneous (cue-TAY-knee-us): pertaining to the first layer of the skin.

Cytology: the study of cellular structures.

Decussate (deh-CUSS-ate): a crossing action that results in an X formation; usually applied to nerve groups of the central nervous system.

Deferens (DEAF-er-ens): that which carries away from the center; usually applied to nerves or ducts.

Deglutition (deh-glue-TISH-un): the act of swallowing.

Dendrite (DEN-drite): the portion of the neuron that carries stimuli toward the cell body, usually a short portion.

Diaphragm: a large muscle of respiration that separates thoracic and abdominal cavities.

Diaphysis (die-AFF-i-sis): the portion of a growing bone called the *shaft*.

Diarthrosis (die-are-THROW-sis): a freely moving joint such as the elbow, wrist, shoulder, etc. (also, *diarthrodial*).

Digastric (die-GAS-trick): double-bellied muscle of mastication located near the floor of the mouth.

Distal (DIS-tull): away from the point of attachment, away from the midline.

Dorsal: toward the back or rear side.

Dorsum: The superior and rear surface of a portion, especially of the tongue.

Ectoplast (EK-toe-plast): the outer layer of the protoplasm that forms a cell membrane.

Efferent: that which conveys away from the center; usually applied to motor nerves.

Embryology: the study of cell growth and the development of an organism.

Endo-: prefix meaning within, or inner.

Epi-: prefix meaning upon, above, or upper.

Epiphysis (ee-PIFF-i-sis): the ends of a growing bone that form the boundaries for the diaphysis or shaft.

Epithelium (epeh-THEE-lee-um): the cellular, outer substance of skin and mucous membrane that is without blood supply.

Esophagus: part of the digestive system; the tube connecting the pharynx and the stomach.

Eustachian tube (you-STAY-kee-un): the tube that leads from the middle ear to the pharynx; named in honor of Eustachius, Italian anatomist of the sixteenth century.

Falciform (FALL-si-form): sickle-shaped.

Fascia (FASH-ee-ah): a band or sheet of fibrous connective tissue that encloses muscles and some organs.

Fasciculus (fas-IK-you-lus): a bundle or cluster of nerve or muscle fibers that gather to make up whole nerves or muscles.

Fauces (FAW-seez): the space between mouth and pharynx.

Fenestra (fen-ES-tra): window or opening; usually applied to the opening found in the middle ear which leads to the inner ear.

Fissure: a groove or sulcus; usually applied to those clefts found in tissues.

Fixate: the act of making static, fixed, or relatively immovable.

Flaccid (FLAK-sid): soft, inert; usually applied to muscles that have lost their quality or tonus.

Follicle: a small sac or gland capable of excretion.

Foramen (fore-AY-men): a window or hole that is a regular part of a structure.

Fossa (FOSS-ah): a pit, cavity, or depression that is a regular part of a structure.

Frenum (FREE-num): a fold or ridge; usually applied to ridge found in the mucous membrane that connects the tongue with the floor of the mouth.

Fusiform (FEW-zi-form): anything that has a spindle shape.

Ganglion (GANG-lee-on): a concentration of nerve-cell bodies that serve as nervous centers.

Gastric: pertaining to the stomach.

Gestalt (gesh-TALT): usually related to a philosophy or action that is total and wholistic.

Gingiva (JIN-ji-vah): usually applied to the membranous covering of the alveolar ridge; the gum.

Gladiolus (glad-I-oh-luss): body or main portion.

Glossal (GLAH-sull): pertaining to the tongue.

Glottis (GLAH-tis): the opening between the vocal folds that disappears when the folds approximate.

Gyrus (JIE-rus): a rise, hill, or promontory located in membraneous tissue; usually applied to the convolutions located in the brain.

Hamulus (HAM-you-luss): any hook-shaped structure; usually applied to the pterygoid process of the sphenoid bone.

Hiatus (hie-A-tuss): a space, gap, groove, or opening in any structure.

Histology: the study of tissues.

Hormone: a chemical secretion of the ductless glands that is carried in the blood stream and that acts to stimulate the activity of organs.

Humerus: the upper arm bone.

Hyaline (HIE-a-lynn): type of white cartilage commonly found throughout the body.

Hyoid (HIE-oid): the U-shaped bone located below the tongue and above the thyroid cartilage.

Hyper-: prefix meaning in excess of some normal state.

Hypo-: prefix meaning less than some normal state.

Ilium (ILL-ee-um): the hip bone.

Incus (ING-kuss): anvil-shaped bone of the middle ear.

Inferior: below; toward the caudal end of the body.

Infundibulum (in-fun-DIB-you-lum): a funnel, canal, or extended cavity; usually applied to a passage connecting the nasal cavity with ethmoid bone or with the area at the upper end of the cochlear canal.

Inguinal (ING-gwi-null): pertaining to the groin.

Innervate (in-NERVE-ate): to stimulate or to supply with nervous stimulation.

Insertion: point of attachment for muscles; usually applied to the most movable point of attachment.

Integument (in-TEG-you-ment): the outermost surface of the body, or skin.

Interstitial (in-ter-STISH-ull): located in the spaces between cells.

Intrinsic: anything wholly contained within another structure; usually applies to muscles that are exclusively attached to one organ or structure, as intrinsic muscles of the tongue.

Jugular: pertaining to the neck; usually applied to the large vein of the neck.

Karyotheca (kare-ee-OH-thee-kah): term applied to the membrane separating the nucleus from the cytosome of a cell.

Labial (LAY-bee-ull): pertaining to the lips.

Lacrimal (LACK-ri-mull): pertaining to the tears and the ducts from which they arise.

Lacuna (lah-KOO-nah): a small pit or cavity; usually applied to bone cavities.

Lamina (LAM-i-nah): a plate or flat layer of bone.

Larynx (LAH-rinks): the structure responsible for voice; composed of cartilages and muscles; usually called voicebox.

Laryngectomy: surgical removal of the larynx.

Lateral: away from the midline, toward the periphery.

Ligament: tough, fibrous connective bands that support or bind bones and various organs.

Linea alba (LIN-ee-ah AHL-bah): a white line; usually applied to major tendonous structure running down the front of the abdominal cavity.

Lingual (LING-gwull): pertaining to the tongue.

Lobe: a regular part of an organ usually delineated by fissures or cleavages.

Lumbar (LUM-bar): pertaining to the portion of the back located between the thorax and the pelvis, commonly referred to as the loins.

Lumen (LOO-men): a transverse or cross-sectional area in a tubular structure.

Lymph (limf): a clear, watery fluid secreted by the lymph glands in order to expedite the removal of waste from tissue cells.

Malleus (MALL-ee-us): mallet-shaped bone of the inner ear.

Mandible: major bone of the lower jaw.

Manubrium (mah-NEW-bree-um): a handle; usually applied to the uppermost portion of the breastbone and the inferior portion of the malleus.

Mastoid: nipple-shaped; usually applied to a process of the temporal bone.

Meatus (mee-AY-tuss): any passage; usually applied to the passage of the ear.

Media: middle.

Medial: toward the midline or median plane.

Median: situated in the midline.

Mediastinum (mee-di-ah-STIE-num):a median partition; usually applied to the median septum which divides the thorax into two lateral cavities.

Medulla oblongata (meh-DOOL-ah ahb-long-GAH-tah): the most inferior portion of the brain; the uppermost portion of the spinal cord that connects with the pons.

Membrane: a thin sheet of tissue that sheathes or divides organs and surfaces.

Meninges (meh-NIN-jeez): specialized membranes that encase the brain and spinal cord.

Metabolism: the regular chemical modifications of substances that occur in the growth and development of the body.

Modiolus (mo-DIE-o-luss): the central pillar of the cochlea.

Morphology: the study of forms and structure.

Mucus (MEW-cuss): the sticky secretion that covers the membranes of many cavities and passages that are exposed to the external environment.

Muscle: specialized fibers, tissues, and organs that can contract and furnish the body with motive power.

Mylohyoid: a muscle connected to the mandible, the hyoid bone, and median raphe.

Myo-: prefix pertaining to muscle.

Nares (NAY-reez): the anterior openings of the nasal cavities that communicate with the external environment, i.e., the nostrils.

Nasopharynx: the part of the pharynx located above the velum or soft palate.

Neuron (NEW-rone): the basic structural unit of the nervous system; composed of a cell body, axon, and dendrites.

Nucleus (NEW-klee-us): a small round body within every cell that acts as the functional control center; refers also to a mass of cell bodies in the brain or spinal cord.

Occlusion (uk-KLOO-shun): the act of closing or the state of being closed.

Orbicular (or-BICK-you-lar): circular; usually applied to the orbicularis oris muscle encircling the mouth.

Orifice (OR-i-fiss): an entrance or opening into a body cavity.

Origin: the relatively fixed muscular connection.

Oropharynx: the part of the pharynx located between the velum, or soft palate, and the hyoid bone.

Ossicle (AHS-i-kull): a small bone; usually applied to the bones of the ear.

Ossify: the act of becoming bone.

Osteoblasts (AHS-tee-o-blasts): cells that are formed into bone.

Osteology (ahs-tee-AH-low-gee): study of bone.

Ostium (AHS-tee-um): an entrance or opening.

Otosclerosis (oh-toe-sklee-ROW-sis): formation of spongy bone in the capsule of the labyrinth of the ear.

Papilla (pah-PILL-ah): a small elevation on epithelial tissue.

Parietal (pah-RIE-eh-tull): pertaining to the walls of organs or cavities; usually applied to the parietal bones of the cranium or to the lobes of the brain lying near these bones.

Pectoralis (peck-toe-RAH-liss): pertaining to the chest; usually applied to the muscles that form the chest.

Pedicle (PED-i-cull): stalklike process or stem.

Peduncles (pee-DUNG-culls) a supporting part of another structure; usually applied to the bands running between sections of the brain.

Pelvis (PEL-viss): a basin; usually applied to the pelvis bone that forms the hip region.

Pericardium (per-i-CAR-dee-um): the membranous sac that ensheathes and contains the heart.

Perilymph (PER-il-imf): the lymphatic fluid that fills the space between the various labyrinths of the ear, and communicates with the cerebro-spinal fluid.

Periosteum (per-ee-OSS-tee-um): the fibrous sheath that covers all bones.

Peristalsis (per-i-STAHL-sis): a wave of contraction passing along a tube.

Peritoneum (per-i-toe-KNEE-um): the membrane that lines the abdominal cavity.

Pharyngeal: (fah-RIN-gee-ull): pertaining to the pharynx or throat.

Phrenic (FREN-ik): pertaining to the diaphragm; usually applied to the spinal nerve that supplies the diaphragm.

Plasma: the fluid portion of the blood during circulation.

Platysma (plah-TIZZ-mah): a plate; usually applied to the neck muscle connected to the mandible and the clavicle.

Pleura (PLOOR-ah): pertaining to the ribs; usually applied to the chest or thoracic cavity; refers also to the membrane that lines this cavity.

Plexus (PLEK-suss): a collection, concentration, or network of parts of the nervous or vascular systems.

Pons: a bridge; usually applied to that portion of brain stem that is between the medulla oblongata and the midbrain.

Posterior: toward the back or rear side.

Protoplasm: the basic material of every living cell.

Proximal: toward the point of attachment; toward the midline.

Pterygoid (TER-i-goid): wing-shaped; usually applied to the sphenoid bone and to the muscles that are connected beneath the skull to the mandible.

Pulmonary: pertaining to the lungs.

Ramus (RAY-muss): a branch; usually applied to parts of nerves, vessels, or bone.

Raphe: a line formed by the union of two parts.

Rectus: straight; applied to the rectus abdominis muscles connected to the pubis and the lower costal cartilages.

Reticular: like a network; usually applied to the network of fibers passing between the pons and the medulla oblongata.

Risorius (ri-so-ree-us): a muscle connected to facial fascia and the angle of the mouth, and that affects facial expression.

Rostral (RAHS-trull): toward the head end.

Sagittal (SAJ-i-tull): straight; usually applied to the plane that divides the body into right and left portions.

Sarcolemma (sar-ko-LEM-mah): a membranous sheath encasing a muscle.

Scalenus (skay-LEE-nuss): uneven; applied to the muscles of the neck that connect to the first rib and the cervical vertebrae.

Scaphoid (SKAF-oid): a bone or process shaped like a small boat.

Scapula (SKAP-you-lah): the shoulder blade; the triangular bone behind the shoulder.

Segmentation: division into small parts or segments.

Sensory: nerves, organs, or structures related to the process of sensation and carrying stimuli from the exterior toward the cerebro-spinal system.

Septum: a partition or dividing wall, such as the nasal septum.

Sinus: a depression, hollow, or cavity; usually applied to those located in the facial bones.

Sphenoid (SFEE-noid): wedge-shaped; usually applied to the complex bone of the interior skull.

Sphincter (SFINGK-ter): any muscle or combination of muscles that provides a closure for a natural body opening.

Stapes (STAY-peez): a small, stirrup-shaped bone of the ear.

Stapedius (sta-PEE-dee-us): a muscle attached to the stapes bone of the ear.

Sternum: the breastbone.

Striated: streaked; usually applied to a special type of muscular fiber that effects voluntary movement.

Styloid (STY-loid): pin-shaped; usually applied to a part of the temporal bone that furnishes attachment for muscles and ligaments.

Sulcus (SULL-kuss): a fissure or groove in bone or membranous tissue.

Superior: above; toward the head or cephalic end.

Suture (SOO-cher): a seam; usually applied to a juncture of cranial or facial bones.

Symphysis (SIM-fi-sis): usually applied to a line formed by the union of two bones; more definite than a suture.

Synapse (SIN-aps): the junction between the axon of one nerve cell and the dendrite of another.

Synarthrosis (sin-are-THROW-sis): restricted movement or complete lack of movement in a joint.

Synchondrosis: restricted movement of a joint because of cartilaginous connections.

Syndesmosis (sin-des-MO-sis): restricted movement of a joint because of connective tissue attachments.

Synergy (SIN-er-jee): a coordination or cooperation that results in smooth, economical activity.

Synostosis (sin-os-TOE-sis): restricted or lack of movement of a joint due to a bony connection.

Synovial (sin-OH-vee-ull): pertains to a fluid secreted in joints, bursae, and around certain tendon sheaths.

Systemic: affecting the body as a whole.

Systole (SIS-toe-lee): the stage of contraction of the heart muscle.

Tendon: a cordlike, fibrous material connecting muscles with points of origin and insertion.

Therapy: the treatment of a pathological condition caused by malformation, injury, disease.

Thorax: pertains to the region of the body that is located between the clavicle and the diaphragm.

Thyroid: the shieldlike cartilage of the larynx that rests on the cricoid cartilage and furnishes an attachment for the vocal folds; also a gland.

Tonus: a state of partial contraction of a muscle that produces a healthy, resilient quality in the muscle.

Trachea (TRAY-kee-ah): the cartilaginous and membranous tube extending from the larynx to the bronchial tubes, commonly referred to as the windpipe.

Transverse: usually applied to a plane that extends horizontally from one side of a structure to the other; a cross section.

Tricuspid (try-CUSS-pid): having three cusps or heads; usually applied to molars.

Tuberosity (too-ber-OSS-i-tee): protuberance or eminence; usually applied to bones.

Turbinate (TER-bi-nate): any structure shaped like a top and filled with pits, hollows, or swirls; usually applied to bones of the nasal chamber.

Vaginal (VAJ-i-null): pertaining to any sheath or sheathlike structure.

Vein: a vessel that conveys blood toward the heart.

Velum (VEE-lum): the soft palate; the posterior and muscular portion of the roof of the mouth.

Ventral: toward the front or abdomen.

Ventricle: a small cavity.

Vertex (VER-tex): the topmost part; usually applied to the top of the head.

Vestibule: An antechamber; usually applied to special chambers in the nose, ear, pharynx, etc.

Viscera (VISS-er-ah): generic term for the organs of any large body cavity; most frequently applied to the organs in the abdomen.

Xiphoid process (ZIF-oid): the most inferior portion of the sternum; the tip of the breastbone.

PHYSIOLOGIC PHONETICS

BASIC ASSUMPTIONS

The following charts attempt to present primary muscular activity in the production of speech sounds. They are the result of essentially a deduced analysis that is incompletely substantiated by research or clinical evidence. The reader must assume the following:

1. He is dealing with a normal, average speaker of general American speech, who has no known defects or deviations.
2. In all cases, the inspiration of the air to the lungs has been completed.
3. The articulators under consideration are in a dynamically neutral position, with
   a. the mouth closed.
   b. velopharyngeal aperture open.
   c. the tongue blade horizontally flat.
4. Static positions indicated are preceded and followed by dynamic synergic activities such as facial movement or exhalation of air.

In reading the charts, reference to Phonation (Section I) or to Resonance (Section II) must be made at the indicated analysis to complete the description of the articulatory act.

The reader should refer to the text for complete descriptions of the musculature, including origins and insertions as well as neural innervation of the muscles listed. Also, the listed bilateral structures are ordered according to an arbitrary importance of the muscles. Individual differences, among persons as well as sounds, dictate the degree of participation of each muscle in the action indicated. The listing only indicates that a muscle does participate, not the extent to which it contributes to the completed phonetic act. Fixation of antagonistic muscles or muscle groups is assumed to maintain an equilibrium in the articulatory system. Effort has been made to present the essential muscles that effect the movement; in each case, contraction of closely related muscles probably assists the activity.

I. THE PHONATORY PROCESS

ACTION
A. Glottal closure (Vocal fold adduction)

MUSCULATURE
1. Intermembranous adduction
   a. Lateral cricoarytenoid m.
   b. Thyroarytenoid m.

2. Intercartilaginous adduction
   a. Interarytenoid m.

B. Vocal fold tension and lengthening

1. Cricothyroid m.
2. Vocalis m.

C. Vocal fold mass change

1. Vocalis m.
2. Cricothyroid m.
3. Thyroarytenoid m.

D. Increase of air pressure

1. Abdominal group
   a. External oblique m.
   b. Internal oblique m.
   c. Rectus m.
   d. Transverse m.
2. Controlled relaxation of
   a. Diaphragm m.
   b. Thoracic mm.

II. THE RESONANCE PROCESS

ACTION
A. Velopharyngeal closure

MUSCULATURE
1. Velopharyngeal sphincter m.
2. Levator veli palatine m.
3. Tensor veli palatine m.
4. Superior constrictor m.
5. Palatopharyngeus m.

B. Tongue movement[1]

1. Position
   Retraction
   Protrusion

1. Extrinsic musculature

2. Shape (contour)

1. Intrinsic musculature

C. Mouth opening
1. Jaw depression

1. External pterygoid m.
2. Digastric m. (anterior belly)
3. Mylohyoid m.
4. Geniohyoid m.

2. Lip opening
   a. Upper lip

1. Quadratus labii superior m.
2. Zygomatic m.
3. Caninus m.

b. Lower lip

1. Triangularis m.
2. Quadratus labii inferior m.
3. Mentalis m.

[1]For detailed analysis, see specific speech sounds.

III. VOWEL SOUND PRODUCTION[2]

SOUND	ACTION	MUSCULATURE
/i/	A. Slight parting of lips	1. Quadratus labii superior m. 2. Quadratus labii inferior m.
	B. Strong retraction of lips	1. Risorius m. 2. Zygomatic m.
	C. Slight depression of mandible	1. External pterygoid m. 2. Digastric m. (anterior belly) 3. Mylohyoid m. 4. Geniohyoid m.
	D. Strong depression of tongue apex	1. Longitudinal inferior m. 2. Genioglossus m. (anterior fibers) 3. Hyoglossus m.
	E. Strong elevation of posterior tongue dorsum	1. Palatoglossus m. 2. Styloglossus m.
/I/	A. Slight parting of lips	1. Quadratus labii inferior m. 2. Quadratus labii superior m.
	B. Slight depression of mandible	1. External pterygoid m. 2. Digastric m. (anterior belly) 3. Mylohyoid m. 4. Geniohyoid m.
	C. Slight depression of tongue apex	1. Longitudinal inferior m. 2. Genioglossus m. (anterior fibers) 3. Hyoglossus m.
	D. Slight elevation of posterior tongue dorsum	1. Palatoglossus m. 2. Styloglossus m.
/e/	A. Slight parting of lips	1. Quadratus labii superior m. 2. Quadratus labii inferior m.
	B. Slight retraction of lips	1. Risorius m. 2. Zygomatic m.
	C. Moderate depression of mandible	1. External pterygoid m. 2. Digastric m. 3. Mylohyoid m. 4. Geniohyoid m.
	D. Moderate depression of tongue apex	1. Longitudinal inferior m. 2. Genioglossus m. (anterior fibers) 3. Hyoglossus m.
	E. Slight elevation of posterior tongue dorsum	1. Palatoglossus m. 2. Styloglossus m.

[2]Basic assumptions: (a) all vowels are phonated (see Section I); (b) velopharyngeal closure occurs for all vowels (see Section II A).

/ɛ/   A. Moderate parting of lips

1. Quadratus labii superior m.
2. Quadratus labii inferior m.
3. Caninus m.
4. Triangularis m.
5. Zygomatic m.
6. Mentalis m.

          B. Moderate depression of mandible

1. External pterygoid m.
2. Digastric m. (anterior belly)
3. Mylohyoid m.
4. Geniohyoid m.

          C. Slight elevation of posterior tongue dorsum

1. Palatoglossus m.
2. Styloglossus m.

          D. Slight retraction of lips

1. Risorius m.
2. Zygomatic m.

/æ/   A. Considerable mandibular depression

1. External pterygoid m.
2. Digastric m. (anterior belly)
3. Mylohyoid m.
4. Geniohyoid m.

          B. Retraction of angles of lips

1. Risorius m.
2. Zygomatic m.

          C. Strong depression of anterior tongue dorsum

1. Genioglossus m. (anterior and middle fibers)
2. Hyoglossus m.

/a/   A. Moderate mandibular depression

1. External pterygoid m.
2. Digastric m. (anterior belly)
3. Mylohyoid m.
4. Geniohyoid m.

          B. Moderate depression of anterior tongue dorsum

1. Genioglossus m. (anterior and middle fibers)
2. Hyoglossus m.

/ɔ/   A. Slight mandibular depression

1. External pterygoid m.
2. Digastric m. (anterior belly)
3. Mylohyoid m.
4. Geniohyoid m.

          B. Moderate labial protrusion

1. Orbicularis oris m.
2. Mentalis m.
3. Quadratus labii superior m.
4. Quadratus labii inferior m.

          C. Slight tongue apex depression

1. Genioglossus m. (anterior fibers)
2. Longitudinal inferior m.
3. Hyoglossus m.

          D. Slight depression of anterior tongue dorsum

1. Hyoglossus m.
2. Genioglossus m. (middle and posterior fibers)

/o/   A. Slight mandibular depression

1. External pterygoid m.
2. Digastric m. (anterior belly)
3. Mylohyoid m.
4. Geniohyoid m.

      B. Moderate labial protrusion

1. Orbicularis oris m.
2. Mentalis m.
3. Quadratus labii superior m.
4. Quadratus labii inferior m.

      C. Tongue dorsum depression

1. Genioglossus m. (anterior and middle fibers)
2. Hyoglossus m.

/U/   A. Slight mandibular depression

1. External pterygoid m.
2. Digastric m. (anterior belly)
3. Mylohyoid m.
4. Geniohyoid m.

      B. Moderate labial compression

1. Orbicularis oris m.

      C. Depression of anterior tongue dorsum

1. Genioglossus m. (anterior and middle fibers)
2. Hyoglossus m.

/u/   A. Slight mandibular depression

1. External pterygoid m.
2. Digastric m. (anterior belly)
3. Mylohyoid m.
4. Geniohyoid m.

      B. Strong labial protrusion

1. Orbicularis oris m.
2. Mentalis m.
3. Quadratus labii inferior m.
4. Quadratus labii superior m.

      C. Depression of anterior tongue dorsum

1. Genioglossus m. (anterior and middle fibers)
2. Hyoglossus m.

/ə//ʌ/   A. Slight mandibular depression

1. External pterygoid m.
2. Digastric m. (anterior belly)
3. Mylohyoid m.
4. Geniohyoid m.

      B. Depression of anterior tongue dorsum

1. Genioglossus m. (anterior and middle fibers)
2. Hyoglossus m.

/ɝ//ɚ/   A. Slight mandibular depression

1. External pterygoid m.
2. Digastric m. (anterior belly)
3. Mylohyoid m.
4. Geniohyoid m.

      B. Slight lip protrusion

1. Orbicularis oris m.
2. Mentalis m.
3. Quadratus labii superior m.
4. Quadratus labii inferior m.

      C. Tongue border elevation   1. Palatoglossus m.
                                             2. Styloglossus m.
                                           3. Transverse lingual m.

IV. CONSONANT SOUND PRODUCTION

/b/   A. Strong lip compression   1. Orbicularis oris m.

        B. Slight mandibular depression   1. External pterygoid m.
          (on release)   2. Digastric m. (anterior belly)
                                           3. Mylohyoid m.
                                           4. Geniohyoid m.

        C. Velopharyngeal closure   (See Section II-A.)

        D. Phonation   (See Section I.)

/p/   A. Strong lip compression   1. Orbicularis oris m.

        B. Slight mandibular depression   1. External pterygoid m.
          (on release)   2. Digastric m. (anterior belly)
                                           3. Mylohyoid m.
                                           4. Geniohyoid m.

        C. Velopharyngeal closure   (See Section II-A.)

/t/   A. Elevation of tongue tip and   1. Superior Longitudinal m.
          lateral margins   2. Styloglosus m.

        B. Velopharyngeal closure   (See Section II-A.)

/d/   A. Elevation of tongue tip and   1. Superior longitudinal m.
          lateral margins   2. Styloglossus m.

        B. Velopharyngeal closure   (See Section II-A.)

        C. Phonation   (See Section I.)

/k/   A. Elevation of tongue middle,   1. Palatoglossus m.
          from border to border   2. Styloglossus m.

        B. Velopharyngeal closure   (See Section II-A.)

/g/   A. Elevation of tongue middle,   1. Palatoglossus m.
          from border to border   2. Styloglossus m.

        B. Velopharyngeal closure   (See Section II-A.)

        C. Phonation   (See Section I.)

/s/   A. Lips slightly apart   1. Quadratus labii superior m.
                                             2. Quadratus labii inferior m.

        B. Dental occlusion   1. Internal pterygoid m.
          (jaws together)   2. Temporalis m.
                                           3. Masseter m.

        C. Extension of tongue apex   1. Genioglossus (anterior fibers)

	D. Narrow grooving of tongue dorsum	1. Transverse lingual m.
	E. Velopharyngeal closure	(See Section II-A.)
/z/	A. Lips slightly apart	1. Quadratus labii superior m. 2. Quadratus labii inferior m.
	B. Dental occlusion (jaws together)	1. Internal pterygoid m. 2. Temporalis m. 3. Masseter m.
	C. Extension of tongue apex	1. Genioglossus m. (anterior fibers)
	D. Narrow grooving of tongue dorsum	1. Transverse lingual m.
	E. Velopharyngeal closure	(See Section II-A.)
	F. Phonation	(See Section I.)
/f/	A. Slight mandibular retraction	1. Internal pterygoid m.
	B. Slight mandibular depression	1. Digastric m. (anterior belly) 2. Mylohyoid m. 3. Geniohyoid m. 4. Exterior pterygoid m.
	C. Tension of lower lip	1. Buccinator m. 2. Risorius m. 3. Orbicularis oris m. (lower portion)
	D. Slight elevation of lower lip	1. Those listed in C. 2. Mentalis m.
	E. Velopharyngeal closure	(See Section II-A.)
/v/	A. Slight mandibular retraction	1. Internal pterygoid m.
	B. Slight mandibular depression	1. Digastric m. (anterior belly) 2. Mylohyoid m. 3. Geniohyoid m. 4. External pterygoid m.
	C. Tension of lower lip	1. Buccinator m. 2. Risorius m. 3. Orbicularis oris m. (lower portion)
	D. Slight elevation of lower lip	1. Those listed in C. 2. Mentalis m.
	E. Velopharyngeal closure	(See Section II-A.)
	F. Phonation	(See Section I.)
/m/	A. Strong lip compression	1. Orbicularis oris m.
	B. Phonation	(See Section I.)

/n/   A. Slight mandibular depression

1. Digastric m. (anterior belly)
2. Mylohyoid m.
3. Geniohyoid m.
4. External pterygoid m.

B. Strong elevation of tongue apex

1. Longitudinal lingual superior m.
2. Styloglossus m.

C. Phonation

(See Section I.)

/ŋ/   A. Slight mandibular depression

1. Digastric m. (anterior belly)
2. Mylohyoid m.
3. Geniohyoid m.
4. External pterygoid m.

B. Strong elevation of tongue middle

1. Palatoglossus m.
2. Styloglossus m.

C. Phonation

(See Section I.)

/tʃ/   A. Elevation of tongue tip, lateral margins, and central apical portion

1. Superior longitudinal lingual m.
2. Styloglossus m.

B. Velopharyngeal closure

(See Section II-A.)

/dʒ/   A. Elevation of tongue tip, lateral margins, and central apical region

1. Superior longitudinal lingual m.
2. Styloglossus m.

B. Velopharyngeal closure

(See Section II-A.)

C. Phonation

(See Section I.)

/θ/   A. Slight mandibular depression

1. Digastric m. (anterior belly)
2. Mylohyoid m.
3. Geniohyoid m.
4. External pterygoid m.

B. Protrusion of tongue tip

1. Genioglossus m. (medial and posterior fibers)
2. Longitudinal superior lingual m.

C. Flattening of tongue dorsum

1. Vertical tongue m.

D. Velopharyngeal closure

(See Section II-A.)

/ð/   A. Slight mandibular depression

1. Digastric m. (anterior belly)
2. Mylohyoid m.
3. Geniohyoid m.
4. External pterygoid m.

B. Protrusion of tongue tip

1. Genioglossus m. (medial and posterior fibers)
2. Longitudinal superior lingual m.

C. Flattening of tongue dorsum

1. Vertical tongue m.

D. Velopharyngeal closure

(See Section II-A.)

E. Phonation

(See Section I.)

/ʃ/ A. Slight mandibular depression
1. Digastric m. (anterior belly)
2. Mylohyoid m.
3. Geniohyoid m.
4. External pterygoid m.

B. Slight labial protrusion
1. Orbicularis oris m.
2. Mentalis m.
3. Quadratus labii superior m.
4. Quadratus labii inferior m.

C. Flattening of tongue dorsum
1. Vertical tongue m.

D. Depression of tongue apex
1. Genioglossus m. (anterior fibers)
2. Longitudinal inferior lingual m.
3. Hyoglossus m.

E. Velopharyngeal closure
(See Section II-A.)

/ʒ/ A. Slight mandibular depression
1. Digastric m. (anterior belly)
2. Mylohyoid m.
3. Geniohyoid m.
4. External pterygoid m.

B. Slight labial protrusion
1. Orbicularis oris m.
2. Mentalis m.
3. Quadratus labii superior m.
4. Quadratus labii inferior m.

C. Flattening of tongue dorsum
1. Vertical tongue m.

D. Depression of tongue apex
1. Genioglossus m. (anterior fibers)
2. Longitudinal inferior lingual m.
3. Hyoglossus m.

E. Velopharyngeal closure
(See Section II-A.)

F. Phonation
(See Section I.)

/l/ A. Slight mandibular depression
1. Digastric m. (anterior belly)
2. Mylohyoid m.
3. Geniohyoid m.
4. External pterygoid m.

B. Elevation of tongue apex
1. Longitudinal superior lingual m.
2. Styloglossus m.

C. Elevation of tongue borders
1. Transverse lingual m.
2. Palatoglossus m.

/r/ A. Slight mandibular depression
1. Digastric m. (anterior belly)
2. Mylohyoid m.
3. Geniohyoid m.
4. External pterygoid m.

B. Slight protrusion of lips
1. Orbicularis oris m.
2. Mentalis m.
3. Quadratus labii superior m.
4. Quadratus labii inferior m.

	C. Elevation of posterior tongue borders	1. Palatoglossus m. 2. Transverse lingual m.
	D. Depression of tongue apex	1. Genioglossus m. (anterior fibers) 2. Longitudinal inferior lingual m. 3. Hyoglossus m.
	E. Velopharyngeal closure	(See Section II-A.)
	F. Phonation	(See Section I.)
/j/	A. Slight mandibular depression	1. Digastric m. (anterior belly) 2. Mylohyoid m. 3. Geniohyoid m. 4. External pterygoid m.
	B. Protrusion of lips	1. Orbicularis oris m. 2. Mentalis m. 3. Quadratus labii superior m. 4. Quadratus labii inferior m.
	C. Tongue grooved	1. Transverse lingual m. 2. Palatoglossus m.
	D. Velopharyngeal closure	(See Section II-A.)
	E. Phonation	(See Section I.)
/hw/	A. Slight mandibular depression	1. Digastric m. (anterior belly) 2. Mylohyoid m. 3. Geniohyoid m. 4. External pterygoid m.
	B. Strong protrusion of lips	1. Orbicularis oris m. 2. Mentalis m. 3. Quadratus labii inferior m. 4. Quadratus labii superior m.
	C. Velopharyngeal closure	(See Section II-A.)
/w/	A. Slight mandibular depression	1. Digastric m. (anterior belly) 2. Mylohyoid m. 3. Geniohyoid m. 4. External pterygoid m.
	B. Strong protrusion of lips	1. Orbicularis oris m. 2. Mentalis m. 3. Quadratus labii inferior m. 4. Quadratus labii superior m.
	C. Velopharyngeal closure	(See Section II-A.)
	D. Phonation	(See Section I.)
/h/	A. Slight mandibular depression	1. Digastric m. (anterior belly) 2. Mylohyoid m. 3. Geniohyoid m. 4. External pterygoid m.
	B. Velopharyngeal closure	(See Section II-A.)

INDEX

22215 | 299

431   74 75 76 9 8 7 6 5

Books by **Ursula K. Le Guin**

NOVELS
Tehanu
Always Coming Home
The Eye of the Heron
The Beginning Place
Malafrena
Very Far Away from Anywhere Else
The Word for World Is Forest
The Dispossessed
The Lathe of Heaven
The Farthest Shore
The Tombs of Atuan
A Wizard of Earthsea
The Left Hand of Darkness
City of Illusions
Planet of Exile
Rocannon's World

SHORT STORIES
Searoad
Buffalo Gals
The Compass Rose
Orsinian Tales
The Wind's Twelve Quarters

FOR CHILDREN
Catwings Return · *Catwings*
Fire and Stone
A Visit from Dr. Katz
Leese Webster

POETRY AND CRITICISM
Going Out With Peacocks
Hard Words
Dancing at the Edge of the World
Wild Oats and Fireweed
The Language of the Night
Wild Angels